To Brian
   With so mu[ch thanks]
to your input to [this, I hope]
you see from this how valued it is.

VERBATIM
The Fun of Making Theatre Seriously

VERBATIM
The Fun of Making Theatre Seriously
by Mark Wheeller
Design & Layout by Barrie Sapsford

Salamander Street

Published in 2021
www.salamanderstreet.com

© Mark Wheeller 2021
First Edition

The moral right of Mark Wheeller to be identified as the author of this work has been asserted by him in accordance with the Copyright, Design and Patents Act 1988.

All rights reserved. Except as permitted under current legislation, no part of this work may be photocopied, stored in a retrieval system, published, performed in public, adapted, broadcast, transmitted, recorded or reproduced in any form or by any means, without the prior permission of the copyright owner. Enquiries should be made to Wheellerplays@gmail.com

VERBATIM - The Fun of Making Theatre Seriously by Mark Wheeller.

ISBN: 9781914228124

VERBATIM - The Fun of Making Theatre Seriously by Mark Wheeller

Author's Acknowledgements

Rachel Wheeller: The great woman behind the barely adequate man.
Mum and Dad (John and Jean Wheeller) for my stable home and supportive, creative background.

David Bowie for adding all manner of nuanced colour into my creative life.

Graham and Marie Salmon for their friendship, inspiration and trust in us (Epping Youth Theatre) as a fledgling company.
The writing and researching team from Epping Youth Theatre 1983 for the original production of **Race To Be Seen**: Matthew Allen; Lisa Beer; Zara Chapman; Frances Jackson; Barrie Sapsford. Assisted by: Dawn Baker; Bernadette Chapman; Laura Dove; Jan Farringdon; Nicki Harris; Jon Hicks; Rebecca Mallison; Paddy Mallison; Luke Nyman; Sara Record; Alis Stylianou; Tracy Tee & Steve Wyatt.

Barrie Sapsford for his incredible design ideas (especially the pixies) and his ongoing support in my work. Barrie has been a friend from 1984 when I met him in a 4th year in a drama class in St. John's School, Epping. This book could not haver happened without Barrie's understanding and support.

Matt Allen, Lisa Andraeae, Johnny Carrington, Bernadette Cleere, Robbie Currie, Rachael Dennett, Nigel Dyer, Jason Eames, Paul England, Ali Garner, Dave Goldring, Simon Guppy, Mike Mears and Claire New for their memories specifically written for this book.

All the sources of the plays I have written over the years for generous permission to use their testimony.

The performers from Marlwood School, 4R & Stantonbury/Epping/Oaklands/Oasis/Romsey School Community Youth Theatre.

Tony Key for inspiration, support and piano through my college years.

Roy Nevitt and Stantonbury Campus Theatre for introducing me to documentary theatre and a general theatre education.

Various newspaper reviewers/adjudicators who have allowed more people to hear about my plays.

Danny Sturrock for his unique support and friendship throughout my OYT years (starting with his involvement as an active member in **Happy Soap**) which has been barely touched upon in this book. Not only did he help with technical aspects of productions but he was also a powerhouse behind the Wheellerplays digital presence which continues into the future.

Cathy Hudson (Therwood School) and Tim Ford (Eastleigh Borough Youth Theatre) for their directorial ideas for the post-2000 versions of **Race To Be Seen**. Sophie Gorell Barnes and all at MBA Literary Agency for continued belief. Ape, StopWatch, Wizard and Tie It Up Theatre Companies for their professional productions of my TIE plays.

Dawn Boyfield, Evie Efthimiou and Lynda Taylor from dbda (later Zinc Publishing) who put their trust in Wheellerplays and set so many balls rolling.
George Spender for rescuing Wheellerplays in the 2020 pandemic and for working so closely with me to make my work available more widely than ever before. With thanks to Richard Kitchen, a former collaborator on **Kizzy** (a 1982 Wheellermusical), for his proofreading skills throughout this book and his sensitive editing skills applied to my Lincoln Cathedral School experiences.

Photographs/Images

Cover: Salamander Street

Page 8, 10, 15, 18, 19, 21, 22, 23, 25, 26, 28, 31 (bottom), 33 (bottom right), 36, 37, 38, 39, 44, 45, 47, 49 (middle), 50, 52, 55, 58, 59, 62 (top), 66, 67, 68, 70 (bottom), 71, 72, 73 (middle), 74, 76, 77, 78, 84, 86, 92, 93, 96, 98, 106, 111, 112, 113 (right), 141 (bottom), 142, 150 (bottom), 152, 154, 163 (bottom) 164, 166, 167, 171, 185, 187, 190, 195, 201, 203, 204, 206, 207, 208, 209, 213, 215, 234, 250, 251, 254, 255, 256, 257, 259, 261, 263, 290. **Mark Wheeller's personal collection**

Page 9, 12, 13, 14, 16, 34, 45, 47, 48, 51, 53, 70 (middle), 82, 85, 97, 104, 109, 111/112, 113 (top), 116, 117, 1118, 119 (bottom), 120, 121, 122, 124, 127, 131, 132, 133, 135, 139, 143, 144, 151, 155, 157, 158, 159, 161, 163 (middle), 165, 175, 181, 182 (top), 183, 186, 196, 197, 198, 200, 207 (top), 209, 224, 233, 239 (middle), 265, 271, 276, 279. **Barrie Sapsford**

Page 11: Steve Wood (Express) (Public domain)
Page 17: Visit Lincoln (Public domain)
Page 7, 32, 41, 179: Shutterstock (Licensed)
Page 24, 27: Dave Goldring
Page 29, 31, 33, 35, 40, 43, 65, 146, 170, 173: Everypixel (Licensed)
Page 49 (top): Londontopia.net (Public domain)
Page 54: Epping Gazette
Page 61: Amazon (Public domain)
Page 64, 72, 150 (middle): Ebay (Public domain)
Page 69: dreamtime.com (Licensed)
Page 70 (Top): Steve Crisp
Page 119 realbuzz.com (Public domain)
Page 141 (right): Edinburgh Festival Fringe Twitter (Public domain)
Page 156: Southampton City Council (Public domain)
Page 239: Manchester Evening News (Public domain)

Page 149, 257 (top): Clipart (Licensed)
Page 45: Longman Group
Page 66: Harry and Maud Salmon
Page 81: West Essex Gazette.
Page 90, 91, 105, 108, 131, 155 (Quenchers/Punch images): John Rowley
Page 160: Brian Price
Page 163 (top): Steven Holloway
Page 163 & 176: poster designs - Chris Vaudin
Page 168, 169: Jason Eames personal collection.
Page 181 (middle), 239 (bottom), 243, 244, 259 Salamander Street
Page 182 (middle), RoSPA
Page 184: Ape Theatre Company Photographs by Derek Jones
Page 188: Martha Whittingham
Page 192, 193: Ali Garner personal collection 191
Page 206, 207 (bottom), 213, 236 : Dbda
Page 210, 216, 217, 220, : Danny Sturrock
Page 240: Dbda/OUP/Salamander Street.
Page 244: Samuel Ward Academy
Page 243: Pping Publishing (Hazel Howlett)/Sonia Oliver Photography
Page 246: Methuen drama (top left)
Page 246 & 254/256 (bottom), 263 & 290: Chris Webb photography.
Page 246: Daniel Spargo-Mabbs Foundation (image of Daniel)
Page 247 & 254: Pping Publications (Helen Green illustration)
Page 247 (bottom): Alison Clarke
Page 248, 257: Salamander Street
Page 256: Barrie Sapsford & Bleu Wheeller
Page 258: Tie It Up Theatre Company
Page 264: Courtney Bryant @mashdesignstudio

Note: Every effort has been made to acknowledge and credit the originators and copyright holders of the images used within this book.

VERBATIM - The Fun of Making Theatre Seriously by Mark Wheeller

Content

7:	Chapter 1:	Expertise ? Ha ha ha
49:	Chapter 2:	Seeing Beyond The Blackout
62:	Chapter 3:	Meeting My Storybook Man
70:	Chapter 4:	Developing The Script
89:	Chapter 5:	Page To Stage
113:	Chapter 6:	At Last… Performances… And Reviews!
144:	Chapter 7:	EYT Race To The Fringe
156:	Chapter 8:	Race At Oaklands
170:	Chapter 9:	The Graham/Race Legacy
195:	Chapter 10:	Special Friends
204:	Chapter 11:	A New Millennium - A New Play
207:	Chapter 12:	Therfield School - Where The Stars Aligned!
211:	Chapter 13:	OYT 2008 Graham Production
225:	Chapter 14:	OYT 2008 Competitive Festival Performances
239:	Chapter 15:	Legacy and The Fun Of Being a Serious Playwright
257:	Afterword:	Race To Be Seen (2021 edit)
260:	Appendix 1:	School Report - From my Head of House 50 years on
262:	Appendix 2:	Magic Moments by Johnny Carrington
265:	Appendix 3:	Director's Commentary - Race To Be Seen 1984 Epping Youth Theatre (VHS)
271:	Appendix 4:	Director's Commentary - Race To Be Seen 1987 Oaklands Youth Theatre (VHS)
276:	Appendix 5:	Writer's Commentary - Graham - World's Fastest Blind Runner 2000 Eastleigh Borough Youth Theatre performance (VHS)
279:	Appendix 6:	Director's Commentary - Graham - World's Fastest Blind Runner: OYT at the AETF Final 2008 - Thameside Theatre.
287:	Appendix 7:	Where Are They Now? What happened to the contributors?

VERBATIM - The Fun of Making Theatre Seriously by Mark Wheeller

Chapter 1: Expertise? Ha ha ha!

When I introduce myself to groups of young people I often say:

'I am a playwright who has had some success but I am actually a failed rock star. I wanted to be Ziggy Stardust.'

I've realised in writing this book, it's actually wider than that.

I'm a failed celebrity. An astronaut, a footballer and then a rock star. I failed but my determined quest to become successful inadvertently led me to become a playwright, despite having rarely seen any plays!

My creative and artistic background was in music.

> "You can't connect the dots looking forward; you can only connect them looking backwards. So, you have to trust that the dots will somehow connect in your future.
>
> You have to trust in something — your gut, destiny, life, karma, whatever.
>
> This approach has never let me down, and it has made all the difference in my life."
>
> Steve Jobs
> Stanford Commencement Address (June 12, 2005)

Inspiration

I cite my main inspirations as my dad, David Bowie, Tony Key and Roy Nevitt. I imagine you may only know of one of them. Sorry to Brecht and all those others who probably should be a playwright's influences (I only heard about them as I progressed through my career) though I know they would have been an influence on Roy.

My dad was a choirmaster, organist and music teacher. I was a choirboy (in his choir) and classical music was all around me as a child.

At the age of nine I was packed off to boarding school to become a chorister at Lincoln Cathedral (more on this later). We sang every day (and three times on a Sunday) in services and practiced every morning for an hour, apart from Wednesday.

VERBATIM - The Fun of Making Theatre Seriously by Mark Wheeller

Discipline

The discipline of being in a professional choir with responsibilities to produce quality every time we performed has left its mark (with a small m).

I have always been driven by passion. My passion at Lincoln was football.

I was good.

I thought I was the best!

I wanted Lincoln City to see me and thought, if they did, they would have no hesitation in signing me.

One day, we played a match in a school next to Sincil Bank (the Lincoln City Stadium). I was convinced there'd be a scout there. I was in goal. We lost 12-2. No one approached me at the end of the match but...

...I did get the man of the match award. Yes I'm serious, I was told, if it wasn't for my goalkeeping skills we would have lost 24-2!

Me with my prized Footballer of the Year award from the Cathedral School 1971.

VERBATIM - The Fun of Making Theatre Seriously by Mark Wheeller

Motivating Passion

I lived for break times where I organised a termly league between two teams. It gave our break and lunch-time matches meaning. I always like to create a motivation... a reason for doing things better and with more enthusiasm.

Everyone shared my passion. My league mattered. The context I created made it matter to us... much more than the cathedral choir!

Entertaining Myself

As an only child at home in the school holidays, in a neighbourhood where, because I was at boarding school and my parents had moved, I knew no one. I remember conducting interviews with myself playing both interviewer and interviewee.

Initially, the 10-year-old interviewee me was in my back garden, pretending to be a (famous) footballer, proudly reviewing goals I'd scored in a grandiose FA Cup Final at Wembley. Ha ha, even I didn't imagine myself as a World Cup Finalist!

I played Subbuteo football (google it if you're not of a certain age) on my bedroom floor and created extensive leagues which I kept up to date religiously. I commentated on all my matches (with me being both teams) and recorded some on our reel-to-reel tape recorder.

As I approached my teens I started to two-time football and eventually embarked on a serious and lasting affair with pop music. Football was relegated.

VERBATIM - The Fun of Making Theatre Seriously by Mark Wheeller

When my parents bought a stereo radiogram cabinet for our front room they passed their smaller Dansette-style record player on to me.

Suddenly, I had independence in my music choices.

At first I played brightly coloured singles by Pinky and Perky but, these soon became black 45rpm singles with MUCH more interesting music such as Middle of the Road, Slade, Sweet, T Rex and then... David Bowie.

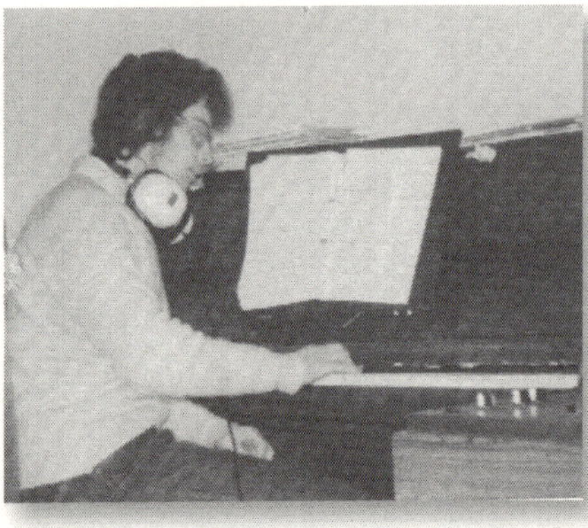

This new passion inspired me to write my own songs.

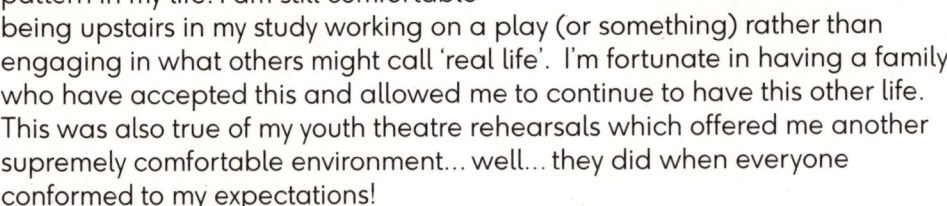

I had been having piano lessons and, although I hated any form of practice for my long-suffering teacher Mrs Heaney, the piano became my companion at home. I spent long hours in my dad's office at his piano writing hundreds of songs obsessively.

I am aware of this obsession becoming a pattern in my life. I am still comfortable being upstairs in my study working on a play (or something) rather than engaging in what others might call 'real life'. I'm fortunate in having a family who have accepted this and allowed me to continue to have this other life. This was also true of my youth theatre rehearsals which offered me another supremely comfortable environment... well... they did when everyone conformed to my expectations!

I continued to interview myself in my teens as a much loved songwriter, talking about my early songs that in reality no one had heard. Playing them in this fictional interview setting, and recording them on the trusty reel-to-reel tape recorder gave them a purpose for me... albeit a make-believe one.[1]

Sadly (for me) these tapes (and the commentaries) were binned by my parents, unaware of what a treasure trove of my early voice this would have been.

I remember doing these commentaries and interviews privately and was embarrassed if my parents caught me at it. I could have been up to far worse things!

---

[1] I have recently started to upload performances of some of my songs onto my YouTube Channel... I shan't be doing football commentaries though!

VERBATIM - The Fun of Making Theatre Seriously by Mark Wheeller

Introducing - The Magic Of Theatre

In the 4th year (Year 10) June 1973 I experienced what I refer to as the 'magic of theatre' for the first time as David Bowie/Ziggy Stardust appeared on stage before my eyes. People of my age were all around me screaming and fainting. I realise now this was hysteria but at the time it seemed like a mystical spell.

I needed no encouragement to suspend my disbelief and, without understanding the process, Bowie became 'Ziggy.' Something blatantly not true became 'real'. I wanted to conjure this magic.

Bowie had created a consciously faked rock star. He generated Ziggy's importance by hyping him. Before he (or Ziggy) was famous he employed bodyguards to escort him (or was it Ziggy?) to and from concerts, interviews etc.

Making something seem more important than it actually was, in the light of this, offered even more exciting possibilities.

The theatricality of Bowie's presentation was extraordinary and utterly absorbed my teenage incredulity. I was determined to see a flaw in this mirage, just as I'd always enjoyed trying to see the strings on the Bill and Ben puppets, or the wrist of Sooty's hidden puppeteer. I wanted to see a speck of humanity through Bowie's painted idol. I was obsessed by the possibility of seeing behind the image... seeing the real David Jones. I never could, and so the spell was cast.

Attributing the magic incorrectly to the music, rather than to the words, image or theatre that contextualised it, I decided I would become a tunesmith. It was a long time before I understood how important the words, images and context were to my being drawn into the spell.

The theatre I have been involved with throughout my adult life mirrors what Bowie did with Ziggy. There is limited trickery. My plays make no pretence at being real; they are clearly plays. The mind of the audience, I have realised, is better at achieving an illusion than any flash effects I might find to employ.

11

VERBATIM - The Fun of Making Theatre Seriously by Mark Wheeller

That is not to say my (or Bowie's) work is not theatrical... it is.

In my early teens, at around the same time as David Bowie came into my orbit, I became involved in the Thornbury Amateur Operatic Society. I did this to please my dad who was the Musical Director but I soon discovered I LOVED it and it introduced me to a theatrical world I could step into in a very real sense.

I started off as a call boy... (not what you're thinking), whose role was to run between the dressing rooms and the stage to check people arrived on stage in time. I took it very seriously and loved the variety of characters who filled the dressing rooms with their sometimes eccentric personalities.

That role lasted for one production, after which I became a singer, actor and dancer (in that order) for the next four years! It became the part of my week I most looked forward to and offered me some limited knowledge of (musical) theatre.

I was now quite happy to become Andrew Lloyd Webber (or Lionel Bart) if Ziggy Stardust didn't work out. I had a Plan B!

VERBATIM - The Fun of Making Theatre Seriously by Mark Wheeller

Collaborations - For Serious Fun

In the 5th year (Year 11) at school I befriended a new boy, Simon Guppy, who had moved from Basingstoke and seemed equally enthused by all things music. Somehow I talked him into becoming my lyricist.

This served two purposes.

It saved me from having to do the hard work of writing lyrics...

...and...

...suddenly I had an audience... a motivation to impress someone... and keep him on board.

Writing songs became even more of an addiction.

We moved fast (after only two collaborations) from individual songs to rock operas.

> In 1973, my parents relocated from Basingstoke (Hampshire), to Thornbury (near Bristol). I was 15, and I had to change schools. I ended up at Marlwood School, in Alveston.
> I can't say I enjoyed my time at Marlwood. I never felt I fitted in and I just wanted my days to be over, and to move on with my life.
> However, one person who I befriended (or who befriended me - I can't remember which way round) was Mark. We were in the same class for at least one subject.
> What struck me immediately was Mark's infectious love of David Bowie. Although I knew of Bowie, Mark's enthusiasm spread to me. Before long, I wasn't just listening to Bowie records, but also Lou Reed and Mick Ronson.
> On stage early in 1974, Mark asked [...] tried songwriting. I'[...] give it a go. M[...]

cont...

VERBATIM - The Fun of Making Theatre Seriously by Mark Wheeller

At some stage early in 1974, Mark asked me if I had ever tried song-writing. I hadn't, but I was willing to give it a go. My task was to write the lyrics, and Mark would set them to music. I can't remember much about those early attempts, although Mark showed me some of my handwritten manuscripts, when we met up a couple of years ago.

After a while, Mark revealed he wanted to write a rock opera based on George Orwell's 1984. I went off to Thornbury Library, borrowed a copy of 1984, and started to read it. And, while I was supposed to be revising for my O' Levels, I was writing lyrics for our version of 1984.[2]

I left Marlwood in the summer of 1974, moving on to the local technical college. Mark and I stayed in touch for a year or so, while he was still in Thornbury, and I remember going to see Eed Sud and the band rehearsing our songs once or twice.

Despite not liking Marlwood, I remember enjoying my work with Mark on these songs.

Simon Guppy

Two things on this:
- Our version of 1984 had 27 songs in it... quite a mammoth effort in three months. I also added a booklet of notes on performance.
- Simon refers to Eed Sud. This needs some explanation.

David Bowie was Ziggy Stardust.
Mark Wheeller was Eed Sud.

---

[2] The Orwell estate famously denied David Bowie permission to adapt 1984 so he turned his ongoing songs into a very successful album **Diamond Dogs.** We completed ours without permission but no one, apart from us, ever heard it, until in 2021 I put a few extracts on my Mark Wheeller YouTube channel.

VERBATIM - The Fun of Making Theatre Seriously by Mark Wheeller

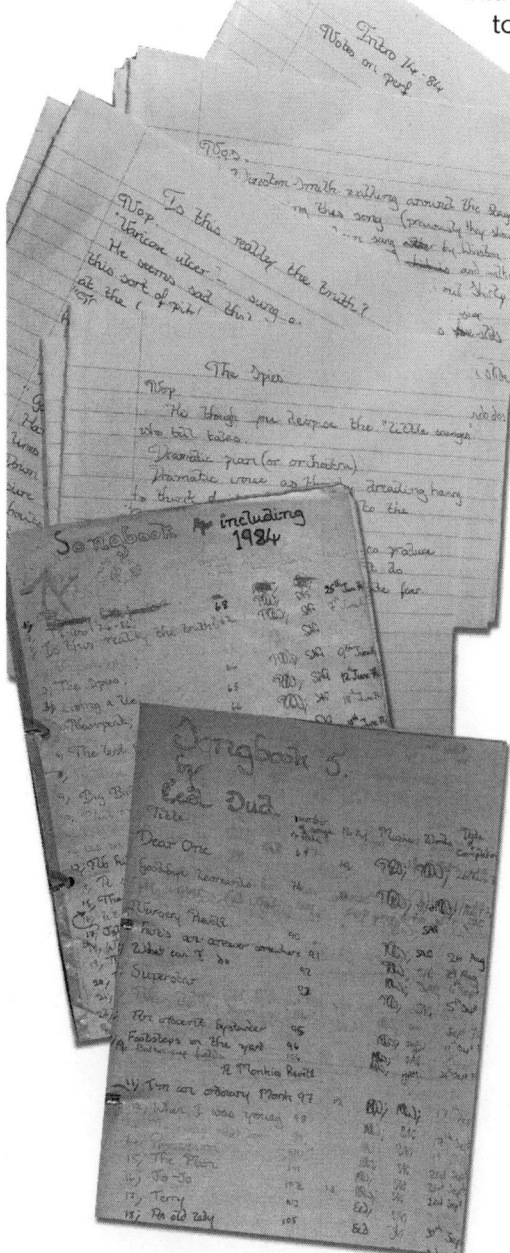

Initially my (fictional) backing band were to be called **The Eclipse** but later I rebranded them as **The Luminous Earwigs,** a name I'm still very proud of, despite appropriating it from the fabled **Spiders From Mars.**[3]

There was a band at school (**Stonewall**, a pun on 'rock', long before it referenced something more political) who needed a vocalist. I could sing so, we struck a deal. I would sing, as Eed Sud, if they played two of my songs in their set.

The arrangement lasted for only 2 gigs as it became abundantly clear: no one wanted to hear my (and Simon's) songs. (My impression was that the audience was no more interested in **Stonewall**'s cover choices either.)

Simon and I had, by this time, written another rock opera about a monk who got a nun pregnant (two of these songs were performed by **Stonewall**) and then Simon suddenly stopped providing lyrics. I can't think why![4]

---

[3] The original idea was that Eed Sud would appear as some kind of superstar releasing the Luminous Earwigs from their bubbles (soap suds) so that they could play. It was all fantasy. We had no way of doing this and no budget. On the plus side, it did show some imagination on my part.

[4] I was flattered to receive an unsolicited Facebook message from an old Marlwoodian (the brother of one of the Stonewall band) saying:
"My brother can remember the lyrics of your **Ordinary Monk** song and I can remember the whole of the first bit too. It made an impression on us 50 years ago!"
So nice to know it has been remembered by more than just me and Simon. You can hear it too on my YouTube Channel!

VERBATIM - The Fun of Making Theatre Seriously by Mark Wheeller

I befriended Kevin Rimell (pseudonym Dave Kent). At my instigation we atempted to write a rock opera called:

The High Road To Stardom of Eed Sud.

I can see that after 2 months of work and 11 songs, we gave up. It says 'Project cancelled'.

I continued to write songs with Kevin and occasionally my then girlfriend, Jane Falconer.

I progressed into the sixth form and assembled a group of students from our 'House' (Harwood) to organise something to bid farewell to Mr Cooke, a favourite teacher and our head of house who, back in the 4th year when he was promoted to this role, had shown belief in me. He had to see all the "naughty" pupils under his pastoral care. I was one. I anticipated a standard rollicking. Instead, he simply said:

'I don't believe this is the real you.'

I wanted to rise to his expectations of the real me so I changed... just like that! It was basically pretty much that simple with a little added nuance!

Mmm... perhaps now is the moment to delve into the murky world of my own schooldays and offer the context for this 'naughty boy' that Mr Cooke had been asked to talk to. Somehow, going into this detail felt wrong on the opening page of the book, when I initially mentioned boarding school. My schoolboy experiences proved to become the foundations of how my philosophy as a teacher developed and also, arguably, sheds some light on the main themes and content of so many of my plays...

If I were doing this as a drama presentation in school I would ask everyone to do a wobbly-bodies thing[5] to denote a flashback. If you are able to see these words as a film in your mind, this next section should be shown in black and white.

---

5 A crass representation (for comic effect generally) of the way in which films at one point showed a scene going into a flashback by making the screen wave down the screen and then straighten out.

VERBATIM - The Fun of Making Theatre Seriously by Mark Wheeller

Cue narrator...

My life has been blessed and I have had little to trouble what I consider to have been a charmed life. If creativity derives from difficult experiences, I've had little to inspire me aside from what follows. I'm going to write about that in detail as it explains how some aspects of my education became a barrier which I would have to overcome. It may also explain why I have chosen to tell people's real life stories in my work.

I was forced to live apart from my parents from the age of nine (1967), when I was packed off to boarding school. My parents did this for my benefit, although my dad's background of being denied (by his parents) the opportunity to pursue a musical education when he left school also came into it.

I was touted around various cathedrals doing voice trials to become a cathedral chorister. I remember this as an exciting experience which led to enjoyable overnight hotel stays with my mum and dad in various beautiful English cities. I failed to get into the first few choirs but was never made to feel any sense of failure by my parents.

At Lincoln however, I was awarded a vocal scholarship. This meant my school fees would be partially paid by the cathedral.

Nevertheless, my parents would still make financial sacrifices for me to benefit from the private education they valued, alongside what they imagined would be a solid musical education.

I remember them being very happy but I was non-plussed. I was content at (my state Junior) school but I made the most of the fuss around the scholarship with congratulations coming my way from everywhere. Friends and relatives seemed incredibly impressed. It particularly pleased my parents and that felt wonderful.

I didn't understand the implications AT ALL!

My trunk (to take all my stuff to school) was bought (also exciting) and the following September I didn't go back to my Junior School with my friends. Instead, I had a few extra days' holiday... amazing!

VERBATIM - The Fun of Making Theatre Seriously by Mark Wheeller

Soon we were in Lincoln and I was abandoned. That's how it felt. The separation from my parents played on my mind: what if they died? I would be left alone forever. I was beside myself with confusion and upset.

My first two years at Lincoln Cathedral School were blighted by two people who left me with a deep mistrust of formal relationships and 'authority'.

One was a matron who lacked all empathy and seemed to me hostile and cruel, so different from my loving and protective mother. I was so scared of her that I wet the bed and she berated me front of everyone else in my dormitory.

The other was Roy Griffiths, the deputy Headmaster and our Housemaster. He was 'Mr' Griffiths to me of course but I use his first name now to defuse his authority, for reasons that follow. He was exactly the kind of teacher I would not wish to become.

Bare bottom caning was standard practice in schools back then but Roy literally ruled by the rod: we were caned so frequently it became the norm. Again, how different from my humane father. Imagine this adding to the feelings of isolation I was plunged into.

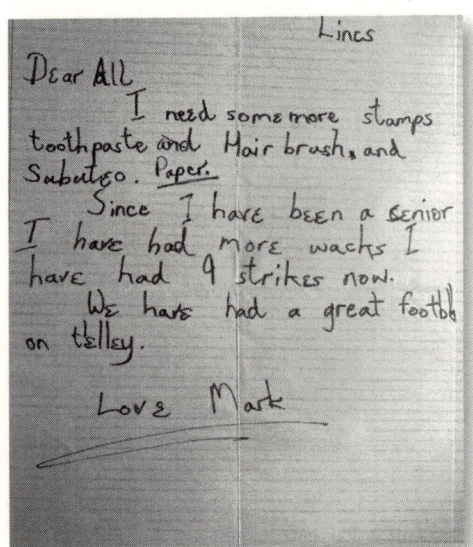

It's interesting to see my bland acceptance of the caning in this (very demanding) weekly letter home. What must my parents have thought?

It's galling now to think that Roy may have got some private pleasure out of our punishments, for he was also a paedophile... and I was one of his victims, although far less so than some.

One of the privileges he granted to his favourites was to watch TV in his room. One night all the seats were taken and he invited me to sit on his lap.

VERBATIM - The Fun of Making Theatre Seriously by Mark Wheeller

I felt proud to be 'chosen' by this man who was normally so scary.

At some point I became aware he was stroking my groin through my pyjamas. I thought he was just tickling me, but my body reacted in a way that to an innocent ten-year-old meant only one thing.

'I need to go to the toilet,' I said.

When I returned I sat on the floor, ashamed that I had let us both down. He was being so nice to me! He undoubtedly realised that his boys wanted his approval so much, and he exploited it to abuse not only us but his position of authority.

Later, when other boys reported him, the penny dropped and I spoke up too. And we were listened to, which for the late 1960s was impressive.
But, appallingly, the cathedral authorities covered it up and Roy kept his position until the end of term.

Had I reported the abuse to my parents they simply wouldn't have believed me. Roy was a senior teacher in the school, a Christian and sang in the cathedral choir. The perfect cover. As a three-year-old I had told my parents I could see pixies in our garden: they would have thought the existence of pixies substantially more likely than him doing any of this.

So I didn't tell them. I felt guilty about the financial sacrifices they had made for me and they were so proud of me. I couldn't smash the illusion. They, as much as me, had been deeply let down.

I have included this photo because the barrister acting on my behalf in the 2018 court case against Roy Griffiths (historical abuse) said she wanted the judge to see me as a little boy, rather than the man who was to appear in the witness stand. It is important to show how little and innocent I was at the time Roy Griffiths was abusing children at our school. This photo was taken by my mum when I first tried on my new uniform. For my parents it represented pride in what I had achieved in getting a singing scholarship. For me looking back, it represents a dark secret that has finally been brought to the surface. The court case and sentencing of Roy Griffiths brought some closure for me but I still feel my parents had their efforts to improve my life thwarted by people in authority who they would have trusted above almost anyone else in society.

VERBATIM - The Fun of Making Theatre Seriously by Mark Wheeller

However, in 2015 I was given a good reason to tell them the whole truth.

The Lincolnshire police contacted me. I said immediately: 'I know exactly why you are calling me. You want me to talk about Roy Griffiths.'

There was media coverage of the case in the wake of the Jimmy Savile revelations. It was tough for my parents to face what had really happened. They found it difficult to accept that I'd never talked about it but they understood why. It's sad they became so disillusioned with those they had put so much faith in.

Nearly 40 years after these events, Roy was jailed. I was not a victim to the same extent I now know others were and I would have appreciated a 'sorry' from him more than anything else. That said, the timing of his 'guilty' plea (only an hour before the trial was due to start) fails to suggest much regret for, or understanding of, the severity of the situation he had trapped us in.

I recently watched a programme about the unravelling of the historical abuse scandal in the F.A. and one of the victims commented: 'Doing something you find deeply meaningful in your life is good for you.'

In this respect I believe my theatre work has helped me to acquire strong feelings of self-worth as well as helping others. The relationship between parents and children is a key feature of many of my plays, though always in a more extreme and dire situation than my own. Have I been dealing with my own story by living out their experiences second hand? It's an interesting thought.

The feeling of inferiority and inability to achieve academically lived with me for many years after Lincoln and I still have few formal qualifications. My approach to teaching is undoubtedly influenced by my own experiences as a student.

My unhappiness in those first two years had halted my progress. I was made to repeat a year, which did my confidence and motivation no good at all - why hadn't they just moved me back earlier? I found solace in football and making people laugh. I became the class clown - and I certainly achieved top grades at that!

Tony Defries (David Bowie's former manager) said Bowie used his music to create a way for people to love him following his loveless childhood. My boarding school life in those years was somewhat comparable and I wonder whether the accolades I receive from my theatre work are my own opportunity to gain others' love and/or approval. I might be similar to Bowie after all!

But back to the '70s. At thirteen, when most of my peers went off to the next stage of their private education, I was moved to the local state school which was about to become a new-fangled 'comprehensive school'.

If you want to avoid being bullied, my advice is that this is how you should avoid appearing!

I had an awkward transition in the 3rd year (13 years old) as I moved from a boarding school to a state school where I was considered posh. This was identified nowhere more clearly than in my 'snobby' accent. This alternative background gave anyone of that inclination a reason to bully me. I wasn't good at fighting back, which made me an easy target. I now had the task of avoiding peer beatings which, although different, were just as terrifying as teacher ones. I also discovered that I had to remain silent about these too.

I tried to speak to my tutor about them once and was given the 'man up' type response. This unsympathetic man became another on my tick list of teachers I didn't want to become.

Once again, I called on my class clown role to rescue me, affecting a further year of any worthwhile educational progress. My silly behaviour was simply a means of coping with bullying. When I did stupid or funny things people laughed and seemed to like me more. The consequence, which I was certainly prepared to live with, was that I became irksome to teachers... but more popular with my peers.

At the end of my third year (my first year at Marlwood - Year 9 in modern terminology) the school was re-organised and a pastoral house system introduced along with mixed ability tutor groups. Both of these, in their different ways, saved me.

VERBATIM - The Fun of Making Theatre Seriously by Mark Wheeller

In the mixed ability tutor groups I mixed with a wider range of pupils... not just the lower ability range (within a fading Grammar School setting) that I had been placed alongside in my late 13+ admission. This had a huge impact on my self-esteem and affected my aspirations instantly. Prior to this, I felt almost unworthy of associating with "A" formers as they were known.

It was at the end of my first year there (3rd year/ Year 9) that I had the 'naughty boy' meeting I mentioned previously, with Mr Cooke, our freshly minted pastoral head of house.

The following two years were so much happier. The bullies mysteriously dissolved as we moved into this new comprehensive school way of organising our lives.

I worked(ish) but was put in the (lower ability) CSE classes for most subjects as opposed to the O level ones. Most teachers expectations of me were low and academic work didn't capture my imagination. Drama wasn't offered as an exam subject so my only exposure to that was what I was doing with my dad at the Thornbury Operatic Society.

Myself aged 17 (third from the left) with my first speaking/solo singing part in The Pajama Game with TAOS

VERBATIM - The Fun of Making Theatre Seriously by Mark Wheeller

Exam-wise I did ok, passing enough exams to allow me into the sixth form... just.

Towards the end of my lower sixth year it was announced that Mr Cooke was leaving for a promotion. I remember being very pleased for him but it was potentially devastating for me. Mr Cooke was THE teacher I really connected with.

I suggested to some friends that we put on a lunch time entertainment to thank him. I wrote some songs with Kevin and asked Jane (an original 'A' former so obviously clever enough) to write a script around them. I presumed this would be way too difficult for me with my low grade in CSE English Literature!
Hardened Criminals was born.

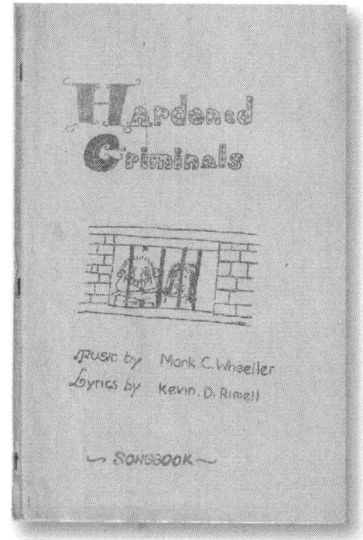

To get this musical performed I had to organise and direct it. I discovered I enjoyed directing and, importantly, had a talent for bringing people together and making them feel capable enough to have a go at moving about on stage in a vaguely appropriate manner given the scene they were in.

This served to fulfil another motive: to get my songs performed and heard! It was such a fortuitous merging of ideas to create an opportunity. The cast had to learn the songs and then, I am pleased to report, came to like them more often than not! I also discovered that, in the context of these performances, the audience actually listened more attentively rather than carrying on conversations which had happened in **Stonewall** gigs.

I also organised a **This Is Your Life** assembly for Mr Cooke's last day in school. I arranged this with his wife in complete secrecy. I came to know her as I had been their babysitter. He had absolutely no idea about it. All he knew was that I was doing an assembly at the end of the term. Then his wife, children and a few friends turned up after having been hidden somewhere in school! It was wonderful!

Inspired by the success of **Hardened Criminals** I decided to mount follow-up projects, on a larger scale, involving more pupils. I was appointed House Captain, largely on the basis of my theatre work and awaited the news as to who would be appointed in place of Mr Cooke.

VERBATIM - The Fun of Making Theatre Seriously by Mark Wheeller

Then came the news that Mr Goldring had secured the role. He was an established teacher at the school who had been on a sabbatical for a year and returned to take on a pastoral head responsibility.

I wasn't optimistic.

Nor was anyone else.

He was a biology teacher and, to my knowledge, had no specific interest in theatre or music. He was a scientist and serious. I knew he had published science materials which were used in schools. This impressed me and was something to aspire to but it had academic connotations... and that was very different to what I felt I was about.

He was also into athletics and had trained a fellow pupil (Nigel Gossedge) to international standard. He had the reputation as a hard task-master.

Everyone was saying how he wouldn't like me and that:

'He doesn't suffer fools.'

I was a fool... and he'd remember that because, despite never having taught me (thank heavens!), his wife worked with my dad at nearby Filton High School. They did a car share. My name would have rung a bell whenever it came up... and it would have done.

What would he think of me and my crazy ideas of putting on original Harwood House musicals?

I was called to a meeting with him and approached it with due trepidation. As soon as I arrived, he did something that was so surprising and so significant... especially as he had a reputation of being an austere figure.

He said this, pretty much as his opening gambit:

'If we're going to work together Mark, as we need to, I don't want to be Mr Goldring. You should call me Dave.'

I was staggered. I admit, at first, it felt a bit awkward.

VERBATIM - The Fun of Making Theatre Seriously by Mark Wheeller

This was so different to what anyone else had suggested about him.

It disarmed me and came to play such an important part in the my teaching career, where I was always Mark, rather than 'Sir' (I haven't been knighted... yet) or Mr Wheeller. The use of first names symbolised so much. An egalitarian start and a feeling of a truly authentic relationship. I didn't put all this together in my mind at the time but deep down I understood it and liked whatever it was that I felt it represented. It was seismic. It got us off to a perfect start.

I owe so much to Dave's trust in my work. He let me get on with it but was always there if there were a problem... booking rooms or other organisational aspects. We could all see he respected what we were doing and he was also clearly excited by it.

It seems bizarre to think that without a drama teacher we just put musicals on so, I checked with a friend of mine from school who was also involved and I'm right; it makes us look supremely resourceful but, to be honest, we were having fun... and carving out our respective careers without knowing it!

> I first started to get to know Mark at Thornbury Operatic Society; I helped out with the lighting. In 1972 the school had moved to new premises and boasted a new drama hall with well-equipped stage lighting. However, none of the teachers seemed to have taken responsibility for the lighting so, when the parent/teacher association wanted some lighting for their first event in the new School Hall, they asked me to help because of my Operatic Society experience. Consequently, I ended up being the lighting person in Mark's team when he put on his productions.
> Looking back, I have little recollection of teachers being involved. My memory is of Mark and his team, including myself, identifying what needed to be done and getting on and doing it. We needed additional stage lighting equipment so we organised lunch-time discos which kids paid to attend in order to raise money. The lighting circuits had not been wired correctly so I (and some friends) rewired them. It is like remembering an Enid Blyton "Famous Five" story where the children got on with the adventure in hand with adults as some background characters who just provided tea to eat at the end of the day. No teachers came into the lighting box in the whole time I was involved.
>
> My memories are of a very collaborative, organic way of working. I have no memories of long detailed discussions of what needed to be done. I would be given a script with some lighting ideas scribbled on and I would do what I could with the equipment that was available; getting on with the stuff that I was responsible for.
> I have been fortunate that I have been able to work in this way through much of my subsequent career, because that is how I had learnt to do things.[6]
> **Nigel Dyer**

Nigel and myself probably being interrupted planning a new production.

---

[6] Nigel spent 25 years in telecommunications research and development followed by 15 years in genetics research; continuing to work out how best to follow the vague direction given to him by the people he worked for.

VERBATIM - The Fun of Making Theatre Seriously by Mark Wheeller

In that final year of my sixth form, supported by Dave, I put on two major productions: **Snow White** and **Pierrot**. Different friends (Jane Falconer, Kevin Rimell, Nick Tranter and David Wrench) wrote the book and lyrics which I still considered to be beyond my meagre ability. These were bigger productions with a cast of over 50 in the final one. The sense of achievement in putting on **Snow White** is something I have tried to rekindle in all my subsequent work. It's never been possible to match that feeling but I have had many incredible close seconds.

Paper Bag Song (Snow White) and me wedging myself in as an Elvis style pop star - the advantages of being in control of the content.

Pierrot: Andy Falconer and Nick Tranter

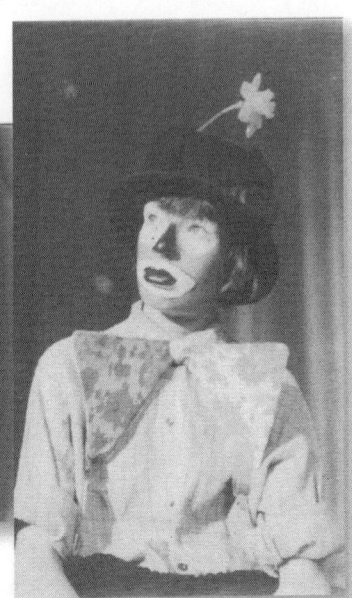

... and Tim Rowland.

VERBATIM - The Fun of Making Theatre Seriously by Mark Wheeller

I cannot remember any cross words between Dave and myself in that final joyous year. We spent many a happy hour just chatting informally. He offered for me a model of how an informal relationship between student and teacher can lead to the very best results with high expectations being a central part of that relationship.

Dave and I worked superbly throughout that year and he remains the only teacher I have remained in frequent contact with.[7]

These productions led to a sort of celebrity within the school which I (obviously) adored!

I also managed to secure my first piece of national coverage during this time which encouraged me enormously! I had written a song advertising the International Stores (a supermarket of the time) where I worked as a Saturday boy. I managed to wedge this into our **Snow White** production (Xmas 1975).

---

[7] I have included, in the Appendix section of this book, an account sent to me by Dave Goldring, who wanted to say his piece, and perhaps he sheds some light on how he as a teacher saw Mark Wheeller the pupil. It's a kind of school report... nearly 50 years on.

VERBATIM - The Fun of Making Theatre Seriously by Mark Wheeller

My store manager heard about this and informed the 'International News' (the store's national magazine) who did a feature. How easy was that?

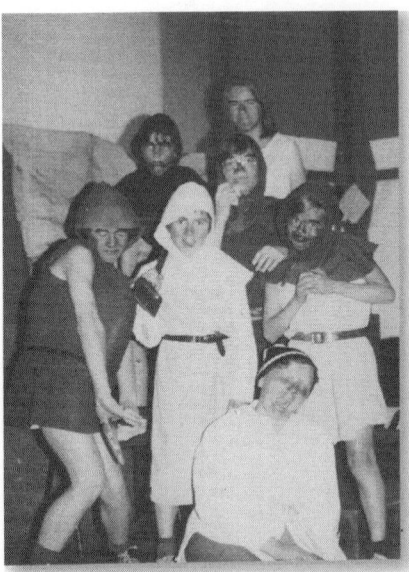

The seven dwarfs from my Harwood House Snow-White production

The Paper Bag Song

JUST BEFORE CHRISTMAS the boys of Harwood House, Marwood School, Alveston, near Thornbury, put on a pantomime 'Snow White and the Seven Dwarfs' in aid of the National Heart Foundation.

Mr David Goldring, head of Marwood House writes: 'We have a twelve-year-old first year boy in the National Heart Hospital, London, where he has undergone extensive major heart surgery and has now been in intensive care for two months.

'It is this association that has led us to support the Heart Foundation's Appeal. To date we have raised £55 from Snow White and a Revue just before Easter. We plan another show for July at which the entertainment will be extracts from our past shows and will include the Paper Bag Song'.

The Paper Bag Song was featured in the Snow White pantomime, sung by eighteen-year-old Mark Wheeller, who wrote the words and music, with backing from the Seven Dwarfs

'I got a little paper bag in a store today. It cost no money so I took it away. My little paper bag.

In the International Stores in Thornbury the bags that you get are really ... Better ... Oh, better than Lipton's better than the Co-op or the Great Yate Gateway.

CHORUS

Tell all the folks that we got nice bags, got nice prices, got nice people, we're The International Stores.'

I wedged in a few more songs for a variety of products into future productions, ranging from Colgate toothpaste to Johnson's Baby Powder in the hope of achieving more interest. Nothing more happened... but I was now aware: national coverage was possible. I thought I could be on the path to fame and fortune!

Reality soon kicked in and normal life resumed.

VERBATIM - The Fun of Making Theatre Seriously by Mark Wheeller

This back story is important and shows how I made my way into my theatre life through enthusiasm, not over theoretical or academic knowledge. Enthusiasm enabled me to achieve whatever it is that I am now deemed to have achieved.

The peak of this acclaim was an invitation to perform two songs (by David Bowie) as the guest vocalist for the legendary guitarist from Marlwood School, Andy Skirrow, who put a band together for an end of term event.

My performance of **Hang Onto Yourself** and **Ziggy Stardust** remain to this day a highlight of my life.

Of course, I appeared as Eed Sud (what must Andy have thought?) but I felt like

I WAS actually Ziggy Stardust!

... and...

... for that day (in my own mind), a proper celebrity!

Petrol was poured on my ambition to become super-famous.

I thought:

It's only a matter of time.

Is it odd to have these thoughts?

Are we all like that?

Oh no... I've just remembered... I should have come out of the wobbly-bodies flashback section a while... back... so... we'll do that now. Apologies.

We can also return to full colour images in the film in your mind... though they will be in the style of 1970s heavily pixelated images; 1976 to be precise.

VERBATIM - The Fun of Making Theatre Seriously by Mark Wheeller

Becoming a Teacher

I was destined to fail my A' Levels due, in part, to the exceptional commitment I'd given to the productions I'd organised. The other part was comparative disinterest in the subjects I had taken - Religious Knowledge (chosen purely because that was what Mr Cooke taught and I trusted I would be more focused) and History (I was infatuated by the teacher - Miss Ross - sadly she left after one term) but real life beckoned and I needed to formulate plans for my future.

Aside from being a rock star, I had wanted to be a teacher like my dad before me and had enjoyed (and been good at) my work experience in a Special School.

I felt I had a good idea how to be an effective teacher.

I had always internally assessed my teachers for the way they behaved towards me as a pupil.

My problem was....what subject could I teach?

Music seemed the only option because that was my passion...

... but... and it's an enormous **BUT** ...

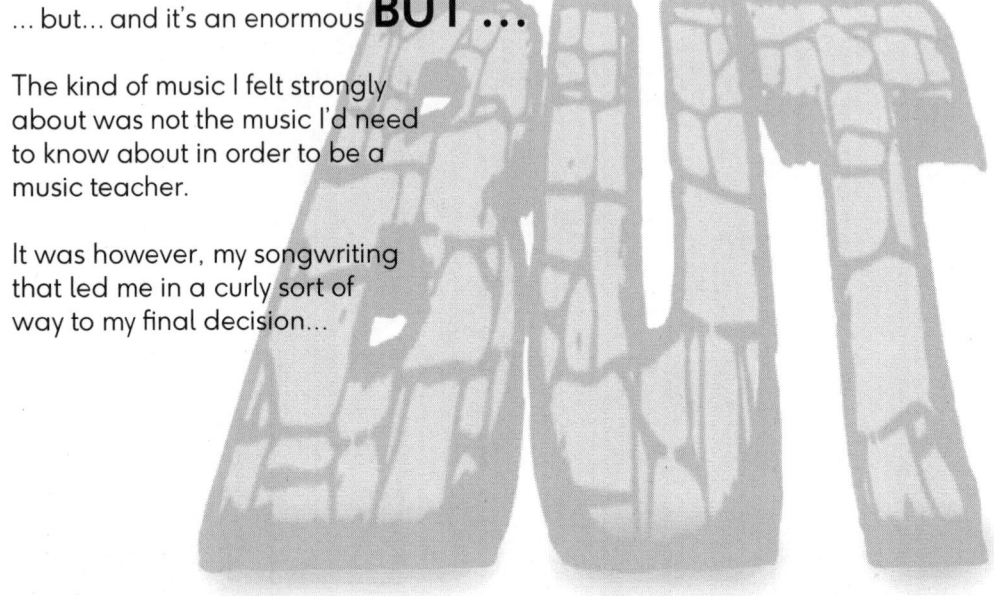

The kind of music I felt strongly about was not the music I'd need to know about in order to be a music teacher.

It was however, my songwriting that led me in a curly sort of way to my final decision...

VERBATIM - The Fun of Making Theatre Seriously by Mark Wheeller

The Curly Path to Become a Drama Teacher

I knew that to become a rock superstar I had to get my songs performed/heard. The easiest way to make this happen was to take control and mount productions featuring them.

Inadvertently, I was becoming a 'director' and that, surely, was part of what a drama teacher did... the other bit was, I thought, probably not that hard.

I duly ticked the drama teacher box, despite never having seen many plays (I can remember my parents taking me to see **Blithe Spirit** or **Time and the Conways** - whichever it was made so little impression) nor having read any books about theatre. I hadn't even had any drama lessons!

I signed up to train as a drama teacher at Goldsmiths' College!

You're probably asking yourself...

What has this got to do with verbatim?

So far... **NOTHING!**

I assure you, I am trying to tell this part as fast as possible... but what I must stress again is; I had very little experience of theatre.

The fact I made it up as I went along worried me for many years until I discovered that most people 'fake it' no matter how important they are... just look at the pandemic... or the Brexit so-called strategy! In many ways, not knowing anything about theatre but needing to make it forced me to invent my own approaches out of necessity.

A series of odd coincidences and lucky opportunities led me to make my own (verbatim) theatre.

VERBATIM - The Fun of Making Theatre Seriously by Mark Wheeller

The Curly Path To Verbatim

At Goldsmiths' I had to study Drama and Theatre as part of my course.

I didn't like much of what they offered me.

I was introduced to plays with no songs in them!

When we put on a production that included songs they asked an ex-(favourite) student of theirs to come in and write them. They missed a wonderful opportunity to totally win me over.

The one writer who did interest me was Harold Pinter. I really enjoyed the dialogue (and the narrative) of both **The Room** and **The Birthday Party** and could imagine them being very effective on stage.

Our studies focused on **The Birthday Party**, which I found intriguing.

I was fascinated by Pinter's attempt to achieve authentic dialogue.

For the first time I became aware of 'craft' in the construction of scripts.

I was so disappointed when I went to see a production of Pinter's latest (at that time) production, **Betrayal**, at the National Theatre. I found it inaccessible and not real at all![8]

My exposure to Pinter sowed two important seeds:

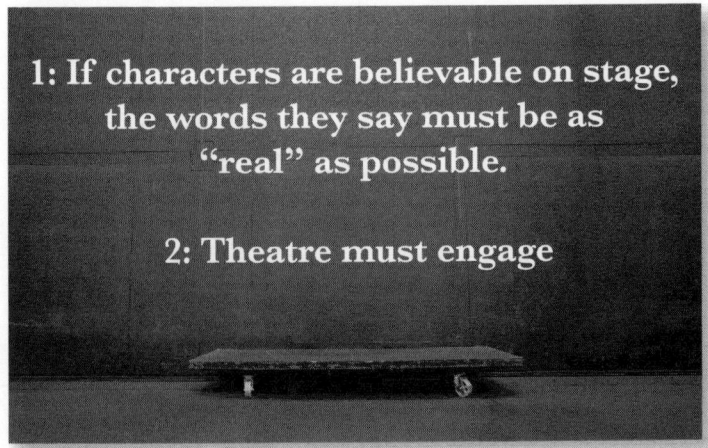

1: If characters are believable on stage, the words they say must be as "real" as possible.

2: Theatre must engage

---

[8] I saw a production of **Betrayal** at the Salisbury Playhouse recently and really appreciated it, especially the backwards telling of the story.

VERBATIM - The Fun of Making Theatre Seriously by Mark Wheeller

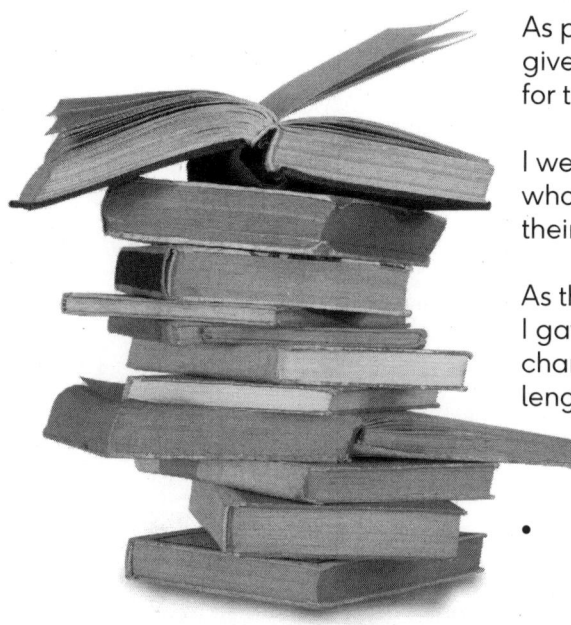

As part of my drama course, I was given the task of finding a short scene for two people, which I had to direct.

I went to our local library and spent a whole afternoon searching through their tired looking plays!

As the library was about to close, I gave up and took a play with two characters that was roughly the right length for our project. This frustrating afternoon taught me another crucial lesson.

- If I create my own play, I will save myself the bother and waste of time spent on this soul-destroying search.

My innate laziness generated a need in me to be creative!

My 'studies' at Goldsmiths' were quickly relegated to the background when I discovered that Tony Key, my Movement Education Lecturer who I saw for only an hour every week, ran a community theatre group in nearby Lewisham.

Tony had already impressed me. He was immensely likeable and hilarious. I was far from a natural in terms of movement and had dreaded the first session but came out of it inspired. Tony made us all feel able. I remember the buzz after his classes.

Amusingly, this dreadful photograph was taken on the morning I met Tony Key. I know that because I was late for my very first lecture with him, as I woke up late and also had to get to a photo booth to sort this for my student union card.

It was so different from the more aloof/academic approach of the staff in the drama department who made me feel like I was not really the sort of student they wanted in their class.

33

VERBATIM - The Fun of Making Theatre Seriously by Mark Wheeller

The posters for Tony's Christmas production on his Dance Studio walls looked impressive and captured my attention.

I created an opportunity to chat to him after a lecture one day and unsubtly let him know I wrote songs. Without blinking, he invited me to a production meeting and there he introduced me as the songwriter for his next project, **Blackout**, a tribute for the Queen's Jubilee of 1977.

Amazing!

Such trust. Tony knew little about me... other than I was a bit cheeky to speak to him about my songwriting. For him that was enough.

He expected me to rise to his expectations... and I did!

Nick Mason, one of the parents of a 4R member at that first meeting offered to become my lyricist. Nick was the Sports Editor for the Sunday Times. A proper wordsmith (who was a lot further on in his life) was choosing to work with me as my lyricist!

Tony bought a piano so I could write the songs in his house and gave me a door key.

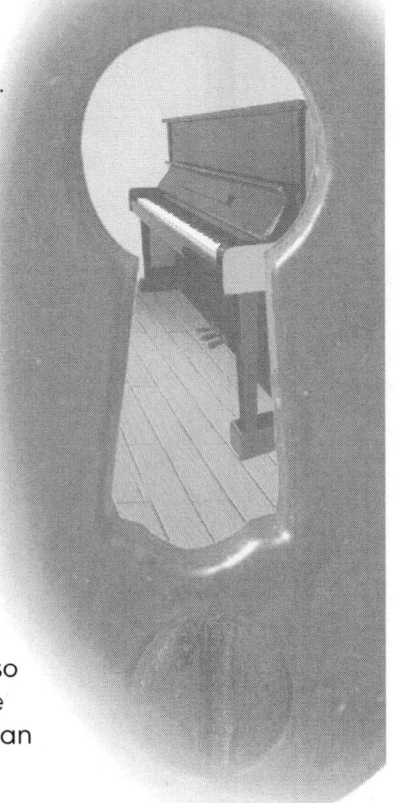

Unbelievable!!

I worked on five productions over the three years I was at Goldsmiths'.

Friends from the outstanding Goldsmiths' music department supported me voluntarily. Andy Fox arranged all of my songs for a small orchestra (his friends, all aspiring professional musicians) so my songs were fully orchestrated when they were performed at the Lewisham Concert Hall. It was an incredible and very special experience.

As at school, this extra-curricular work became far more relevant to me and my future than the formal curriculum I was meant to be studying.

Tony, like David Bowie, hyped his work, making it seem more important.

VERBATIM - The Fun of Making Theatre Seriously by Mark Wheeller

Hype as a Motivating Force

Tony was a massive influence on me and consolidated the idea (which I had already begun to assimilate) that a sure-fire way of motivating people was to make what you were doing **seem** special, just as David Bowie had managed so successfully with Ziggy. Simple hype!

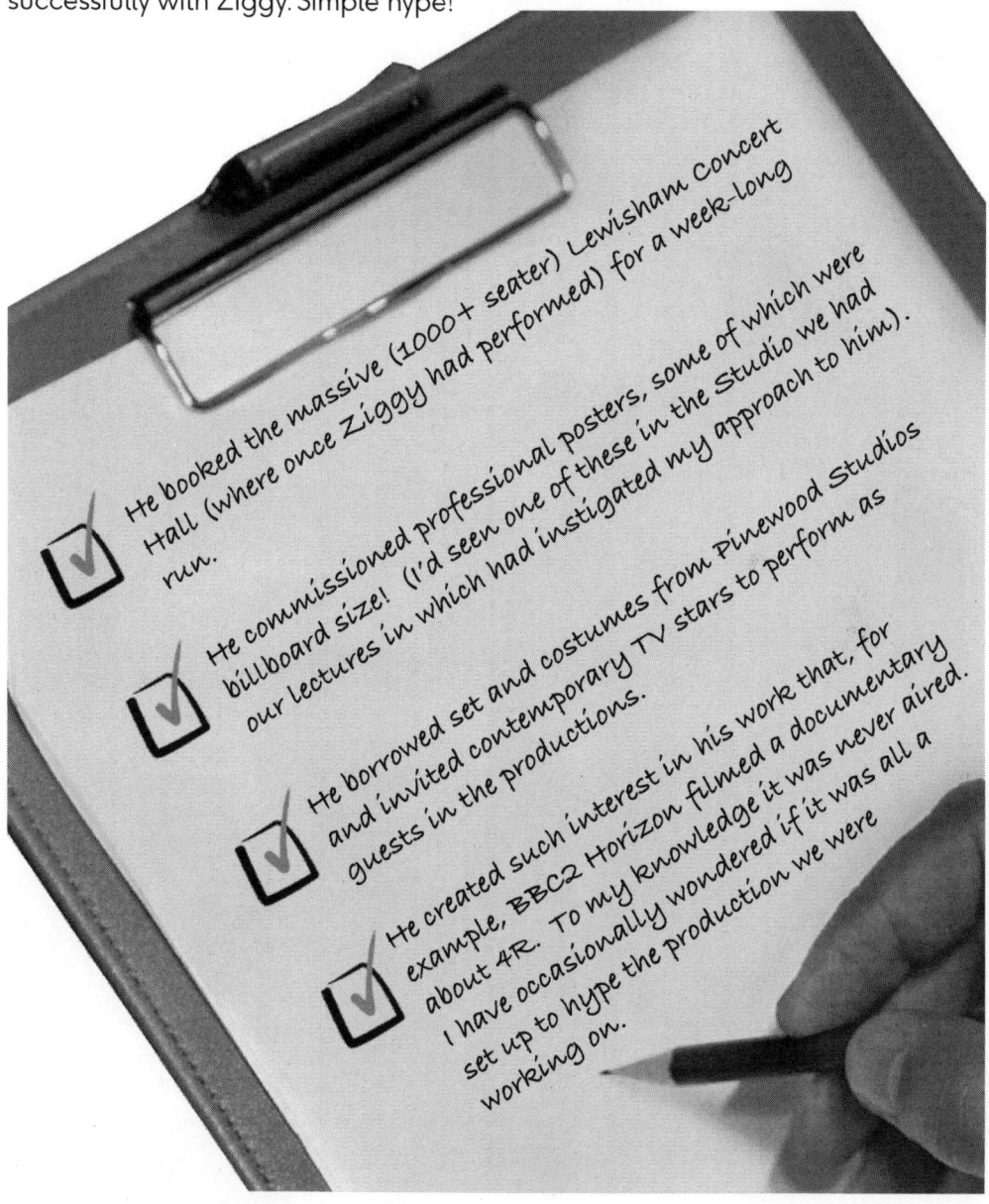

- ✓ He booked the massive (1000+ seater) Lewisham Concert Hall (where once Ziggy had performed) for a week-long run.
- ✓ He commissioned professional posters, some of which were billboard size! (I'd seen one of these in the Studio we had our Lectures in which had instigated my approach to him).
- ✓ He borrowed set and costumes from Pinewood Studios and invited contemporary TV stars to perform as guests in the productions.
- ✓ He created such interest in his work that, for example, BBC2 Horizon filmed a documentary about 4R. To my knowledge it was never aired. I have occasionally wondered if it was all a set up to hype the production we were working on.

I would put all this to use as I became a teacher.

35

VERBATIM - The Fun of Making Theatre Seriously by Mark Wheeller

Directing or Curating

Tony staged sections of a production without telling any of the (non-auditioned/open access) cast what to do.

He set tasks and the cast were expected to respond with great ideas.

Of course, they did!

Images from the 1977 4R production Beyond The Rainbow. I can be seen in the image on the top right as a singing caveman!

For example:

- In choreographing a song he would get me to sing the song to everyone, with the cast seeing the lyrics on a lyric sheet.

- He would ask all 100 people (a cast of 7 to 70 year olds) to form small groups and to create movements for the lyrics as I repeatedly sang the song.

- After a given time, every group showed their work, then everyone discussed what they liked and a final version of the staging emerged.

I would love Tony to have known how crucial he was to me at this early point in my career. It will not surprise you that I kept in touch with him, bit his unexpected death in the early 1990s meant that some things I should have said were never spoken.

VERBATIM - The Fun of Making Theatre Seriously by Mark Wheeller

Over the years many people have talked about and tried to explain how I work. There's a fairly unified version of this but they probably have no idea where it came from... a good proportion was from Tony Key and his work with 4R. I was able to soak up Tony's friendly approach and genuinely democratic way of working.

To me, who KNEW nothing, it offered a tried and tested way forward that was philosophically sound and inclusive.

In recent months I have had my verbatim style adaptation of **Silas Marner** published and, in the support materials, two former cast members talk about my approach in 2014. They could have been talking about Tony!

> Throughout the years of working with Mark, I've realised he only knows one way of directing, which is simply not to direct. Instead, he acts as a curator to the ideas in the room, shaping, evolving, destroying, rejecting and embellishing them. Mark as a director and as an educator is more of a guide. He is a curator not a director.
> **Simon Froud**

> Mark is probably one of the most laid-back directors I will ever meet. "This could work. Let's try it" is, I think, the best way to explain the process of Silas Marner.
> Every suggestion is discussed and tried, whether it be from a chorus member or the protagonist. Quite often, the original idea doesn't work, but another suggestion will stem from that and the process continues with the entire cast having the chance of an input. What is suggested by one person won't be the complete answer but it starts the process off and, as more and more cast members add suggestions, with Mark's guidance, the idea is transformed into this amazingly clever piece of theatre.
> As the rehearsals go on, there are more and more amazingly clever moments of theatre created until suddenly, at the dress rehearsal, we realise we have tweaked and pasted everything together into one amazingly clever play.
> **Charlotte McGuinness Shaw**

VERBATIM - The Fun of Making Theatre Seriously by Mark Wheeller

Learning to be a Teacher in my First Job

Once I had completed my training I applied for Drama teaching jobs.

I was so fortunate.

I was appointed to, what was then, an exemplar progressive comprehensive school, Stantonbury Campus in Milton Keynes.

I have often spoken about my three years here which seemed, for all the right reasons, more like a hundred and three!

I'll try to reduce the huge impact this establishment made on me to a few bullet points... but I could write a whole book about this.

Uniform was never an issue. These photographs were both taken in school time and they seem entirely 'normal'.

1. Stantonbury teachers were all called by their first names. It seemed entirely natural. It was unfettered by status and dignity which helped to develop more authentic inter-relationships. I have often said it was the foundation upon which all the other things I did were built. I was always 'Mark' and this period, in a school setting, consolidated everything I had seen in Tony Key's successfully practice.[9]

---

[9] Geoff Cooksey, the founder of Stantonbury, once said:
"It's always struck me as rather strange that people called Stantonbury Campus radical. It always seemed to us as immensely normal. You treated children in the same way that you treat your own kids and you treated parents in the same way that you treat your neighbours. The school didn't belong to you, it belonged to everybody and, if you're out to get the best out of life, you could do it by cooperation. If you wanted people to cooperate then you would use every skill, every trick, every guile to ensure people do cooperate."   cont...

VERBATIM - The Fun of Making Theatre Seriously by Mark Wheeller

2. The Drama Department, with five full time teachers, was unique. Three were very experienced and two were baby teachers, one of which was me. I was only 21 years old!

3. The Head of Curriculum Drama (Luke Abbott) was an advocate of Dorothy Heathcote's teaching. I had (shamefully on Goldsmiths'!) never been introduced to her. This led to my discovery of a curriculum teaching methodology with a philosophy that married perfectly with what I had learnt from Tony. It served me well throughout my career and ensured that Drama was popular with most students my departments encountered.

4. Luke was timetabled to work with me every week in one of my lessons (in my probationary year) and I observed him teach as part of my timetable. I was never placed in the position of being judged or belittled... just encouraged.

5. The Director of Drama across the Campus and in the community was Roy Nevitt who also worked with me in lessons and ran demo sessions for me.

Me on a the famous concrete cow sculptures in Milton Keynes

6. Luke and Roy taught me how to teach.

7. Roy also ran a Community Theatre group. They presented original and well-respected documentary plays. He was, unbeknown to me, a pioneer of the Documentary Theatre form, using true stories from the different villages that made up what had become the seemingly rootless Milton Keynes. Roy's idea was to 'dig where you stand': stories from the community, told by the community to the community. I loved the philosophy but didn't get involved as I was so busy with my own productions which continued to determinedly focus on being a vehicle for my songwriting. By the end of my time at Stantonbury I had started to use the cast to devise the scripts. Again, I say this to emphasise my lack of confidence in doing this myself, although I reluctantly wrote some lyrics. My shows were proving popular but, if I'm honest, there was little development from what I'd been doing in my sixth form.

9 ... cont
Today (17/11/2020), on Facebook, I saw the dreadful news that Stantonbury (now International School), taken over by The Griffin Schools Trust (who threw out all the innovative features I have referred to), have been served by the Government with a "termination warning" following a disastrous Ofsted report. One of the many comments that appeared beneath this Facebook post was from a student from Youth Theatre back in 1979:
"When it stopped being Geoff Cooksey's vision, it stopped being Stantonbury Campus. It became just another secondary school, churning out young people and forcing them through the awful system that so many wonderful teachers are now forced to work in. How many adults can say they have a number of the secondary school teachers who are now very dear friends? I know we can."
Caz Tricks.

VERBATIM - The Fun of Making Theatre Seriously by Mark Wheeller

My Introduction to Documentary Theatre

Before I saw Roy's plays I prejudicially mis-judged them to be overly academic (I am generally suspicious of academia), purely because Roy was an Oxford graduate and taught A' Level Theatre!

I imagined, like much of what I was introduced to at Goldsmiths', documentary plays would be difficult for me to understand.

When I looked beneath the surface of this off-putting label, I discovered how wrong I was.

Documentary theatre was very much of and for 'the people'.

Peter Cheeseman (Victoria Theatre, Stoke on Trent 1962-1998) had been a major influence on Roy's work. He conceived that:

> Repertory Theatre should be like the local football team. The community know the actors by name. The stories they tell should derive from the community. The spearhead of all our work at Stoke is the Documentary. Our writers lead the research and uncover the documents and memories on which the shows are based.
> The material used on the stage must be primary source material. Words or actions deriving from the events described or from the participants in those events are the only permitted material for the scenes of our documentaries. If there is no primary source material available on a particular topic, no scene can be made about it.
> We can't approach the material as historians, but as entertainers. We must say something that could not be said in a book.
> My hope was that these shows would really intensify our relationship with the district and give this relationship a concrete form on the stage. They have done.
> **Peter Cheeseman** - Director, Victoria Theatre Stoke-on-Trent.

Although songs were included this form, it brought content to the fore rather than existing merely to serve the songs and it was the possibility of including songs that particularly delighted me...

I could do these plays **AND** have an exciting new vehicle for my songs!

VERBATIM - The Fun of Making Theatre Seriously by Mark Wheeller

Historical and Documentary Plays:

- Historical plays have existed as long as theatre itself.

- 492 BC the ancient Greek playwright Phrynichus produced *The Capture of Miletus about the Persian War.*

- 427 BC Aristophanes wrote **Diatals** (Banqueters), a satire on the latest fashions in education. His play **Clouds** took up the story of the trial and execution of Socrates.

- The genre continues through to European medieval mystery plays and Shakespeare's historical tragedies and French revolutionary patriotic dramas.

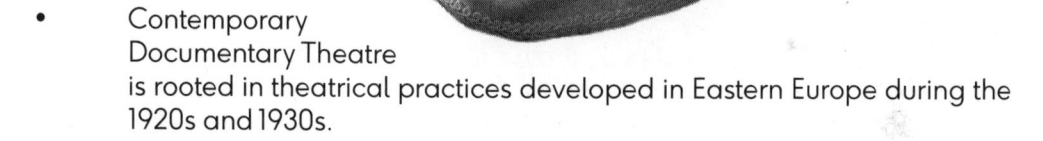

- Contemporary Documentary Theatre is rooted in theatrical practices developed in Eastern Europe during the 1920s and 1930s.

    In the years after the Russian Revolution, the USSR's Department of agitation and propaganda employed theatre troops known as the Blue Blouses (so-called because they wore factory workers overalls) to stage current events for the largely illiterate population.

    The Blue Blouses dramatised news items and current events through song, dance, and staging. By 1924 these performances were standardised into the form of Zhivaya Gazeta or Living Newspaper.[10]

- Peter Cheeseman at the Victoria Theatre Stoke on Trent pioneered the use of Documentary Theatre. His plays (e.g. **The Fight For Shelton Bar** about the closure of a local steelworks) used exclusively the words spoken in interviews or found in transcripts/letters etc. to become the utterance of the performer on stage.

---

[10] Source - wikipedia.org - Documentary Theatre. I remember Roy referring to the Living Newspaper productions with great reverence.

VERBATIM - The Fun of Making Theatre Seriously by Mark Wheeller

My First Experience of a Documentary Play

The first documentary play I saw was Roy Nevitt's production for Stantonbury Campus Drama Group of *Your Loving Brother Albert*. This was based on the letters from an underage World War I soldier, Albert French, in the trenches to his sibling, which were discovered many years later. Even the title came from the letters. These words were those he always used to sign his letters off. My decision to attend this (to support Roy and because one of my youth theatre members - Neil Canham - had the main role), in 1980, changed my practice.

Your Loving Brother Albert.

While watching the production:

- I was constantly aware (if only in the back of my mind) that the words in the script were 'real', all direct quotes from Albert French's letters.

- I found myself imagining the real Albert writing them in the original context of the trenches. This image would fade and the theatrical reconstruction replaced it centre-stage in my mind.

- I was internally cutting from one focus to another, which helped my flighty mind to maintain concentration.

- This was more 'real' than any invented script could be... even Pinter! Using real words from real people/letters added weight, reverence and depth to the words.

I remember thinking, after I saw that first production, I was too timid to do such a play on Roy's patch, but when I left Stantonbury I could develop my own documentary plays and put my own spin on them.

Roy's plays were historical stories.

Mine would be contemporary.

At this time, no one had coined the term Verbatim.

Aside from Peter Cheeseman, I only know one other example of verbatim theatre from this period.

VERBATIM - The Fun of Making Theatre Seriously by Mark Wheeller

- 1974 British-American playwright and critic Eric Bentley's play *Are You Now Or Have You Ever Been: The Investigation of Show-Business by the Un-American Activities Committee* was built on testimonies delivered before the US House Un-American Activities Committee in the 1950's.[11]

Wikipedia currently mentions nothing in the period between 1974 and 1992, when American playwright Anna Deavere Smith is credited with 'pioneering Verbatim Theatre' with *Fires In The Mirror* (1992 - about the 1991 Crown Heights riot in Brooklyn, New York) and *Twilight: Los Angeles* (1994 - about the 1992 Los Angeles riots).

For both plays she conducted interviews with numerous people connected to the events and then fashioned the plays by selecting words from her interview transcripts.

I started to develop *Race To Be Seen* in 1983 and performed it in 1984, so there is a gap in public knowledge about this form. It needs to be filled as I'm sure I was not the only person doing this kind of work.

Verbatim Theatre: a definition

- Limited to making dialogue and other forms of dramatic text from the recorded voices of people speaking within or about a particular event.

My Diaries

Throughout my life I've had periods where I wrote diaries, many long since disposed of.

However, three in my early life as a teacher/youth theatre director, I kept.

These focused, in detail, on my first documentary/verbatim youth theatre productions (*Race, Punch* and *Swallow*,).
I suppose I thought I could (or should) become a feted youth theatre director and people would be interested. I never considered it might be because of my approach to writing. That was never an aspiration.

---

[11] Source - wikipedia.org - Verbatim Theatre

VERBATIM - The Fun of Making Theatre Seriously by Mark Wheeller

I could never have written such a complete account of the development of both ***Too Much Punch for Judy*** and ***Hard to Swallow*** without these diaries. The fact I kept in touch with old cast members proved unexpectedly advantageous as they willingly (thank you) offered their own recollections to complete the picture.[12]

My diary for ***Race To Be Seen*** has stood in a hanging file, untouched since 1984, and never opened.

It is significant in a way the other two aren't.

I had never written a play and this would form the template for my approach to most of my successful plays.

Race To Be Seen - Facts and Figures

Graham Salmon's story was in itself an incredible story and I have always wanted it to be told.

It surprises me that ***Race To Be Seen*** is not my most successful play.

Graham's story should be taken up as a subject for a book or a feature film. I live in hope that, one day, it will.

So, why does it sit in my second tier of plays, in terms of popularity?

It is 12/34 in my chart of most performed plays.

It has been licensed only 56 times and around 20 of those were my own productions. (For context, my most performed play is ***Too Much Punch For Judy*** at 6,063 so, it is a **long** way behind that.)

In terms of script sales it features in my top 10... just... #9.

I often ask myself why is it not more popular?

---

[12] A reference to my two resource books also published by Salamander Street, ***The Story Behind Too Much Punch For Judy*** and ***Hard to Swallow - Easy To Digest.***

VERBATIM - The Fun of Making Theatre Seriously by Mark Wheeller

One obvious reason is, it never attracted financial backing in the way my Road Safety plays did, enabling them to be toured by professional companies in schools for years on end.

Are there other reasons?

Were teachers scared off by the challenge of staging the race scenes? In the early 80's physical theatre companies like Frantic Assembly didn't exist to inspire the staging of such epic (impossible) scenes.

Teachers, theatre directors and their students are now so much better at staging epic (impossible) scenes (better than I ever was!) that this can no longer be the reason.

Was it overlooked because Graham Salmon was not a recognisable (celebrity) name?

Race was the play where I developed my organic 'modus operandi' and (unwittingly) a parallel playwright career path.

Race was my first documentary/verbatim play.

Race was my first play to be published. (Thank you Longman Imprint Books.)

Up until **Race**, I had also held ambitions to be a ground-breaking classroom drama teacher (I was not making it as a songwriter).

From **Race** onwards, creating and performing my plays became my central focus.

After I retired as a Youth Theatre director in 2018, I decided to investigate my hitherto unseen diary and write a book about this play which had become the backbone to my career, having revisited it at various key points.

This idea morphed into something broader. I am aware of other books on verbatim theatre which serve to reinforce its academic image. I wanted my book to be accessible for anyone and have been keen to avoid any approach which might dissuade anyone outside academic circles from reading it.

45

VERBATIM - The Fun of Making Theatre Seriously by Mark Wheeller

Tentatively, I suggested this idea to Barrie Sapsford, now a designer, who as a teenage EYT member was in the first Race production. He was equally as enthusiastic as me.

In the initial lockdown in March 2020, due to the sudden and unexpected closure of Zinc Publishing, my catalogue was taken on by Salamander Street Ltd. Early on in our relationship, I spoke to George Spender (the proprietor of Salamander Street) about our work on this book and he expressed enthusiasm about publishing it.

This book will offer a unique and detailed account of how my first documentary/verbatim play came to be. This will offer, from both first hand experience and hindsight, a unique and entertaining narrative that tracks every aspect of developing a verbatim play from the very beginning to final performance.

- Where does the idea come from?

- The procedure around the initial interviews and the ethics of using testimony in a play.

- Translating testimony into script.

- Igniting the words on the page into the fireworks they need to become on stage.

- Finally, developing the initial tentative production into an award winning performance.

It is remarkable that my unfunded youth theatre output (largely with OYT) is represented on the GCSE set text lists alongside works emanating from Shakespeare and the Royal National Theatre! Consequently, I am in the fortunate position of now being interviewed about my plays (but never my songs, or cup-winning goals). I am not ashamed to admit I love these interviews and often think of those 'pretend' interviews in my childhood. They have proved to be supremely useful practice. There now exists the possibility that others will want or need to read it to discover how we worked.

It traces the foundations of our process... and I say 'our' with due acknowledgement... myself and my groups of wonderfully willing youth theatre members.

We were blissfully unaware that we had a methodology... we just did what we did. Looking back I realise there was a way, discovered through the fun of making theatre seriously.

VERBATIM - The Fun of Making Theatre Seriously by Mark Wheeller

I was recently asked in a **Drama Matters** interview

> *What play of yours would you have performed? Which theatre would you have it performed in and... what cast would you have performing in it?*

I didn't have to think about this whatsoever.

These were my answers:

Play: *Race to be Seen*

Venue: Oaklands Community School Theatre

Cast: A selection of Youth Theatre members I have worked with over my time as a Youth Theatre director.

This really would be something special!

There would definitely be people in my fantasy cast represented from each of my three productions of *Race To Be Seen/Graham - World's Fastest Blind Runner.*

I'm related to three of them, my children. Ollie Wheeller would be on lights, Daisy Wheeller would team up with Bernadette to perform the songs and Charlie Wheeller would not only be in the cast but would also be my movement director.

Barrie, who's designing the book, would be in the cast: possibly now as Harry.

The other dream would be for Graham (and Marie) to 'see' (he'd like that) the production in this fantasy form.

VERBATIM - The Fun of Making Theatre Seriously by Mark Wheeller

My eyes water at the unreal prospect of this possibility... but I know it's one dream too far!

While in the land of fantasy I'll also take the opportunity to book a hit single (and of course a **Top of the Pops** appearance) with the title song that Graham and I co-wrote, **Race To Be Seen.**

Back to reality.

I will enjoy revisiting this play in all its different forms as I research and write this book.

I know I will also relish the contact it will generate with former cast members who are always so willing to offer their memories.[13]

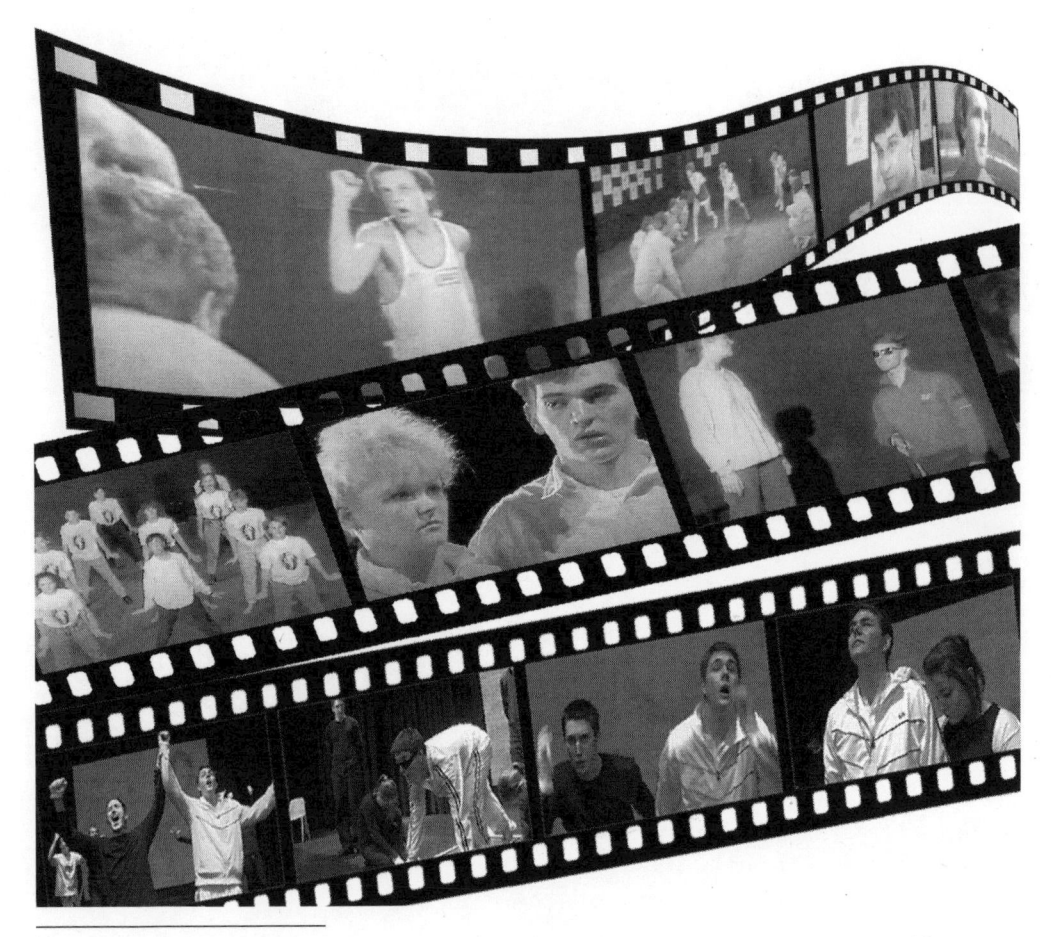

---

[13] This proved to be a highlight of the project... and a big thank you to all who contributed fascinating and funny memories.

VERBATIM - The Fun of Making Theatre Seriously by Mark Wheeller

Chapter 2:
Seeing Beyond The Blackout

Everyone was pulling together, and really wanted to know about things and really wanting to put our hearts and souls into it to create something together. We did everything together like a little band of people. It was a magical time.
Judy Cornwell - Actor (*talking about Joan Littlewood's Company at the Theatre Royal Stratford East production of* **Oh What a Lovely War**.)

I arrived at St John's School Epping as a 24-year-old, fresh-faced drama teacher, after three years at Stantonbury being a sponge. I was excited by the prospect of creating my own department rather than being a small cog in an incredibly smooth and well-oiled machine.

I remember being greeted at a post-interview visit by two very enthusiastic 4th year students Matt Allen and Bernadette Chapman. Both had heard of my appointment and would play a key role in the development of Epping Youth Theatre and *Race to Be Seen*.

> Matt and I were good friends and had worked on a school production of HMS Pinafore. We had heard of this new drama teacher but the head of music advised me not to get too involved in the productions she had heard he was planning. Writing this now, I realise I was being warned off because I was an asset to the music department!
> Matt was confident and, when we heard this drama teacher was visiting, we waited in the music room looking out of the window. He turned up in a leather jacket riding a motor bike!
> We walked across the car park and introduced ourselves! That was when we first met "Mark".
> **Bernadette Cleere (née Chapman).**

VERBATIM - The Fun of Making Theatre Seriously by Mark Wheeller

I remember this car park encounter being hugely empowering after I'd been subjected to the last-but-one drama teacher (in again that day as a supply teacher) ranting about how I would burn myself out trying to get drama going here with "these kids". He was really trying to put me off. It was odd!

This really was the polar opposite of Stantonbury, starting something from nothing but that was just the challenge I wanted... a perfect fit!

By introducing one of the Stantonbury trademarks, being addressed by my first name, I would ensure my arrival didn't go unnoticed. I did this with the full consent of Head Teacher, Stan Dixon, who appointed me to 'bring a bit of Stantonbury to St John's'.

The symbolism of first name use instantly communicated my approach. It would also make me stand out as different, even special. This would be good for my profile in the school... amongst the students at least. Some suggested this approach could have the opposite effect as they thought students might take advantage of me.
I countered that, saying:

'It's easier to be rude to someone using their last name than their first.'

I stand by that and, if there was one change I could make to improve schools, it would be the way students address staff... oh, and I'd ban any form of school uniform or dress code!

One of my tutees from my first year at St John's, Lisa Beer, also became involved in the **Race to Be Seen** development team. She remembers being put in my tutor group at the start of her 3rd year (Year 9 nowadays)... with a fond (I think) smile.

> Okay, brutally honest: I remember being rather irritated at first. I liked where our form room was and our form teacher, Miss Rogers, seemed kinder than some, although (apologies to her) not a huge bundle of energy.
> Suddenly, it was all change and it really was a change. Of course, the huge talking point was that we were to call you 'Mark'. What??! I remember a tangible buzz circulating around the school - a mixture of fear of the unknown and mounting excitement that something different was afoot. You definitely seemed different and no-one could accuse you of lacking in energy.
> *cont...*

VERBATIM - The Fun of Making Theatre Seriously by Mark Wheeller

> ...cont
> Even at my young age, I remember thinking that you must be ruffling some feathers in the staffroom. It was unsettling and I wasn't sure if I liked it, and you, or not. Would you be all hot air and exaggerated "trendiness" from Milton Keynes, (which seemed like another planet at the time) or would you drive some positive, genuine change? It was obvious how upbeat you were; young, enthusiastic, alternative and wearing jeans and jumpers!
> Pretty quickly it was clear. The dynamic of our form, and to an extent, I suspect the school, changed. The physical space of the Drama Studio (which was also our form room), and how you used it had an impact on that, but also your approach. You were actually quite strict and demanding of respect but not for respect's sake.
> Your inclusive, mostly non-confrontational approach blurred the super-formal lines between teacher and pupil and gave a chance for many pupils to be seen, and see themselves, in a different, more beneficial light.
> **Lisa Andreae (née Beer)**

The Drama department was in a mess. The previous incumbent had been on gardening leave after some 'dodgy' behaviour with a court case pending. There had been a succession of increasingly exasperated and often non-specialist supply teachers in the two terms leading to my arrival. Lisa didn't remember any drama lessons prior to mine.

> There was no theatre or drama before unless the First Form (Year 7) French play counts. I was involved in out of school Dance School performances. Sheila Douglas is forever etched in my memory in her black leotard, amazingly wide hips atop her long fish netted legs, and invariably sporting a fag hanging out of the side of her mouth! Doesn't sound that promising but she was a true force and joyfully orchestrated ballet, tap and "modern" dance lessons and fabulous shows with even more fabulous costumes for a gaggle of random girls of all shapes and sizes!
> I was also a member of a relatively serious gymnastics club plus the school team.
> I regularly performed routines and entered national competitions, so I definitely had a taste for, and enjoyed, being 'on stage'.
> When you spoke about EYT starting, it felt so exciting for many reasons. Let's face it, the extra curricular offerings at St John's were not overflowing.
> One of the great things about EYT was that it brought students together who would never have mixed in other circumstances. The classic "Glee" factor. I had only just moved to the area so didn't have those buffering friendships from Junior School, and I was definitely more geek than glam; seen as being too 'brainy', wearing glasses, with dodgy fashion choices largely thanks to my mother - thanks Mum!
> Your vision for EYT opened up so many possibilities and encouraged confidence, inclusion, independent thought and action. It offered a safe way to push the boundaries of comfort (and discomfort!) zones. It was vital for my young mind at that point with limited access to similar outlets at the school and in the town.
> **Lisa Andreae (née Beer)**

Lisa was typical of the EYT membership. No one had much experience. The slate was enticingly clean.

VERBATIM - The Fun of Making Theatre Seriously by Mark Wheeller

Putting My Foot Gently Into The Water

In my first term, I mounted and developed a production I had put on with Stantonbury Youth Theatre a couple of years before. Blackout, loosely based on the wartime experiences of my mum as an evacuee, had used three songs I had originally written for the 4R Jubilee production as my starting point. The Stantonbury script was based on the outline story with cast improvisations providing the basis for my dialogue.

One of the Stantonbury Youth Theatre cast members, 13-year-old Rachel Waugh, had an incredible insight, which began to shine a light on what both she and I were actually doing.

We were standing in the queue awaiting fish and chips mid-rehearsal (yes, as well as a bar, supermarket, newsagent, church and leisure centre, Stantonbury had a proper fish and chip shop on the campus!) and she said:

'This play is actually about me isn't it?'

I was baffled and obviously made a face communicating my feelings all too clearly as she went on to explain:

'It's about my situation with my parents separating and me having to choose between them.'

Rachel had improvised the words the evacuee would say in the script in response to the situation that Rachel was thrown into. She realised she must have been subconsciously using her own experience to help make the evacuee real.
(I loved the authenticity!)

'I suppose it is.'

Spellbinder at Stantonbury!

MARK COOK reports

THE TITLE of Blackout, the latest production of the Stantonbury Campus Youth Theatre Group, did not give any real indication of what the audience was in for.

It gave no clue as to the life and enthusiasm that came from the campus stage last week.

And if the quality of the performance itself was not enough, the group managed to write the musical play themselves.

Blackout has as its main character, Rachel, a young girl who is pushed from pillar to post and emotionally torn apart as an evacuee in the Second World War.

But far from being presented with a sombre entertainment, the audience were treated to rousing chorus numbers, some beautifully wistful solos and some very touching acting scenes.

The actual staging of the play was very simple and I think this worked in the production's favour as there was plenty of talent on stage without it being cluttered by complicated scenery or lavish costumes and musical arrangements.

The force and directness of the performers enabled them to put over their message thoughtfully and effectively.

The cast of about 80 obviously enjoyed themselves and they had some excellent material to play with in the music by producer Mark Wheeller, which ranged from catchy songs with snappy lyrics to roof-raising choruses and the wonderful finale.

Fragmentary

My only criticism would be that some of the scenes towards the end of the second act were rather too rushed and fragmentary but by the end this was completely forgotten.

I don't think it is really fair to pick out individuals as there were so many excellent performances but credit should go to those who wrote their own parts, especially 13-year-old Rachel Waugh who was remarkable as Rachel and Mark Eagle, aged 15, who played her father.

I was enthralled by the production and was suitably moist-eyed at the appropriate places. Blackout was one of the most enjoyable things I have seen for a while — a fantastic achievement by the Stantonbury youngsters.

● Rachel Waugh, aged 13, who wrote her own part.

● Mark Eagle, aged 15, who played Rachel's father.

VERBATIM - The Fun of Making Theatre Seriously by Mark Wheeller

Her revelation made me think of something my mum had said to me:

'We could never have evacuated you at the age (8) my parents did to me given the same situation.'

Until that moment I had failed to spot the irony of my being sent to boarding school aged 8! I don't think mum ever realised it, bless her. The separation from my loving family compounded by the treatment I suffered there opened a vague awareness of my exploring interrupted parent/child relationships which was to continue in so many of my plays.

My involvement in exploring these stories has perhaps offered me a way (a therapy?) of looking at my situation from different perspectives and perhaps helped to lay some ghosts to rest... as I hope it might also have done inadvertently for 13-year-old Rachel.

This insight was so profound... particularly as it was made in the ordinary context of a fish and chip shop queue! Thank you Rachel... one of many times a young person's understanding of what we are doing outshone my own.

Returning to Epping 1983: and knowing I intended to develop a documentary play I put out an advert to interview former evacuees from Epping to trial the idea within this pre-existing musical. I placed their memories next to scenes to mirror the memories of my part-fictional evacuee. It worked a treat and upgraded the musical beyond recognition, leading the TES to write this in their review:

> **THE TIMES Educational Supplement**
> The evocation of the period was so good that I spent the first act waiting for Vera Lynn's entrance.
> **Hugh David - Times Educational Supplement.**

I had proved, to cast and audience alike, that it was possible to create original work and reach a very high standard. I am proud to say **Blackout - One Evacuee In Thousands** proved its point and received a long standing ovation.

VERBATIM - The Fun of Making Theatre Seriously by Mark Wheeller

Epping Youth Theatre had arrived.

People were taking notice of what we were doing.

The big question was:

What will our next production be?

It wasn't only others who were asking this.

I had no idea!

Life in the blackout

Ideas for Our First Documentary/Verbatim Play

I was determined that:

1. The decision-making process about the subject matter of this play would be democratic.

2. We would make a play based on something from real life... a documentary play.

And... here begins the story of **Race To Be Seen** and my writing verbatim plays.

The first entry in my diary for this production (written a little while afterwards, once I decided the project was worth recording) was:

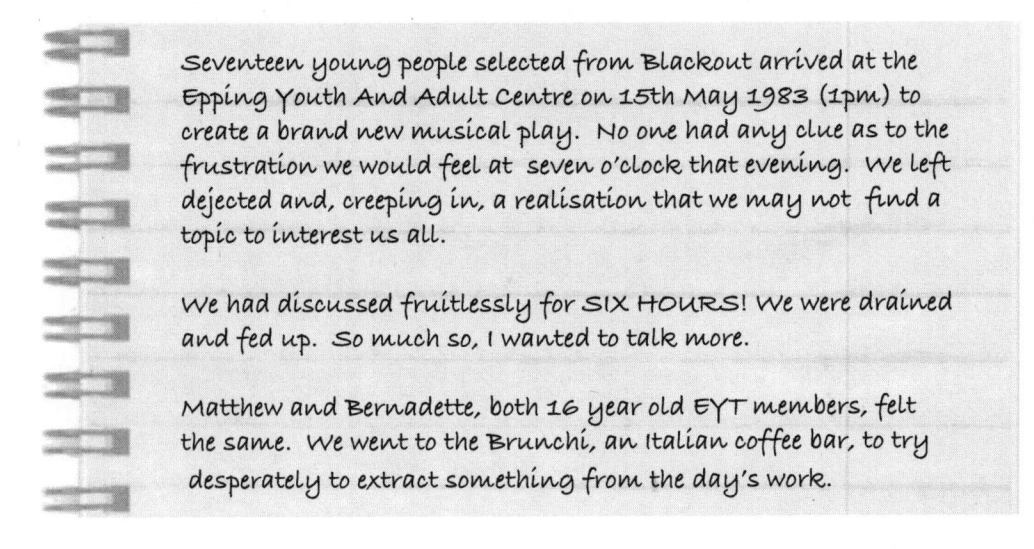

> Seventeen young people selected from Blackout arrived at the Epping Youth And Adult Centre on 15th May 1983 (1pm) to create a brand new musical play. No one had any clue as to the frustration we would feel at seven o'clock that evening. We left dejected and, creeping in, a realisation that we may not find a topic to interest us all.
>
> We had discussed fruitlessly for SIX HOURS! We were drained and fed up. So much so, I wanted to talk more.
>
> Matthew and Bernadette, both 16 year old EYT members, felt the same. We went to the Brunchi, an Italian coffee bar, to try desperately to extract something from the day's work.

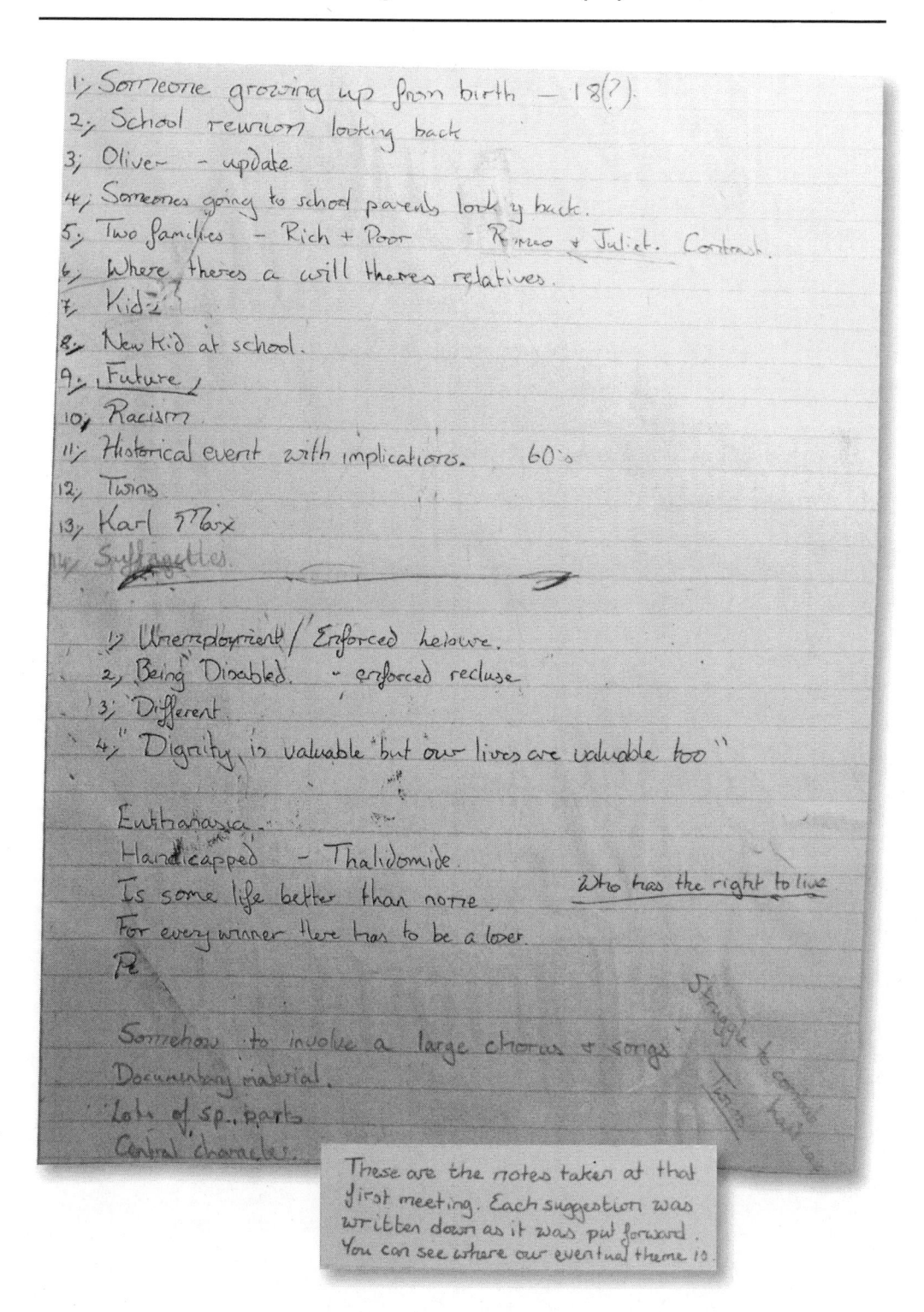

VERBATIM - The Fun of Making Theatre Seriously by Mark Wheeller

1. Someone growing up from birth — 18(?).
2. School reunion looking back
3. Oliver - update
4. Someones going to school parents look g back.
5. Two families — Rich + Poor — Romeo + Juliet. Contrast.
6. Where theres a will theres relatives.
7. Kidz
8. New kid at school.
9. Future
10. Racism
11. Historical event with implications. 60's
12. Twins
13. Karl Marx
14. ~~Suffragettes~~

1. Unemployment / Enforced leisure.
2. Being Disabled. - enforced recluse
3. Different
4. "Dignity is valuable but our lives are valuable too"

Euthanasia
Handicapped — Thalidomide.
Is some life better than none.   Who has the right to live
For every winner there has to be a loser.
Re

Somehow to involve a large chorus + songs
Documentary material.
Lots of sp. parts
Central character.

These are the notes taken at that first meeting. Each suggestion was written down as it was put forward. You can see where our eventual theme is.

55

VERBATIM - The Fun of Making Theatre Seriously by Mark Wheeller

Even as it begins, I see something that couldn't happen today. I spontaneously took two 16 year olds out for a coffee. Today, I'd need to complete risk assessments, get permission from parents, the school and possibly get a 'trip' approved by the local council! This spontaneity allowed so much of our project to happen and this coffee was the tip of an entirely moral iceberg.

Matt remembers the impact on him of EYT.

> When Mark arrived in Epping I was in the fifth form at school and he asked me to help him set up a Youth Theatre. I told him it would never work in Epping. However, once we got it going, not only did everyone want to be in it; lots of people came to see the shows. We had such a great time.
> At Guilford School of Acting, my special project was on Community Theatre. I explained how at EYT we found stories from our community, which that same community would be interested in watching - such a great starting point.
> **Matt Allen.**

I was so frustrated by Matt. He was enthusiastic but hadn't opted for Drama because it had such a poor reputation in the school! It was seen as a 'doss', as he put it. He wasn't in my 5th form (Year 11) CSE Drama class but he went on to be a crucial part of this project and then to have a career in TIE setting up his own company, The Ape Theatre Company, who established their outstanding reputation in the 1990s using my plays **Too Much Punch** and **Legal Weapon**.

Bernadette was another 5th year non-optee and a key member of EYT. She had the most incredible singing voice, proved beyond doubt in the **Blackout** production with a standout performance of my song **Eyes Of A Child**. Tony Key once told me his friends in Boney M might record it. That never happened but it did make me feel very excited. Tony-style hype?
For me as an aspiring songwriter Bernadette was gold dust!

> Working on *Blackout* gave me a great sense of purpose, helping rewrite dialogue was like a dream to me. Working on any follow up project was a natural progression. If I'd only been involved with EYT from a younger age. I might have had the confidence to follow my dreams. This is why I encouraged my Liam (Cromby) to sing, be confident and go for it. Liam went on to become a professional rock singer, achieving incredible success with *We Are the Ocean*.
> **Bernadette Cleere** (née **Chapman**).

So, back to the Brunchi Bar in Epping. The three of us reflected on the six frustrating hours but were determined to pull something positive out of it...

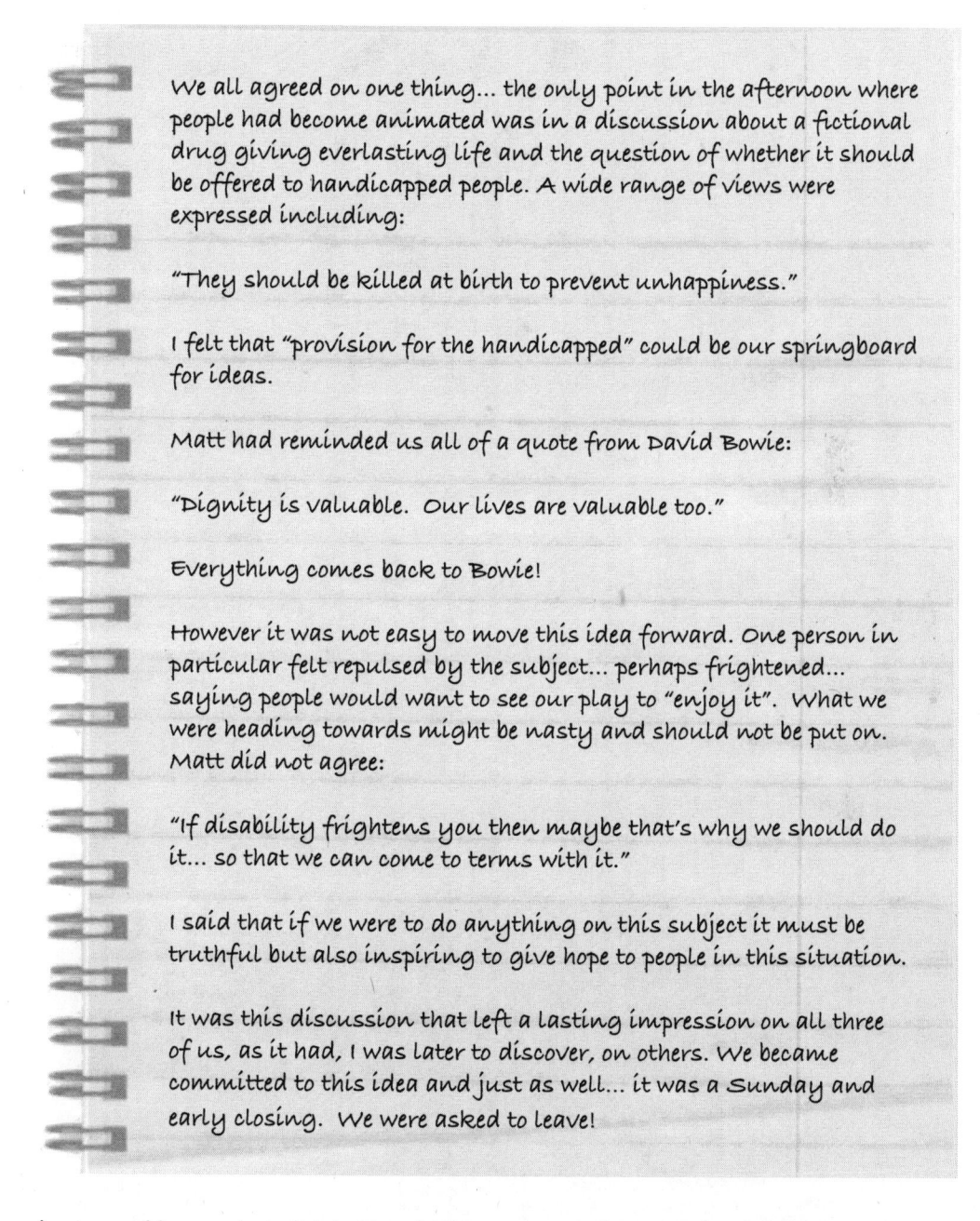

VERBATIM - The Fun of Making Theatre Seriously by Mark Wheeller

> We all agreed on one thing... the only point in the afternoon where people had become animated was in a discussion about a fictional drug giving everlasting life and the question of whether it should be offered to handicapped people. A wide range of views were expressed including:
>
> "They should be killed at birth to prevent unhappiness."
>
> I felt that "provision for the handicapped" could be our springboard for ideas.
>
> Matt had reminded us all of a quote from David Bowie:
>
> "Dignity is valuable. Our lives are valuable too."
>
> Everything comes back to Bowie!
>
> However it was not easy to move this idea forward. One person in particular felt repulsed by the subject... perhaps frightened... saying people would want to see our play to "enjoy it". What we were heading towards might be nasty and should not be put on. Matt did not agree:
>
> "If disability frightens you then maybe that's why we should do it... so that we can come to terms with it."
>
> I said that if we were to do anything on this subject it must be truthful but also inspiring to give hope to people in this situation.
>
> It was this discussion that left a lasting impression on all three of us, as it had, I was later to discover, on others. We became committed to this idea and just as well... it was a Sunday and early closing. We were asked to leave!

I returned home, but didn't stop thinking about what we should do.

I phoned the headteacher of a nearby special school (also a parent of one of my students) to see if he had any stories we could use. He was encouraging which was "just the ticket"!

VERBATIM - The Fun of Making Theatre Seriously by Mark Wheeller

The group, as it was on 15/5/83 BEFORE the six hour discussion about what we should do.
I wonder how many will last the project?

58

VERBATIM - The Fun of Making Theatre Seriously by Mark Wheeller

As the evening wore on I started to think that the best thing would be to use a story of someone famous... Helen Keller or Louis Braille rather than someone local which had been my original plan.

Knowing these stories had already been used, I thought we could perhaps augment them with verbatim accounts from parents of children from Ben's dad's school and their parents, following the format used in Blackout. When I said this the following day, a couple of the sixth form YT members spent one of their spare lessons researching (in an encyclopaedia – no internet in 1983!).

They gave me all their findings as I stood in the dinner queue! Lunch was more important to me but their enthusiasm and commitment was unstoppable and truly affirming.

Graham Salmon

Stan Dixon, the headteacher, approached me during lunchtime to find out how our meeting had gone. I explained and he offered the silver bullet!!!

"I've heard of a man from Loughton (very near our school in Epping) who is a blind athlete and he holds various records. I think he might even have been on television. Graham Salmon. It might be worth a conversation?"

It didn't take long to find his phone number. I phoned him, discovered he was a world record holder and, amazingly, he agreed to meet me that Friday evening.

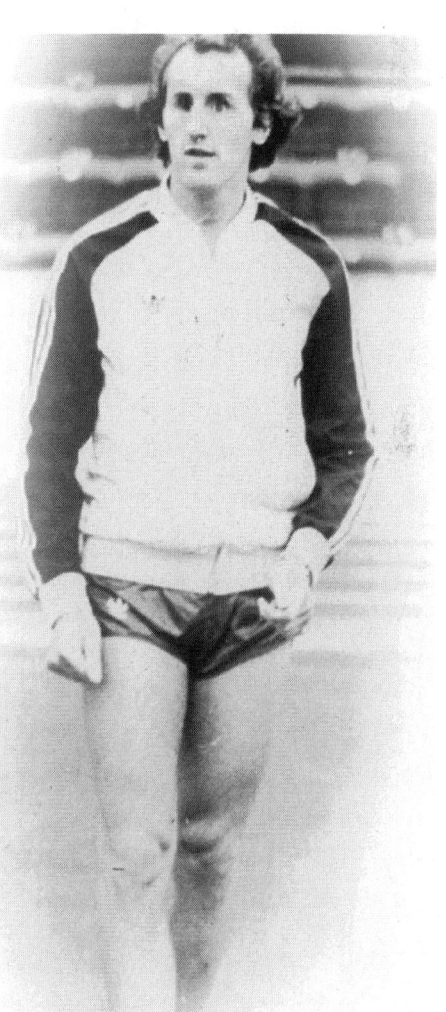

VERBATIM - The Fun of Making Theatre Seriously by Mark Wheeller

> *I had just returned from a training session and was still recovering from running up some of Loughton's longest and steepest hills, when the telephone rang. Mark's voice sounded friendly, perhaps a little nervous, but sincere, and I was keen to meet him to discuss his proposal further. It may have been vanity but the thought of having a play written about me appealed very much. I was grinning broadly as I told Marie. She expressed some reservations about people intruding on our privacy, and I must admit to a few doubts myself. I could not imagine how a bunch of kids could write a play that would be anything more than an amateurish school production. I was to discover my worries were entirely unfounded.*
>
> **Graham Salmon,** written for the introduction for the original *Race To Be Seen* script published by Longman

I was incredibly excited. This idea fulfilled everything (and more) I could ever want for my new project. I was certain the young people would adore it and be motivated by it too.

Assuming Graham would agree to being our 'subject', we could interview him, his friends and family and use their words to tell his story in our script.

My life had kept famous people away from me and in my childhood (the '60s and '70s) famous people were distant. That distance added to their enigma. George Best and Bobby Charlton from the football world. David Bowie and Marc Bolan from the world of music. All were completely inaccessible and despite my having seen Bowie live, the idea that any of them were human seemed as bizarre as a pixie invasion.

I remember being at university with a girl who lived near John Cleese (from Monty Python's Flying Circus, a popular TV comedy show). The idea that a real life Python lived in a house in a 'normal' street with other people completely shocked me.

VERBATIM - The Fun of Making Theatre Seriously by Mark Wheeller

The fact that Graham appeared in the Guinness Book of Records (I checked in my own copy!) gave him that enigmatic status.

Yet I was to meet him.

I may have the opportunity to interview him and hear first-hand of his experience, as I saw it, of being a super-successful person (who was also totally blind!).

This guy lived in a normal house, in a normal street too...

,,, and in a neighbouring town.

I had made an appointment to see an enigma... a myth... a storybook man.

I remember that week building up my hopes about this opportunity to develop a play about him and how amazing it could be... amazing for me and for all of us in our youth theatre. People would be genuinely intrigued in seeing his story. Perhaps I would even be interviewed about it!!!

The big problem was that I had no control over Graham's decision to let us (a mere youth theatre group) tell it.

I'm an enthusiast.

I remember talking animatedly to absolutely everyone about the possibility.

Everyone I told was another person I'd have to inform if Graham turned me down... and then what?

What other project could ever be this exciting?

Please... please Graham... please agree, so we can show you we can do this.

I lived through that whole week thinking of virtually nothing else...

... just willing Graham to say yes!

I needed to ensure I was on time for our meeting.

Being on time was the least I could do to evidence my commitment.

61

Chapter 3: Meeting My Storybook Man

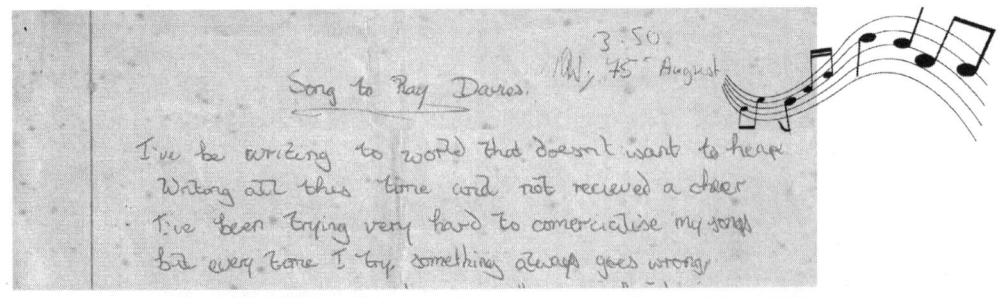

Song to Ray Davies. 3.50. (W, 75 August)
I've be writing to world that doesn't want to hear
Writing all this time and not received a cheer
I've been trying very hard to comercialise my songs
but every time I try something always goes wrong.

Song to Raymond Douglas (Snow White) by Mark Wheeller (1975)[14]

Leave in good time...
Arrive on time...
Make a good first impression...
Hhhmmmmm...

Half an hour after I was due at Graham's house I pulled my motorbike into a lay-by and lifted my drenched visor to look at my fast disintegrating handwritten directions in the gathering storm.

I might have arrived faster had I waited for Sat Nav to be invented (still about 25 years away). I was completely lost.

The threadbare directions didn't help much either.

---

[14] You can hear me singing the whole of this song on my Mark Wheeller Youtube Channel 'Wheellersongs 8'.

VERBATIM - The Fun of Making Theatre Seriously by Mark Wheeller

I did have Graham's phone number.

Mobile phones in 1983 were like the Sat Nav, a distant dream.

My best bet was to find a call box.

Coins?

Yes. Phew!

I can't recall exactly what happened in the next half hour.

What I do know is that I did arrive, nearly an hour late.

I heard later Graham was feeling annoyed that some crank had made him the subject of a stitch up. So, for both of us, my arrival was a huge relief.

I was absolutely drenched!

That was Graham's first impression of me... not what I'd intended at all!

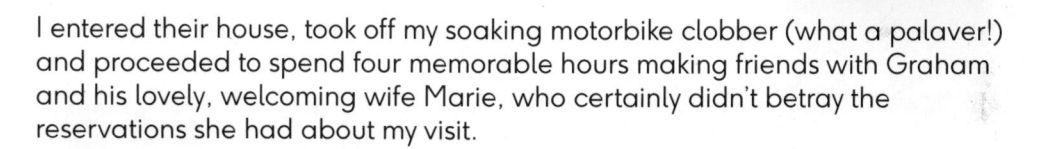

I entered their house, took off my soaking motorbike clobber (what a palaver!) and proceeded to spend four memorable hours making friends with Graham and his lovely, welcoming wife Marie, who certainly didn't betray the reservations she had about my visit.

> *I was impressed by Mark's enthusiasm and ideas, particularly that of using the actual words spoken in interviews, which helped to allay any fears regarding the quality of the script.*
>
> **Graham Salmon,** written for the introduction for the original ***Race To Be Seen*** script published by Longman

I remember our meeting started with Graham showing me the TV documentary[15] called ***Just To Have Taken Part***, which showed him and two of his friends as they prepared for the Winter Olympics back in the mid-1970s.

---

[15] You can see this on my Mark Wheeller YouTube Channel

VERBATIM - The Fun of Making Theatre Seriously by Mark Wheeller

It was a wonderful way of getting a basic understanding of who Graham was and is the way I always introduce him to students exploring the play.

> Graham was happy for me to record his words so I took my portable cassette recorder with me.
>
> He had been totally blind from the age of eighteen months and had fought to combat his disability by becoming a dedicated athlete, breaking the 100 metres world record for a blind person (11.4 secs).
>
> I left his house with an hour-long interview about his early years on tape and a firm commitment to attend our next EYT meeting, scheduled for Sunday week.

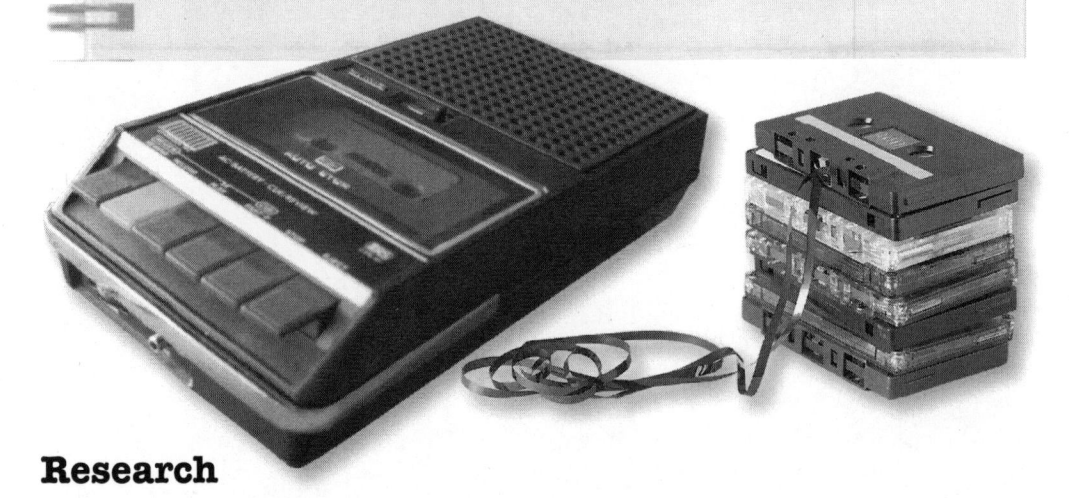

Research

Something I chanced upon in this instance became a template for all my verbatim play interviews.

I did no research.

Asking all the 'dumb' questions led Graham to describe each part of his life fully which would in turn make the play as clear as possible to the audience who, in turn, would arrive knowing nothing about him.

I also realised it would help me with the play if I pushed Graham to remember and replay conversations in detail. This became crucial to create any dialogue. I often went back to him and asked for elaboration.

VERBATIM - The Fun of Making Theatre Seriously by Mark Wheeller

Lesson:
Never research your subjects until you have talked to them.

Ethics

This project also established the ethics I would adhere to in mounting my future verbatim/documentary projects.

- Graham would share rights with me regarding the final script.
- We would, assuming he was willing, involve him in every aspect of the production, encouraging him to visit us in rehearsal and attending any performances as and when he wanted.
- We would listen to, discuss and resolve any reservations he had about the presentation.
- I would not allow Graham to change the lines of any of the other contributors without their permission and nor they his lines.
- Should the play ever make any money he would be paid a percentage of any royalties.
- Other contributors would make their contributions for no financial gain but each had the same editorial rights i.e. over the inclusion of their words. They would also be welcome to rehearsals, though the practicalities regarding where they lived made that less often/likely.
- In the event of us not being able to resolve by mutual discussion any aspect of the script or presentation I or EYT would bow to Graham as having a casting vote on any aspect. (This never had to happen).

VERBATIM - The Fun of Making Theatre Seriously by Mark Wheeller

This whole process was agreed without any contract (I didn't even consider it). It was the obvious and respectful way to proceed.

I wanted to honour the truth, as close as mutual memory offered. Graham and the various other contributors knew far more about that than I did.

I am always annoyed by films which alter the truth for 'dramatic purposes'. I do not understand why this may ever be deemed necessary. I was watching a documentary about Dominic Cummings, the British political strategist, and they said how the film about his contribution to the Brexit vote had 'dramatised' the way they arrived at the three-word quote BRING BACK CONTROL. The real story was completely different and arose from an equally interesting/dramatic situation. I felt cheated by the ego of the writer to needlessly invent.

Graham "Watching" Us

I clearly remember (no need for the diary here) the meeting just over a week later when Graham and Marie were due to see our first efforts.

I decided to do something that was very risky but I thought nothing of it.

I split the cast into groups and using a short part of the interview as our resource they prepared short improvisations.

This was based on Graham's knowledge of how his parents were told their eighteen-month-old baby son was to lose his eyesight.

It was an emotive scene.

I wanted to throw the cast in at the deep end and show I trusted them.

It barely crossed my mind that anything they produced might be less than exceptional and they all lived up to my expectations.

The final photograph Maud and Harry had taken of Graham with both his eyes. They commented to me how they were unable to "line his eyes up properly".

There was no plan B.

VERBATIM - The Fun of Making Theatre Seriously by Mark Wheeller

We met at 2pm.

Graham and Marie were due to join us at 4.

Everyone was focused with one eye firmly planted on the rapidly advancing clock.

There was a real determination to succeed from the outset...

... and great excitement about meeting Graham and Marie.

I was so proud to introduce them to my cast, and indeed the cast to Graham and Marie!

Graham sat and "watched" the scenes intently. Everyone was looking at him furtively to try and gauge his reaction. He gave nothing away until Zara made a simple mistake.

"... making a mountain out of a molehАll"

Everyone saw him laugh.

The tension was burst.

Everyone laughed and continued laughing longer than normal.

The ice had been broken.

Graham then proceeded to entertain us for three wonderful hours helped by his memory book he had typed out and brought with him.

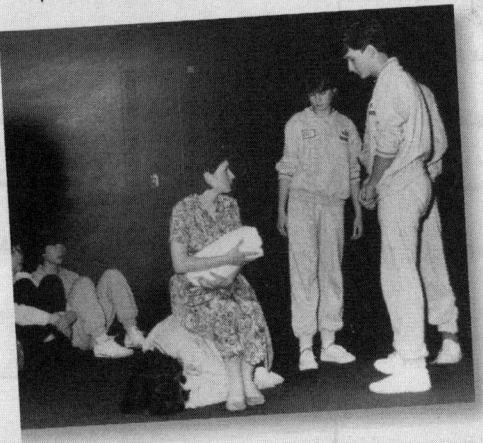

67

VERBATIM - The Fun of Making Theatre Seriously by Mark Wheeller

I didn't need to ask if people agreed. It was obvious from their excitement.

Graham Salmon was to be the subject of the next EYT play.

Our improvisation proved we would not get everything right.

Graham was very amused that we called his parents James and Laura when, in real life, they were Maud and Harry. In his interviews Graham had not mentioned their names.

It was a perfect vehicle for a documentary play... with music.

... of course 'with music'... how else was I to become a famous songwriter?

The idea of developing it as a documentary play was greeted with enthusiasm.

> I was a little apprehensive at first :) but once I was involved I really embraced it. Coincidentally, my mother worked at a school for blind and partially sighted children, so I had spent some time with the children there, but it still all seemed rather scary. I was in awe of Graham's achievements /spirit and, as our process unfolded, so did my admiration and understanding of him as a man and the challenges he faced.
> I remember both him and Marie very fondly. Graham had a wicked sense of humour and appeared to be modest but so determined. Marie was clearly his rock - she came across as an amazing woman with much strength and a vital no-nonsense attitude.
> **Lisa Andreae (née Beer).**

VERBATIM - The Fun of Making Theatre Seriously by Mark Wheeller

None of us had experienced parenthood, let alone a child losing his sight.

We would never have to question 'is this the right line?' because everything said in our play would be the memory of someone who was there!

If a line was missing I could simply ask the person I had interviewed to recall their feelings at the time or even ask them to approximate the words they said.

> *Everyone made us feel so welcome and I was soon at ease in their company. By the time I left that afternoon I was 99% sure I had made the right decision.*
>
> *The eighteen months that followed proved to be amongst the happiest and most enjoyable of my life. I became more involved with the youth theatre and still found the time to train and I really appreciated the support they gave me at race meetings. I could sense their excitement and that gave me extra motivation!.*
>
> **Graham Salmon,** written for the introduction for the original ***Race To Be Seen*** script published by Longman

Over the next few weeks we went to see Graham training and started to conduct some of the interviews. Two of the sixth form girls, Sarah (Record) and Laura (Dove), came with me to interview Maud and Harry. They went in Laura's impressive sports car with me leading the way on my rubbishy motorbike (Honda 125).

Maud and Harry really couldn't understand how anyone would ever be interested in their experiences.

There was a direct link to my boarding school situation in one scene. The awful thing for Graham's parents was, they had no choice in where he went to school. He had to be sent to boarding school because he was blind... from the age of four!

I remember being consciously keen to offer their words 'regarding this situation,' a platform long before I had ever spoken to anyone about my experiences.

Their memories of ordinary people being hurled into an extraordinary situation were fascinating.

I knew we were onto a winner!

Chapter 4: Developing The Script

> "With no family at that time, I threw myself into unbelievable hours of commitment to this "voluntary activity" and expected the same from EYT members. We worked hard, perhaps obsessively together and gave it our all. The quality of our presentations mattered to us above almost everything else."
>
> Mark Wheeller - from
> *The Story Behind Too Much Punch For Judy*

Our writing process was divided into two, research and assembly.

There wasn't much we could assemble until all the research was done, so everything apart from research was put on hold (frustratingly) and we engaged in another fundraising production. This helped bond the group and had everyone developing self-devised work of a light hearted/comic nature. Looking back, we were incredibly resourceful and productive. I record Matthew saying that he was glad it was over so that we could 'focus on the job in hand properly'!

VERBATIM - The Fun of Making Theatre Seriously by Mark Wheeller

Structuring the Outline of the Story

Meanwhile, I discover from my diary, I appointed a small group of sixth formers to become a structuring group alongside me. Following extensive interviews with Graham we held late night meetings at Matthew's parents' front room (larger than my flat!) working from 9pm til midnight to create a skeleton of Graham's story. This highlighted who we needed to interview. I recorded that we were all 'very pleased by our efforts'.

A younger group travelled up with me to Stantonbury to hear Roy Nevitt talk through the ground rules of creating a documentary play. My diary describes the evening as inspiring and 'it released us from some self-imposed chains'. I say little more.

We also had our first idea of what the title might be.

Runner on a String.

This referenced one of my favourite Eurovision winning songs (**Puppet On A String** by Sandie Shaw) and also Graham who, when running any race involving bends, would be attached to his guide runner by a small length of string... well, rope. - #dramaticlicense

Graham was very busy training for the European 400 metres due to be held in Bulgaria later in the year just before our proposed premiere performance. I remember saying to him:

'That will be the end of our play... regardless of how you get on.'

Once again I expected nothing less than he would win the gold medal (his first).

I did vaguely wonder what exactly we would do if he didn't win so was rooting for him.

There was no Plan B!

Roger Wray (guide runner) with Graham.
Roger is holding the guide rope in his hand. You can see how short it is.

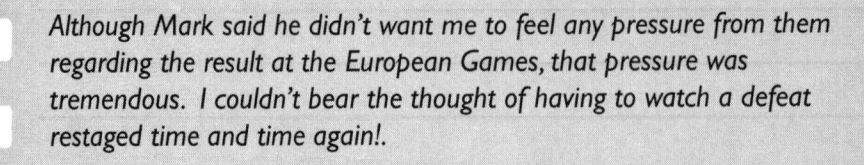

VERBATIM - The Fun of Making Theatre Seriously by Mark Wheeller

> *Although Mark said he didn't want me to feel any pressure from them regarding the result at the European Games, that pressure was tremendous. I couldn't bear the thought of having to watch a defeat restaged time and time again!.*
>
> **Graham Salmon,** written for the introduction for the original **Race To Be Seen** script published by Longman

Research

It was at this point (25th July, the start of the summer holidays) that my diary becomes live and, after another structuring meeting (lasting 11 hours!!!), we began to make real progress.

25th July 1984

None of the work we did could be called inspiring. It was more a process of sifting and sorting into sections. We decided we needed about twenty five files to store our testimony / documentary evidence into chronological order. The purchase of these will make life far simpler.

With Graham's help we are now armed with telephone numbers to arrange interviews. We plan to have every interview transcribed and filed by the end of the summer holidays.

We have agreed on an ending (suggested by Matt) which added to John Rowley's starting gun start gives us a couple of certainties to work from.

The last line of the play will now be:

"I would rather people think of me as Graham first and as being blind very much second."

cont...

VERBATIM - The Fun of Making Theatre Seriously by Mark Wheeller

> ...cont
>
> Or will it? (It wasn't... but the starting pistol start did remain in place). As I write this I realise the contradictory nature of this statement.
>
> It is of course Graham's ability to compensate for this handicap which is of interest to spectators of this play.
>
> I am surprised to report that two sets of students' parents have described this project as being in "bad taste".
>
> What a frightening attitude! I hope they come to see it!

This was to become a feature of my work. I remember (minority) parental concern at a few of my future plays. It was rare for these feelings to be expressed to me... but they were reported by the YT members!

Oh, and we had another title possibility:

Graham - A Life Worth Living?

The next day we were working again (long hours too), I report that we didn't finish till after midnight.

I phoned Graham's contacts and made (inept) attempts at securing sponsorship. It had become clear that research alone would be cost-prohibitive.

Eek!!

When not doing this, I was transcribing Graham's original interview tapes by hand. This was incredibly time consuming but I was like a dog with a bone, describing it in my diary as, 'a well worth-while task.'

That same week the other interviews began.

73

VERBATIM - The Fun of Making Theatre Seriously by Mark Wheeller

> Visited the Abbey National in Moorgate where Graham works. We were given a fabulous morning by the women who work with Graham.
>
> They obviously have a great laugh. I am impressed by how seriously we are being taken. People are keen to support us because Graham is considered to be a worthwhile subject.
>
> One of the women said this play could become "very big" which was encouraging. It's all great fun but tiring. It's the best project I've been involved in.
>
> What will we do when it's all over?

I returned home to complete more transcription, It was non-stop.

It wasn't only me committed to the transcription.

On the 8th August I reported that Lisa (aged 14) had completed 33 sides of A4.
(Lisa on right)

> I remember lots of transcribing, discussions, brainstorming, small groups working on sections possibly? It was a thrill to be piecing together the story in the words of all the crucial people in Graham's life.
>
> My parents remember us gathering a couple of times at my house to write the play and that you asked to borrow a thesaurus to be horrified that we could only find our dictionaries! I have little recollection of this, but it emphasises the community approach that you took over the course of writing *Race*.
> I am still very proud to see my name on the first page of the script. *Race to be Seen* was a world away from the musicals we had done (and I loved). It flexed the TV researcher and writer in me - the TV producer as it turned out. My involvement with EYT and Drama at St John's led me to my career choice. I feel it isn't a huge coincidence that I ended up producing documentaries and television focusing on social experiments and human experiences - peoples' lives always at the forefront.
> **Lisa Andreae (née Beer).**

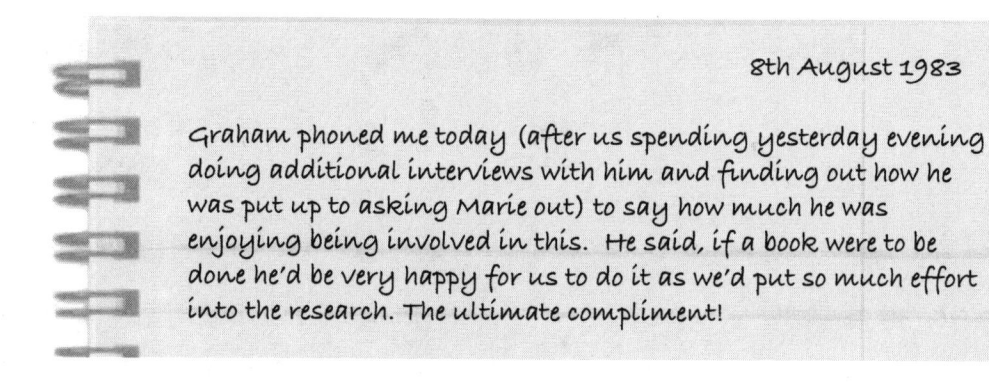

VERBATIM - The Fun of Making Theatre Seriously by Mark Wheeller

> **8th August 1983**
>
> Graham phoned me today (after us spending yesterday evening doing additional interviews with him and finding out how he was put up to asking Marie out) to say how much he was enjoying being involved in this. He said, if a book were to be done he'd be very happy for us to do it as we'd put so much effort into the research. The ultimate compliment!

On the 9th August I heard that Epping Forest District Council were so impressed by our plans that they wanted to publish the script!

Also, Graham's former PE teacher had suggested we take the play up to the Edinburgh Fringe to make all our efforts more worthwhile and... he would put us up in his school for the blind (The Royal Blind School, Edinburgh) where he was now Headteacher. That offered us a huge financial saving.

Edinburgh became a really worthwhile consideration that was now within our grasp! Huge thanks to Bill Aitken!

There were amusing moments too...

> **11th August 1983**
>
> Matthew and I went to Moorfields Eye hospital to interview a top consultant. We discovered that, had Graham been born now, they would be able to save his sight.
>
> In the middle of the interview, while the consultant was talking about glass eyes, Matt slid off his chair, seemingly in slow motion to the floor and stayed there.
>
> The consultant said:
>
> "Does your friend always do this?"
>
> cont...

VERBATIM - The Fun of Making Theatre Seriously by Mark Wheeller

>...cont
>
>He certainly didn't... but we all saw the funny side of it and, after drinking some water, Matt was back to normal and didn't want a fuss made of it at all!
>
>After that, Matt and I went to eat in a little burger bar. I walked into the Ladies loo by mistake!
>However, unlike Matt, I had no scar from my accident!

Matt outside the grand entrance to the Moorfields Eye Hospital on the day he passed out during the interview.

Reading through my diary, I become all too aware of how supportive the EYT members were. I describe Bernadette's work as being like a secretary. She worked with me on the fundraising side of things.

Meanwhile Fran (Jackson) and Matt were off to Scotland (by train on their own - they were 17 and today this would never be allowed) to interview Bill Aitken. They went because it saved on expenses to have them on the train!

On the 17th August we went to see Graham at a race meeting.

>A significant evening as Matt, Laura and I went to watch Graham competing live in a 400m race. It proved to be a powerful evening.
>
>All the other competitors (and it was a big race meeting) were sighted! Graham did a fabulous first 300 metres and it looked as though he may win!
>
>However he felt he "died" in the last 100 metres and he came last with a poor time (for him) of 57.5.
>
>   cont...

76

VERBATIM - The Fun of Making Theatre Seriously by Mark Wheeller

...cont

We were all shaking with excitement by the end of it.

Two little boys, who were quite happy to take the mick out of him at the start, were stunned to see that he had a competent running style, easily matching the others and ran over to him to get his autograph as the race finished.

Prejudice overturned in under a minute! Unfortunately my tape recorder didn't function properly so I wasn't able to record his analysis of the race once it had finished.

I rode home thrilled!

These race meetings at Haringey were a regular feature of that summer holiday. There was a market stall on the way to the track which sold cherries and I'd always stop to buy some. I still think of those days when I see cherries on sale.

I loved the unbelievable challenge of our blind friend taking on fully sighted, fully trained athletes. These were the most exciting sporting events I had ever seen.

Graham also did the high jump. He was the British Champion for blind people no less. It was on one of these occasions that I witnessed the sort of problem Graham had to overcome.

He used the Fosbury Flop which involves approaching the bar in a J shaped run up and then jump backwards over the bar, face up!

VERBATIM - The Fun of Making Theatre Seriously by Mark Wheeller

Graham stood at the bar, then paced five steps back to his start position. Then, using only those five steps, he approached the bar and jumped...backwards! It was incredible. However, under the bar I saw a metal frame holding the cushioned area that makes the landing safe. It wasn't safe if anyone slightly misjudged their run up and landed on the upper part of the frame. That would be incredibly painful.

I asked Graham if he'd ever missed. Of course he had... and, he confirmed, 'It was bloody painful!'

I remember him telling me that on his way to work one day, he had fallen part way down an open manhole cover that was unprotected by any barrier for the few moments he happened to be walking past. He had really hurt himself. He made it into work and, after a short time sorting out his injuries, continued his normal day. Frightening.

> 18th August 1983
>
> Matt followed Graham into work, without Graham's knowledge. His objective was to observe Graham's "behaviour" as research for his acting role.
>
> Matt was unable to answer a man who was rude to him about putting his feet on the seat so he didn't give himself away. We all found that hilarious...
>
> Matt always wanted to answer back. It must have taken huge self control! Matt said he thinks he's got the rhythm of how Graham uses his white stick.
>
> cont...

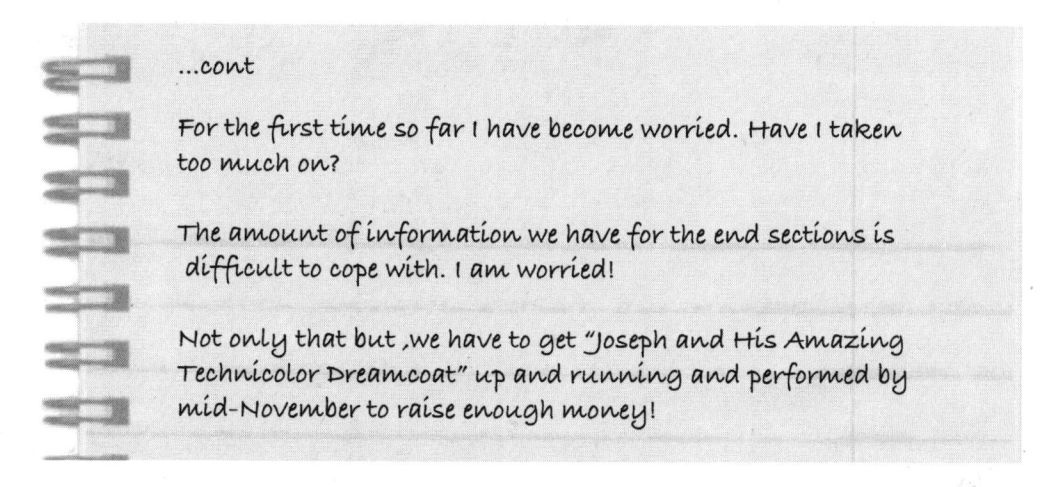

VERBATIM - The Fun of Making Theatre Seriously by Mark Wheeller

> ...cont
>
> For the first time so far I have become worried. Have I taken too much on?
>
> The amount of information we have for the end sections is difficult to cope with. I am worried!
>
> Not only that but, we have to get "Joseph and His Amazing Technicolor Dreamcoat" up and running and performed by mid-November to raise enough money!

I have mentioned all of this because, throughout this period, many of us immersed ourselves in Graham's life. It was an invaluable aspect of our research period. This thorough approach wasn't undertaken unwillingly. It was part of the commitment to the project and led to us all (including Marie and Graham) becoming, quite naturally, a close knit group.

Writing The Play

My diary is abruptly suspended while we are busy with the fundraising production but Bernadette remembers the development of the play and describes it in a wonderfully simple manner showing how we took on the task in-front of us.

> When it came to start writing the play, after gathering masses of hand-transcribed text, it seemed relatively straightforward. We knew the story because over the months we had come to know the man. The time-line, the frame, was all there for us in chronologically ordered files. It was a case of what needs to be in and what we classed as irrelevant.
> Looking back that was a huge decision, which I for one didn't worry about too much. I never felt any pressure. By the time it came to write "his" story, we were writing about a friend.
> **Bernadette Cleere** (née **Chapman**).

During the time my diary went into hibernation my attention switched to our fundraiser: *Joseph and His Amazing Technicolor Dreamcoat*. It was actually pretty good, thanks in no small part to the stalwart efforts of our newly discovered choreographer Alison Burkert, who ended up taking on pretty much everything in terms of directorial duties while I generally swanned around doing... well, I'm not quite sure what I did!

VERBATIM - The Fun of Making Theatre Seriously by Mark Wheeller

It was the first time I'd ever been involved in a production where my heart, honestly wasn't in it. I was constantly projecting forward to being able to focus totally on the Graham Salmon project.

Alison also offered to take on the task of fundraising for the Graham Salmon project. This offer was accepted with much relief and she did a grand job relieving me of something I wasn't good at! Delegation... I was much better at that!

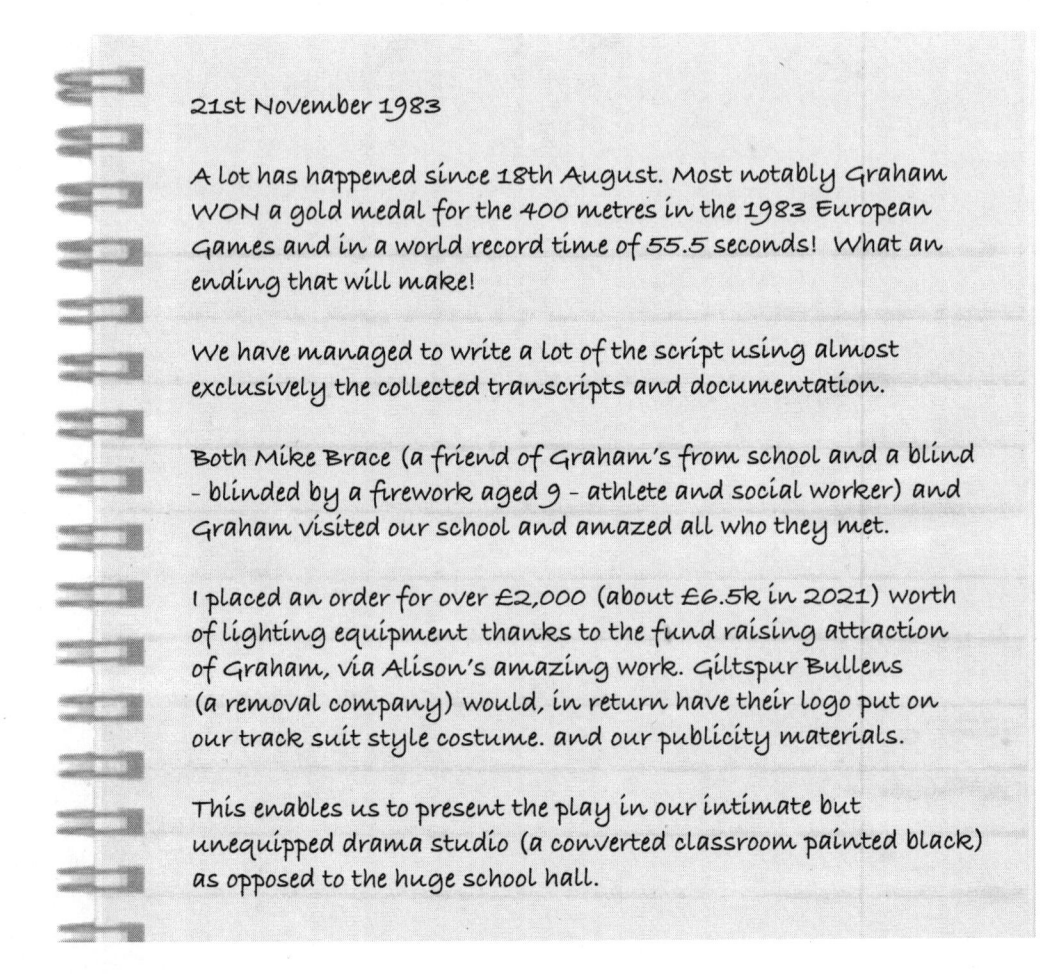

> 21st November 1983
>
> A lot has happened since 18th August. Most notably Graham WON a gold medal for the 400 metres in the 1983 European Games and in a world record time of 55.5 seconds! What an ending that will make!
>
> We have managed to write a lot of the script using almost exclusively the collected transcripts and documentation.
>
> Both Mike Brace (a friend of Graham's from school and a blind - blinded by a firework aged 9 - athlete and social worker) and Graham visited our school and amazed all who they met.
>
> I placed an order for over £2,000 (about £6.5k in 2021) worth of lighting equipment thanks to the fund raising attraction of Graham, via Alison's amazing work. Giltspur Bullens (a removal company) would, in return have their logo put on our track suit style costume. and our publicity materials.
>
> This enables us to present the play in our intimate but unequipped drama studio (a converted classroom painted black) as opposed to the huge school hall.

VERBATIM - The Fun of Making Theatre Seriously by Mark Wheeller

Costumes

We had made the decision by this point to have the cast wearing a uniform. I don't claim any knowledge of costuming a production but this seemed to be an appropriate idea using a sports theme. We contrasted Graham, by giving him an England tracksuit/sports kit (provided by Graham).

Graham's family were kept outside the uniform idea and dressed in clothes the cast found which generally represented people of their age and of that era. Maud wore a dress and Harry a shirt and tie. Graham's sisters wore a skirt, blouse and cardigan.

Giltspur Bullens had, deservedly, a prominent mention as at least half the cast wore the standard track suits throughout the production and were onstage for most of the time. I was very happy to accommodate this and it didn't interrupt the integrity of the production... if anything sponsorship was entirely in keeping with the sports theme.

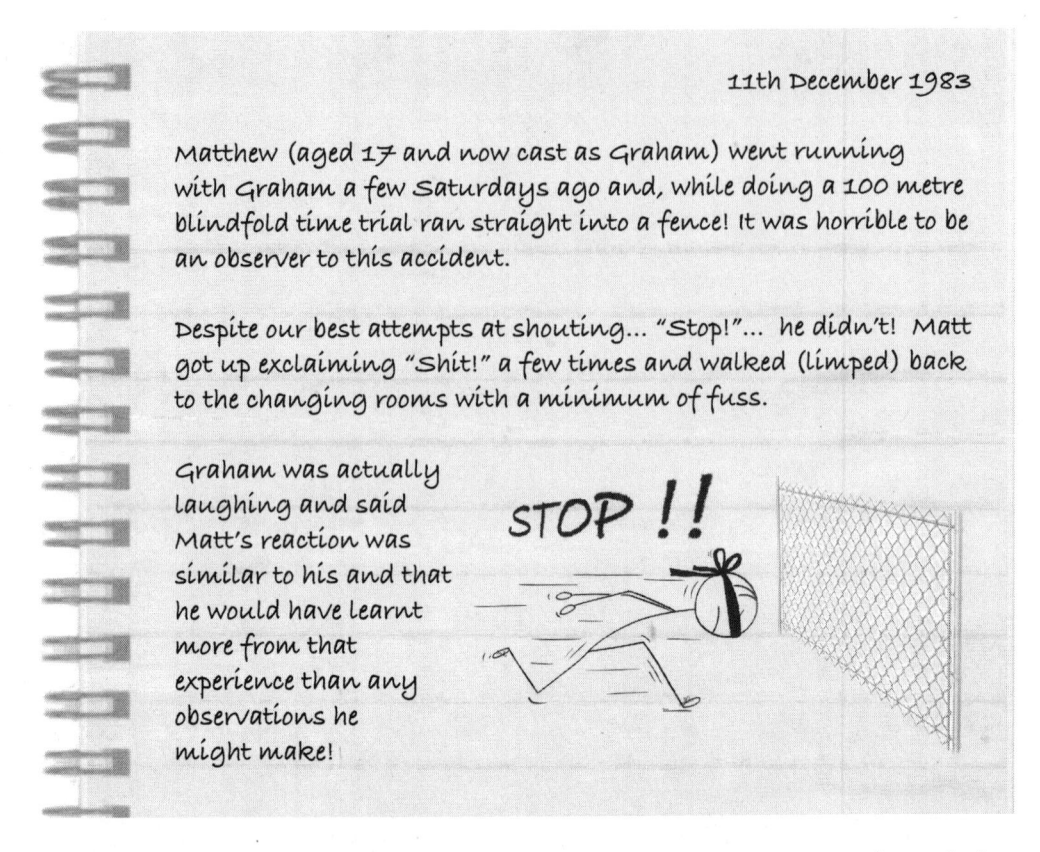

VERBATIM - The Fun of Making Theatre Seriously by Mark Wheeller

> **11th December 1983**
>
> Matthew (aged 17 and now cast as Graham) went running with Graham a few Saturdays ago and, while doing a 100 metre blindfold time trial ran straight into a fence! It was horrible to be an observer to this accident.
>
> Despite our best attempts at shouting… "Stop!"… he didn't! Matt got up exclaiming "Shit!" a few times and walked (limped) back to the changing rooms with a minimum of fuss.
>
> Graham was actually laughing and said Matt's reaction was similar to his and that he would have learnt more from that experience than any observations he might make!

I suspect today I might be taken to court for putting a young person through this without relevant risk assessments being undertaken but Matt took it in his stride and his parents obviously went along with it too! I suspect he didn't tell them too much about it.

We never did find out Matt's time, but he was really going for it.

I wondered what Matt thought about it now…

> It's strange that anyone would need to ask that and, by doing so, misses the interesting and insightful part of the story: Graham's reaction.
> Graham's laughter showed me, first hand, the challenge of disability does not need to make you a victim. Graham would have laughed his head off if he had done it or any of his mates… blind or otherwise.
> Secondly, as Graham pointed out, I learnt more from that experience than any observation. What did he mean?
> Did it hurt? Yes.
> Did it hurt my pride? Yes, a bit.
>
> cont…

VERBATIM - The Fun of Making Theatre Seriously by Mark Wheeller

> Did it stop me wanting to do it again? Of course not. It made me want to do it again but better.
> Disability can hurt physically and emotionally but it mustn't define you and make you miss out on anything.
> People with a disability don't want sympathy; they want a hand to help them up so they can try again.
> The extensive research we undertook was a real luxury. I recognised that at the time and, even in a professional context later in life, I never had the chance to research so thoroughly.
> I didn't tell my parents about it but, hilariously, I remember you being unable to resist telling them, as was your (overly responsible) way.
> They just thought it was all a bit odd but… if I was happy they were too.
> Matt Allen

Interestingly, one thing I have always done with the PE department in my school, is to organise sessions on the field where students can experience a range of blindfold sports, notably running and football.
You will see in the scheme of work (in the new Salamander Street resource to accompany the **Race To Be Seen** script) we undertook various blindfold rehearsals. These really make performers focus!

One disappointing thing about this project is the small number of people who have the commitment to remain with it. Perhaps they lack the vision I have. Perhaps there is not enough action. One of these is in the sixth form and wants to go to Drama School!!!

Another dropped out saying she was finding it boring! Boring? The week before she'd been with us reading the script to Graham's mum and dad. What on earth made her change her mind so fast?

The drop out rate has been high, far higher than anything I've been involved with before, yet I'm convinced it's much more interesting. The drop outs are even causing Matt to wobble. I remain very confident.

I have obviously blocked this from my memory. I think my attitude would always have been to plough on regardless but I couldn't help but feel a sense of personal rejection, not dissimilar to the feelings of being dumped by girlfriends in quick succession. It's not a nice feeling. It is a feature of my productions that people drop out.[16] However, there is always the upside as there was in this instance…

---

[16] Seven out of sixteen who featured in the first meeting photograph saw the production through to its conclusion.

VERBATIM - The Fun of Making Theatre Seriously by Mark Wheeller

Two very powerful and impressive sixth formers have joined our team recently. Nicki Harris and Dawn Baker. It's impressive how Lisa has remained when five of her motivated peers have deserted us.

I have always said the writing team have automatic involvement in the performance. I need to consider this in the casting... particularly as we approach the most complex section... the sporting achievements.

We must avoid this becoming a series of facts and figures. I remain very confident. I will cast in January. I will plug it very hard which will be helped from some interest from the local media: Articles have appeared in the local press (and the Evening Standard) and it looks like we may even get some TV coverage. I remain convinced this is of national interest.

It will be so disappointing if it has no future beyond the performances we do next year.

VERBATIM - The Fun of Making Theatre Seriously by Mark Wheeller

VERBATIM - The Fun of Making Theatre Seriously by Mark Wheeller

At the start of the holidays (19th-22nd Dec) a small team of us (Fran, Matt, Lisa, Zara (Chapman) and Barrie Sapsford)) completed four intensive writing days (clocking up 32 hours) to prepare a script for the highly anticipated January auditions.

Graham helped us with difficult links by offering additional words ("great collaboration - or cheating?" I asked myself in my diary).

Matt put our excitement into words I know I felt as well!:

'Christmas will be an anticlimax after this!'

Graham was equally excited and, on the 22nd Dec, the writing team piled round to his house for a celebratory Christmas meal (always a generous feast) where we shared the completed first draft with him and Marie.

I recorded Graham saying this after we left:

> *It's been great to have such a nice bunch of people to write a play about me. Any of them can feel welcome at my home any time. I have felt so involved in the writing. I would love to be involved in the rehearsals. We must not lose contact. I was so excited at work today about it.*

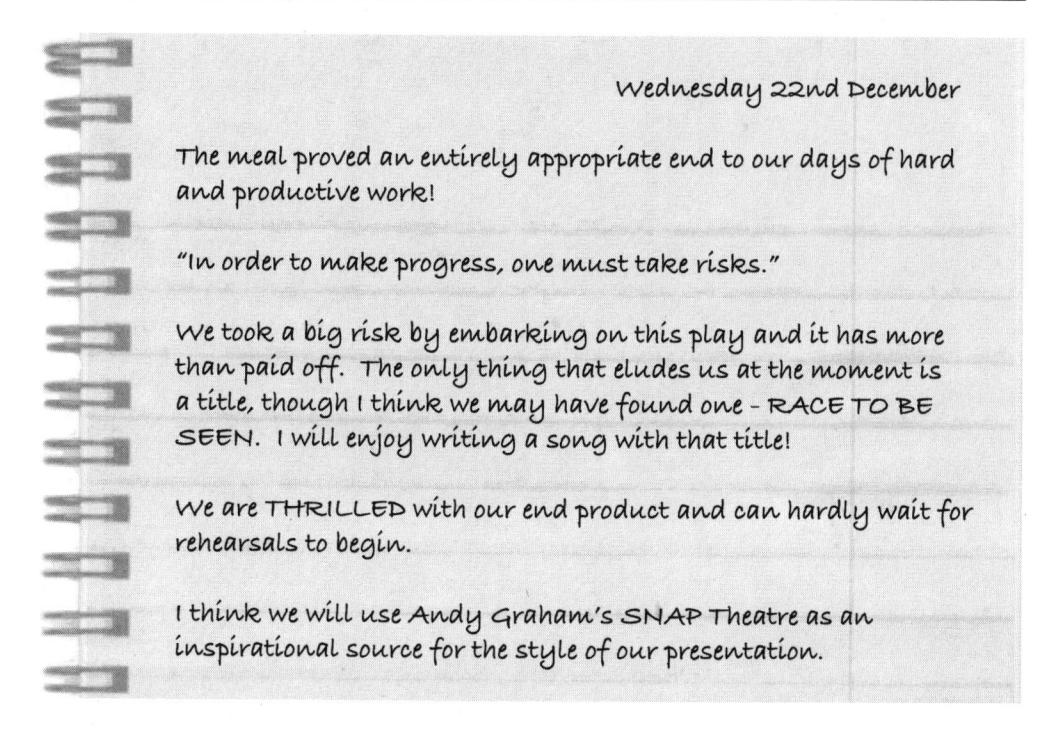

VERBATIM - The Fun of Making Theatre Seriously by Mark Wheeller

Wednesday 22nd December

The meal proved an entirely appropriate end to our days of hard and productive work!

"In order to make progress, one must take risks."

We took a big risk by embarking on this play and it has more than paid off. The only thing that eludes us at the moment is a title, though I think we may have found one - RACE TO BE SEEN. I will enjoy writing a song with that title!

We are THRILLED with our end product and can hardly wait for rehearsals to begin.

I think we will use Andy Graham's SNAP Theatre as an inspirational source for the style of our presentation.

SNAP Theatre Company (My '80s Frantic Assembly - from Hertfordshire!)

I had chanced upon a theatrical production of **Kes** (an adaptation of the **Kestrel for a Knave** book and one of my favourite films) as we started to develop **Race**.

It was totally random. I was in London and a poster advertising Andy Graham's SNAP Theatre Company caught my attention as they were performing very near to where I was standing. Unusually, I made the decision to just go and see it spontaneously!

Then I discovered that SNAP were based down the road from Epping, in Hertfordshire.

I almost walked out, as there were only two others in the audience! I feared it was not going to be very good. I stayed purely because I'd spent money on the ticket and I felt somewhat conspicuous with nobody else there, so settled down to dispose of an hour of my life hoping above anything else that I wasn't going to be embarrassed by any audience participation!

I could not have been more impressed.

VERBATIM - The Fun of Making Theatre Seriously by Mark Wheeller

- The four cast members played not only people, but also props and scenery

- There were so many magic moments and one that was especially spine tingling

Two performers created a pedal bin. A third, playing the young boy searching for his missing kestrel entered and pressed the foot pedal (human foot) on the pedal bin. The lid opened (a pair of human arms) and, as I recognised the little mechanical bounce of the bin lid, I sniggered. This was followed by a silence as we, in the audience, realised what the young lad had seen. The contrast between this moment of humour (from how the scene was presented; not the scene itself) and the high drama of his realisation could not have been more pronounced. His older brother had brutally murdered the kestrel and disposed of it in the pedal-bin.

Like Roy's documentary plays, this presentation worked on different levels:

- The story, which had already won me over

- The clever presentation, which impressed, amused and added to the entertainment

These 'tricks' cost nothing.

I was confident we could emulate this![17]

I spent much of my Christmas holiday copying out the script by hand and simultaneously editing it. I loved doing this.

Graham was working over Christmas too, writing song lyrics. I wrote the music for the title song in an inspired afternoon, made a tape and delivered it to Matt who loved it!

> 8th January 1984
> Graham told me that both he and Marie dreamt of the play. Marie had woken Graham up as she was watching the last race.
> They took a risk letting us delve into their lives but now it seems worth while and they're happy with things.
> This diary is to be read by an old college friend of mine who wants to write an article about the project for a women's magazine.

---

[17] Andy Graham (SNAP Theatre) has contacted me in the lockdown requesting permission for SNAP to embark on a production of my recent play **Game Over**. This will make a wonderful bookend to my career to have the company who inspired me, performing one of my plays!

Chapter 5: Page To Stage

> THE FIRST MURDER THAT ANY SERIAL KILLER COMMITS IS THE REVEALING MURDER.
>
> HE ENJOYED DOING IT AND IT'S THE ENJOYMENT HE GOT FROM THAT FIRST MURDER THAT PROPELLED HIM TO KILL AGAIN AND AGAIN AND AGAIN.
>
> Professor David Wilson - Criminologist talking about Dennis Neilson

> These words sum up my memories of the process we engaged in with you for 'rehearsals':
> - collaborative
> - experimental
> - enthusiastic
> - innovative
> - encouraging
> - inclusive
> - fun
> - demanding
> - perfectionist
>
> Both of the last ones, more positive than negative!
> There was so much involvement, fun and laughter. Lots of moving around the stage - choreography compiled between us. That and you telling me off, quite rightly, for saying one of my lines far too quickly, when I was taking it too literally - now weirdly transfixed phrase in my brain: 'Now they were running (pause) striving to reach maximum speed'.
> **Lisa Andreae (née Beer)**

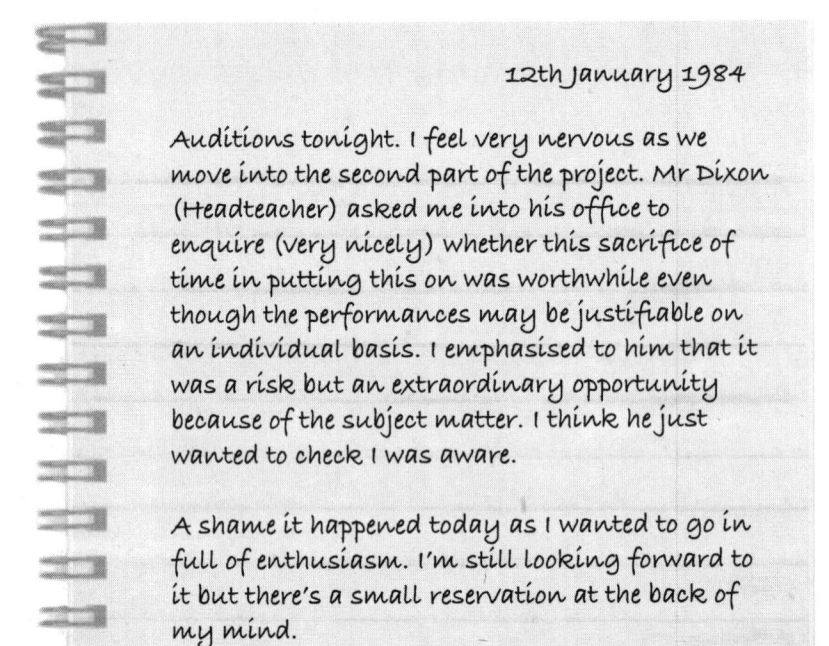

VERBATIM - The Fun of Making Theatre Seriously by Mark Wheeller

> *12th January 1984*
>
> Auditions tonight. I feel very nervous as we move into the second part of the project. Mr Dixon (Headteacher) asked me into his office to enquire (very nicely) whether this sacrifice of time in putting this on was worthwhile even though the performances may be justifiable on an individual basis. I emphasised to him that it was a risk but an extraordinary opportunity because of the subject matter. I think he just wanted to check I was aware.
>
> A shame it happened today as I wanted to go in full of enthusiasm. I'm still looking forward to it but there's a small reservation at the back of my mind.

I decided to have two casts to allow more people to be involved but to have only one (adult) Graham... Matthew Allen. I also cast a young Benjy Shephard (later to become the famous Ben Shephard) as one of the two 'boy' Graham's (the other being Jason Lawrence). Benjy was one of the only people not to attend St John's School. His mum was thrilled about the casting saying soon after rehearsals started:

'He's already got more out of this than we hoped and the effect of meeting Graham was astonishing!'

I would have been so impressed back then to realise that I had spotted a future celebrity!

This said, I was soon reporting that he was a little too stage-school for my liking and wanted him to be more "natural".

VERBATIM - The Fun of Making Theatre Seriously by Mark Wheeller

It should perhaps be noted here that my approach, having run productions successfully prior to any 'training', was to use rehearsals to rehearse. By that, I mean we never did vocal or physical warm-ups or other time-consuming stuff. I have never expected people to take shoes or socks off before they started to act and inwardly laughed when I have encountered it and hated it when it's expected of me! I mean why??? We were very pragmatic and just got on with it.

We never used make up, unless for a very specific effect. It never seemed to have the detrimental effect we were warned this would have under stage lighting... and saved a lot of money!

We never spent any time getting into role or 'releasing the role' after a play. We just got on and did it.

My various casts have always expressed smug amusement when we've watched professional companies arrive and go through what we believe to be 'weird rituals' before they are able to rehearse or perform. We have also enjoyed people's reactions to our low key preparations before our productions.

When someone came in to 'support' (we often benefitted from fantastic interns) who wanted to offer such starters we were respectful and, I hope, open-minded. Some cast members liked the warm-up opportunities, and sometimes they continued to offer this. but it never seemed to catch on fully. There was always something more pressing we needed to accomplish. I can see that, when you are a visitor, it's helpful to have a way of establishing a relationship and a warm-up (or game) can do this... but for every rehearsal?

I have always been always super-proud of our 'no thrills' approach and ability to arrive in a theatre, run on to stage and perform should the situation arise!

Our rehearsals would often lead to major re-writes. This is a feature of all the plays I wrote, where I was the first to put on a production.

So, for me, rehearsals became a period of extended exploration of the script and an indulgent opportunity to see how it transfers from page to stage.

91

VERBATIM - The Fun of Making Theatre Seriously by Mark Wheeller

The Cast Working With Graham

In our second long Sunday rehearsal the cast met Graham and immersed themselves in a number of blindfold activities, including football and cricket. I set the cast the task of teaching Graham how to mime... not as easy as it sounds! The press were there to record it all!

At the end of the rehearsal Bernadette sang **Race To Be Seen**; a perfect end to an incredible afternoon.

VERBATIM - The Fun of Making Theatre Seriously by Mark Wheeller

Exploring the text through Improvisation

We attempted practical improvisations on the themes of the play.

1. Parents being informed and reacting to news of serious health issues for their baby child (not blindness).
2. A child - Feeling different.
3. Overcoming Odds.
4. Trying unsuccessfully to find employment.
5. The determination needed by an Olympic athlete.

The tasks were purposely open ended.

The results were not good.

Only three out of five groups had something they felt able to show.

However, one scene made a lasting impression on me. John Rowley[18] (17) had played a major role in **Blackout** and he demonstrated an innovative idea to show the physical effort of an Olympic athlete.

John stood beside his small group physically exercising and tiring himself out in front of us as his group performed a scene about the determination of an Olympic athlete. Our reaction, as we watched this, was incredible. We found ourselves adopting his breathing pattern and empathising closely with John's physical exertion.

In the versions of the 400 metres race Epping Youth Theatre staged for the final production, we were not experienced enough to exploit this idea. I imagine John must have felt it was lost forever.

---

[18] John Rowley is one of the EYT performers to have made a professional career out of acting, having performed for the famous Brith Gof Company and more recently The National Theatre of Wales.

VERBATIM - The Fun of Making Theatre Seriously by Mark Wheeller

However, I remembered it, realising it was the key to that scene. It became an inspirational stepping-stone to provide the foundation to all the subsequent 400-metre race scenes I staged.[19] It conveyed the essence of the event rather than its physical shape.

Now, I would expect a far higher (5/5) success rate in terms of performances shown. Perhaps this lack of 'judgement' proved supportive and inclusive to put today's jargon onto it. There were six cast members missing without any reason. I don't know how I coped with that but, I must have been disappointed. Despite the low success rate and attendance I seem to have been surprisingly upbeat saying,

> The evening was one of the best first meetings for a production I've experienced. The discussions provoked by the work were invaluable to heightening our understanding of what we are doing… and why we are doing it!

Was that me trying hard to justify a pretty dismal evening?

Whatever is the truth, that one piece of improvisation by John made that evening worth its weight in gold.

By the following week we had a venue booked in Edinburgh but hadn't managed to stage any scenes!

A couple of weeks later I was reporting that Graham and Marie attended a rehearsal and it was 'appalling'.

Progress was by no means what I was expecting. We must have felt worried. I know Matthew was and, as my right hand man, that knocked my confidence. I had 'words' with Matt.

---

[19] An impressive version of this scene using this idea as the starting point can be seen in the OYT production of *Graham — World's Fastest Blind Runner* DVD available from salamanderstreet.com

VERBATIM - The Fun of Making Theatre Seriously by Mark Wheeller

> I was undergoing teenage angst about the meaning of life. I remember it really pissing you off. It wasn't about EYT. You were right to be firm about it. I think I became vegetarian around this time. A teenager searching for personal definition.
>
> Interestingly, I remember talking to you really was just part of exploring the idea of "meaning". Your reaction was so strong and as if you felt a personal attack so I realised I was coming across differently to how I thought I was. Your threat to pull my main helper role from me was like a slap in the face. EYT was one of the very things that was giving my life meaning. So... lesson learned.
>
> Some friends and I had been getting into modern art and reading beginner's philosophy concepts. I think some teenagers are drawn to that stuff. It was EYT that kept my mind busy.
> **Matt Allen**

Rehearsals were turbulent... my diary explains one that worked particularly well and perhaps, shines a light on how I work with my groups... when it's at its best...

25th Feb 1984

We staged the Crystal Palace race (the race against sighted athletes). It worked surprisingly well. The group who staged it produced an excellent illustration of our group decision making process at its best. I was able to take a back seat, contributing as a catalyst/facilitator.

One ace idea I had was to slowly move to silence after the cheers of Graham's success, so the only sound remaining was Matthew (Graham's) panting... an excellent tension creating device. Then we applied the idea of group breaths a lot.

I will need to ask for help. I'm not a very good director but I think my experience is now showing and I am improving. My greatest asset is my ability to facilitate these kids to suggest their views and then frame them into the performance, thus enabling them to develop an "eye" for Theatre.

Zara's unison camera click was Zara at her best.

VERBATIM - The Fun of Making Theatre Seriously by Mark Wheeller

Fran and Emma

There were other entries around this time where we weren't at our best:

4th March 1984

The amount we achieved was negligible. Enthusiasm was low. One cast member dropped out after only two weeks of taking over from someone else. Rehearsals are now well behind schedule. Negativity is creeping in. Only Dawn is giving her all consistently. I am shouting too much. Perhaps this is my way of testing commitment when we're at a bit of a low ebb. Perhaps it gives me confidence that I am in control?

Matt has spoken to Graham about not being able to find a character. This has led to Graham questioning Matt's ability. The pressure is now on Matthew to prove himself.[20]

Even Graham was disagreeing with us when we cut two amusing scenes, saying;

"Without them the play will lack humour."

I'm not sure how to answer that. Perhaps we lack the skills to do this? Some of the cast might benefit from a more prescriptive director. I'm off to bed tonight deflated and worried about the play.

---

[20] I learnt from this that it is important the cast say nothing to the contributors to cause them to develop doubts. This is hard to manage when I am also demanding that relationships need to be authentic!

VERBATIM - The Fun of Making Theatre Seriously by Mark Wheeller

A few days later and I report that Matt voluntarily came up to school (while I was working on another play I was entering for a local drama festival) in the evening to work on his lines and characterisation, saying to me:

'I don't know how you've tolerated me.'

I don't know what I said at the time but I was so grateful for his commitment and felt guilty for my lack of faith.

This project seemed to vacillate from one feeling to another with no warning and was something I continued to experience throughout my time as a Youth Theatre director. I imagine every director/teacher will recognise this... and of course I tended to focus on the worst bits!

A week later I wrote in my diary:

An AWFUL rehearsal today!

Matt took the decision to do some rehearsals in a blindfold. What a fantastic initiative.

I began to see the way in which this project was garnering a reputation outside St John's walls when we entered an imaginative staging of David Campton's fantastic play **Us And Them** in the Waltham Abbey Drama Festival.

The festival organisers had heard of our project. Graham, who was attending as an EYT supporter, was made to stand up by the Mayor to receive an ovation.

A director of a competing group who I'd congratulated said:

'And you're the director of EYT? That is praise indeed!'

I had never had my opinion valued so much and I felt wonderful!

VERBATIM - The Fun of Making Theatre Seriously by Mark Wheeller

Director?

It was magnificent for my sense of self to be seen as an 'amazing director' but the reality was a long way from that.

I have always had serious doubts about my ability.

I was proud of my 'democratic process' but I knew that offered a cover for not having my own original ideas and it saved me from having to plan!

In many ways I could have been accused of 'chickening out' of my directorial responsibilities.

I was totally reliant on the cast for their ideas. I never provide a ceiling to achievements but did become frustrated (and voiced it) when they didn't meet my hopes and expectations.

The incredibly fortunate thing is, I managed to surround myself with young people who consistently rose to the occasion and delivered impressive work because we all cared enormously about what we were doing.

I also offered an iron determination to complete projects I started no matter what befell us on the way!

We were very concerned that **Race** was being deemed the 'serious' side of Youth Theatre, yet Graham was a really funny guy. Were we losing this important aspect of his character in our desire to sell him as a determined athlete?

To resolve this, a number of anecdotes were put into the script, stories from his workmates in addition to the Ringer (copulating dog) monologue. These didn't serve to move the story on but they said so much about Graham.

By Easter, we had staged every scene bar the final one in rough terms but we had never completed a run through.

VERBATIM - The Fun of Making Theatre Seriously by Mark Wheeller

Our process of staging a scene was generally:

- We all read through the scene.

- We discuss ideas people have had during the read through

- We try it out on the floor with cast members guessing appropriate moves to enliven or illustrate the spoken word. Everyone then has the opportunity to review what we have and suggest more ideas before trying to develop this raw idea.

- I might even leave the room (or turn my back) while the cast attempt to stage something more complicated. I return when they are ready and offer my comments.

- Occasionally the cast worked on a particularly difficult scene in small groups and then watch each other's efforts and draw something out of that.

- Occasionally I would tell them what to do.

- More often than not it was a process of me asking open questions like: 'How can we highlight the importance of the employers in this scene?' or 'This scene looks dull on the page as it's just a list of facts... how can we impose a context that might allow us to create some action?'

With the premiere set for May, I pretended I was confident...

...and...

...invited the media.

There is a common belief that when schools put on musicals, they get the best coverage. My gut feeling was this isn't true. Original plays about interesting subjects (in this instance living in our community) were easy to sell.

The opening night sold out a month in advance, hours after they had gone on sale!

The enthusiastic reaction from the media was unexpectedly simple to enlist.

VERBATIM - The Fun of Making Theatre Seriously by Mark Wheeller

Hugh David from the ***Times Educational Supplement*** agreed to write a review. He came to see **Blackout** but chose not to attend **Joseph**.

NATD (National Association for the Teachers of Drama) asked me to write a piece in their ***Drama Broadsheet*** which duly appeared in ***Volume 2 Number 3*** in the Summer of 1984.

Thames TV wanted to film a two and a half minute feature for their ***London News at Six*** programme.

This piled the pressure on for all of us and was to be my first ever TV appearance. I was secretly very excited, though tried to play it cool!

In the end my interview was not included and Matt said:

'I don't know how they got away with that after all the work you've put into it.'

How sweet and empathetic. I was much happier (honestly) to be recognised for what I had done by those in the group. Matt was featured and he spoke so well. He too had put a huge amount into the project.[21]

Around this time I achieved an ambition thanks to the music teacher at St John's School, Epping, Paul Servis.[22] We had a grant to record all the songs from **Race** professionally. Graham played guitar alongside Paul and a young keyboard player, Richard Wood, who had been the runner-up in the Radio 1 Jazz Musician of the Year. Matt and Bernadette did the main vocals and I (with Paul and Graham) offered a few backing vocals.

I felt, for the first time in a while, I was close to my childhood ambition of being a rock star. I adored the day which is etched in my memory. Paul's experience in a studio was invaluable and ensured we have a magnificent version of all these songs (lyrics mostly by Steve Wyatt - English Teacher at St Johns - and of course Graham).

---

[21] The Thames News At Six TV coverage is now on my Mark Wheeller Youtube Channel.

[22] Tragically Paul's life was cut short a few years after this production in an awful car accident. He was a great loss to teaching and to music.

VERBATIM - The Fun of Making Theatre Seriously by Mark Wheeller

Paul was probably able to write better songs than me so it was a great act of generosity that, as he had with **Blackout**, he kept quiet and produced exceptional musical arrangements for us.

I deeply regret not taking taking up Paul's suggestion of using backing tracks during the performances, which I couldn't imagine would work. I wish he had challenged me and showed how it could work but... that wasn't his way. He was a lovely gentle guy! A great collaborator too on the musicals we did throughout my time in Epping. Instead, we had a single, simple, acoustic guitar accompaniment (just like in Roy's Stantonbury documentaries). It was a major missed opportunity!

Our next big problem was how to stage the European 400 Metre Final at the end of the play.

I dedicated a three-hour rehearsal to solving the problem.

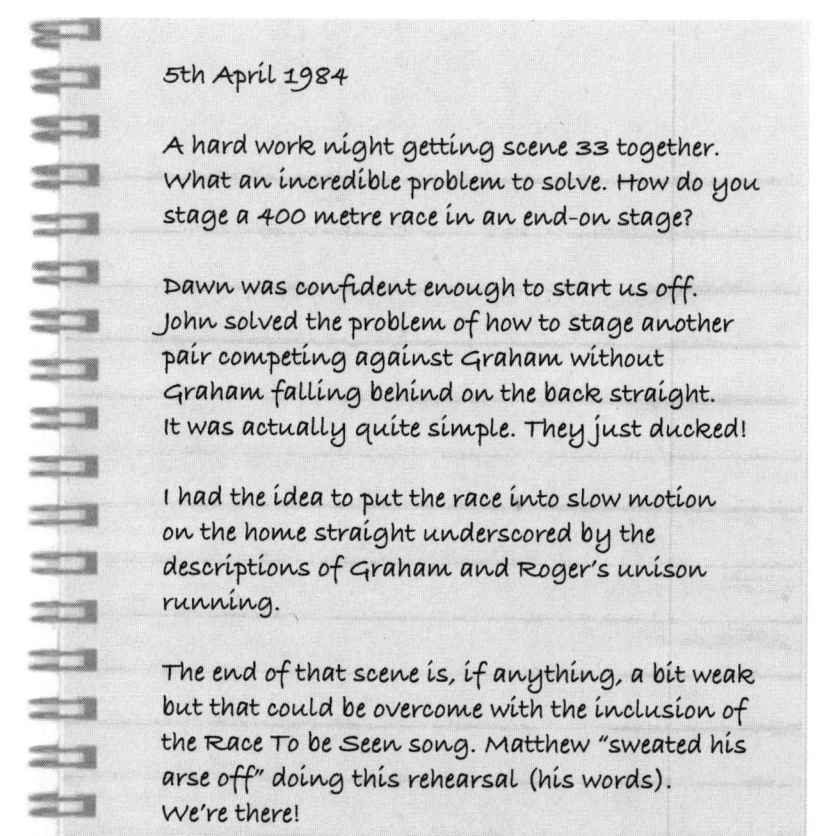

> 5th April 1984
>
> A hard work night getting scene 33 together. What an incredible problem to solve. How do you stage a 400 metre race in an end-on stage?
>
> Dawn was confident enough to start us off. John solved the problem of how to stage another pair competing against Graham without Graham falling behind on the back straight. It was actually quite simple. They just ducked!
>
> I had the idea to put the race into slow motion on the home straight underscored by the descriptions of Graham and Roger's unison running.
>
> The end of that scene is, if anything, a bit weak but that could be overcome with the inclusion of the Race To be Seen song. Matthew "sweated his arse off" doing this rehearsal (his words). We're there!
>
> cont...

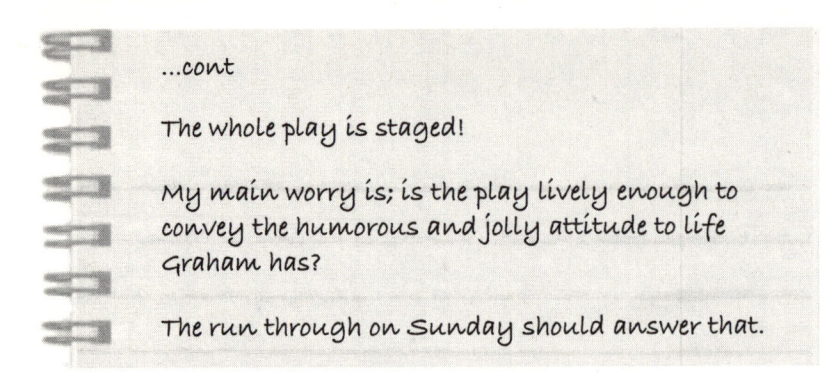

VERBATIM - The Fun of Making Theatre Seriously by Mark Wheeller

> ...cont
>
> The whole play is staged!
>
> My main worry is; is the play lively enough to convey the humorous and jolly attitude to life Graham has?
>
> The run through on Sunday should answer that.

Mmmm... Sunday was not great.

Bill Aitken, Graham's old PE teacher came to watch and, at the end of it, Graham said how embarrassed he was by what we'd done as he'd built it up to be so brilliant. Bill commented how the cast were very mature accepting the criticism I threw at them.

Matt said:

'We're throwing it all away. We might as well have never spent all this time and energy on it.'

It was incredibly disappointing.

My response was to make a series of radical cuts. The ability to chop the script is a huge advantage of presenting original work however, because it is untried and untested, I always find it impossible to establish whether it is the script or the performance to blame for the lack in quality.

The line cull was partly to help those who were struggling with line learning and partly to assist the pace of the play.

> Rehearsals were always never straightforward. Trying to stay focused on what section of the play we were rehearsing always proved a challenge as a scene would suddenly be altered or moved. An image created for the first half would be better used in the second; a song I'd practiced and learnt would get a verse cut or, worse, words changed!
> There was no room for ad libs as these were real words spoken by real people. Mark was always very strict about this!
> The excitement of the ever-evolving production was a challenge for some who took things seriously, but for me, singing... life was amazing!
> **Bernadette Cleere** (née **Chapman**).

VERBATIM - The Fun of Making Theatre Seriously by Mark Wheeller

I also looked at some of the supporting roles and how they might be able to impact on the scenes. For example I made Sister Brown more openly offhand and distant (as the text suggests - "I'm afraid you can't stay! Didn't Mr Mason explain that the children's ward is in quarantine with the chicken pox epidemic?"). This gave Maud more to play against.

There began to be some unrest in the cast. One sent a letter resigning from his role as I had cut so many of his (unlearnt) lines and there were rumours he wasn't to be the only one. That left me feeling uncomfortable but, thankfully, it came to nothing.

We were close to the performance and I was having serious reservations about Matthew's performance...

> 27th April 1984
>
> We may have reached a turning point for Matthew tonight. It happened, strangely, in a moment when Dawn said:
>
> "He wondered where Marie was."
>
> Instantly, I thought of Marie (not Jan (Farringdon) or Zara who were playing Marie). I stopped the cast to ask who they thought of. Some, (frustratingly) weren't thinking at all! Others said Marie or a mixture of Marie and Jan.
>
> I shared my fear that I wasn't seeing Graham through Matt's performance and most people agreed. It took ages to establish why. Finally, we decided there were too many "Matthewisms" in his performance. Matt was (unsurprisingly) not impressed by our conclusion but said he'd try to sort it. It was very tense but, for me, a revelation.
>
> In this style of "demonstrating" theatre, there needed to be a neutrality of performance, uncluttered with characterisation or use of the actors' personal gestures.
>
> cont...

VERBATIM - The Fun of Making Theatre Seriously by Mark Wheeller

...cont

It had to be a simple form of communication supporting the words. The manner should be indicated not impersonated. Matt was concerned this might lead to a flat performance.
Matt observed that "as always", we were spending an inordinate amount of time waffling and getting nowhere.

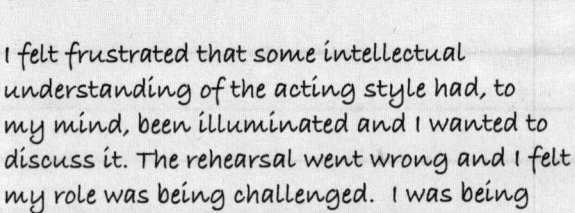

I felt frustrated that some intellectual understanding of the acting style had, to my mind, been illuminated and I wanted to discuss it. The rehearsal went wrong and I felt my role was being challenged. I was being forced to treat Matt with kid gloves.

In the end, I suggested he smiled more as he spoke. He agreed this could be the magic ingredient. Later in the evening we had another argument and I said we should all go home... and we did! It shocked him and he phoned up saying he was just being "him" and that everyone was picking on him. He confided that he was worried and we arranged to have an additional rehearsal. I know Matt will work hard to make it "just right".

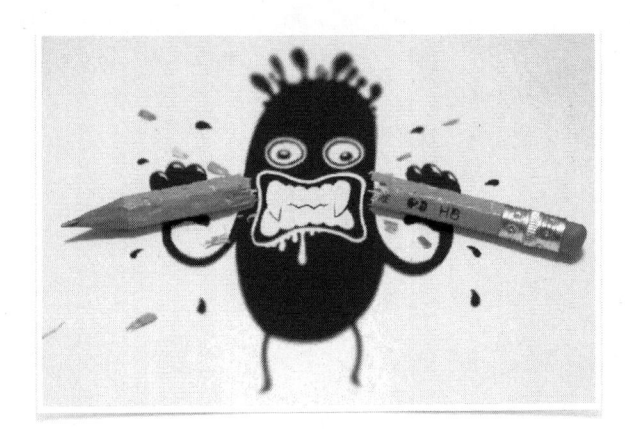

VERBATIM - The Fun of Making Theatre Seriously by Mark Wheeller

The problem with the situation above is that we were all fumbling around in the dark. No one really knew what they were doing. This was fine when we made progress but if we didn't it was incredibly frustrating. I have to confess this scenario was not unique... it became a perennial problem in all my productions. It is a serious downside of me relying on everyone else for an idea and having no back up plan. However, it proved I genuinely had no clue... I wasn't pretending to be ignorant to get a specific response.

The thing that frustrated me was that so many (including Matt) didn't learn their lines!

This made it impossible to see (particularly with a new play) whether scenes were working.

I started to consider replacing Matt with Barrie who was proving a strong and reliable performer. Wow! This would have been a huge and controversial move and risked breaking the whole thing.

The idea remained a private thought. It showed how worried I was.

Some of the cast requested tapes of the real people saying their words in the original interview to help them say the lines as well as they can. I saw this as a really positive and innovative request.

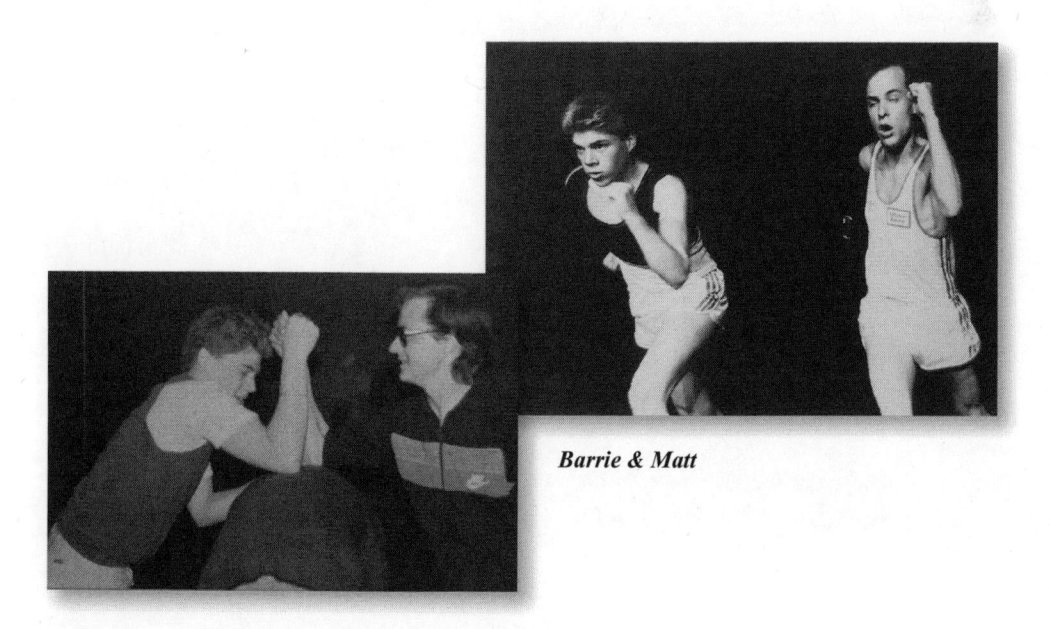

Barrie & Matt

105

VERBATIM - The Fun of Making Theatre Seriously by Mark Wheeller

30/04/1984

I developed a new interest this afternoon... lighting as the new equipment is being used for the first time.

I offered some creative suggestions and, even though it was the simplest of plots, designing the lights and working round the problems that were thrown up proved really fulfilling.

John Fradd from my 3rd year (Year 9) tutor group was excellent to work with. He enjoyed it too, saying how easy this system was to run.

Graham arrived (knocking over Justin's bike in the corridor and laughing) with Marie and our costumes... the sponsored jogging suits. The slides have also arrived this morning so, everything apart from the movie film is here and ready.

I returned home tonight re-motivated, excited and can't wait for tomorrow's rehearsal which I know will be good!

1/5/1984

The rehearsal tonight gave me genuine cause for concern as opposed to tactical. I am worried that lack of confidence on words will spoil what should be an invigorating performance.

I'm very tired so I'll write more tomorrow... however, no one wants to make a fool of themselves so I remain confident it will be very good... if not EXCELLENT!

VERBATIM - The Fun of Making Theatre Seriously by Mark Wheeller

We held an informal preview in our little St John's Drama studio and I experienced a major sense of anticlimax.

> *3/5/1984*
>
> My idealism is fading. I should be happy because the play went well but I hardly felt a part of it last night. The small things I worry about - relationships with individuals in the cast who aren't being as committed as I'd expect are sabotaging my enjoyment.
>
> One comment from an audience member we'd invited really frustrated me. The wife of the SNAP Theatre Company's director went on about how Graham asking Marie out was sexist!!! That is what happened... why would she want to politicise a brilliant, simple and amusing scene?
>
> And that was all she had to say?... Ugh!
>
> Matthew was, at last, very good! So was Neil Chase (playing Harry). What a find!

There were also moments which made us laugh!

> *7/5/1984*
>
> In the Epping Gazette photo session (we are getting great coverage) Graham and Matthew had to run forward towards the photographer with a guide rope linking them.
> Matt completely forgot Graham was blind and they both ran straight into the photographer! Fortunately she wasn't hurt!
>
> A lady was talking to Graham about how people would talk about their deaf son within his hearing and assumed that he was "simple". Then she turned to Marie and said:
> "Does Graham know what a deaf aid is?"
>
> Graham, spotting the irony, said:
>
> cont...

VERBATIM - The Fun of Making Theatre Seriously by Mark Wheeller

> ...cont
>
> "Yes 'he' does."
>
> The programme has been printed and is really impressive!
>
> Tonight, at our rehearsal, we will incorporate some of the suggestions made at the preview performance.

My enthusiasm to introduce other adults into my process was all very well... until they start to offer suggestions I didn't welcome.

One of these was a lighting guy brought in by Alison to help us. He worked for the BBC and was a senior member of a local adult amateur theatre company.

It gradually became clear he wanted to use his involvement with EYT as a recruiting opportunity.

He was confident he could offer our cast a way of moving 'up' to his "adult" group which he clearly felt was better.

Poster design by John Rowley

This really bugged me, as his attitude became progressively competitive and then derogatory towards our/my efforts. That said, he did offer useful help managing to get the cast to speak up... so, for that, I was grateful.

VERBATIM - The Fun of Making Theatre Seriously by Mark Wheeller

7/5/1984 (Late at night)

An excellent and highly productive evening... a magnificent rehearsal. Julie (Knope) and Nic (Jones) planning Maud and Harry tonight really seem to have applied pause and volume to their already good performances. Dawn said that they were "feeling" their lines.

The cast have gained confidence after Saturday's run and are keen to perform, willing to listen and therefore to improve. We worked out a fine ending which will make the audience reach for their hankies!
I feel confident and <u>very</u> excited. Brilliant!

In the final rehearsal in school I realised that the number of races we showed were becoming confusing so, I decided to remove one to clarify the narrative. Of course, this had implications... some of the cast lost chunks of their lines. I don't remember them complaining (to me) about this which was amazing... but...
...they were none too pleased by the frequency of alterations I'd make in the quest for perfection!

VERBATIM - The Fun of Making Theatre Seriously by Mark Wheeller

One of the great things Mark taught me was that, apart from the integrity of our source material, nothing else is sacred. If it didn't work we could cut it, change it, and more than once, within minutes of a performance! I remember being given script changes with the audience in their seats!

> Scenes 1 to 8 (Cut)
> New Lines...
> Enter stage right:
> Scene 9: "Hello"
> Scene 51: "Goodbye".
> Exit stage left:

For me, the story and script were strong. It was the staging and our performances I was less sure about. Not that there was anything wrong with the staging, it was more that I didn't have the experience of physical theatre to bring to any evaluation of what we were doing to the situation.

I dreamed of Theatre of the Absurd, the Theatre of Cruelty and of Antonin Artaud but these were things I had only read about. Of course our performance didn't need all that. A good story will tell itself.

We had collectively fallen in love with the art of theatre and shared a profound need to show it for all its glory. I think we knew the play itself was interesting. Yet the bottom line was: Will the performance be entertaining… or at the very least… not boring?

Without any real knowledge of structure and conceptual style we were, in a very real sense, just playing.

As the first performances neared, the blind experiment was on (pun intended). I remember the writing and rehearsing towards performance being all-consuming. There was a clear sense we were doing something different and new, both with the verbatim style and the subject matter.

It felt important that we got it right. As they say, the proof of the pudding is in the eating and, until we got it up in front of a live audience, we wouldn't know.
Matt Allen

VERBATIM - The Fun of Making Theatre Seriously by Mark Wheeller

As we moved into our performance week we had the most encouraging letter from the Deputy Head at our school, who had attended the preview.

Essex County Council

St. John's School
Tower Road   Epping   CM16 5EN

Headmaster   S Dixon MA
telephone Epping 73028/9
Epping 72194

6 May '84

Dear Mark and Company,

I feel I must put pen to paper to express my sincerest congratulations to everyone concerned for the excellence of "Race to Be Seen". It is too easy for people like me to assume that because we have come to expect such high standards we need to say little!

The script is taut and economical yet realistic and emotional capturing the essence of Graham's life and the attitudes of those with whom he has associated. The music is appropriate and further contributes to the mood of the drama. In all "the book" would in itself be an immense achievement.

I considered the performance to be without a weak link; the characterizations were utterly convincing from everyone. The "deepening process" which inevitably accompanies performance will undoubtedly further enhance the very moving commitment and maturity everyone displays already.

The production was absolutely

> right for the venues you had in mind at the projects inception and the quality of the staging was of the highest order in efficiency and appropriateness, hardly ever appearing contrived or artificial. Astonishing when one considers the extent to which you all invite us to suspend our disbelief!
>
> Lastly, though there is so much more I could say, I can only comment on the extent to which you all _know_ you have a great success on your hands. It shines through your attitudes and performance. If ever confidence was entirely well placed - this is it.
>
> Yours admiringly,
> Ken C Saunders.

VERBATIM - The Fun of Making Theatre Seriously by Mark Wheeller

Chapter 6: At last... Performances... And Reviews!

"It's time to trust my instincts, close my eyes and leap!"
Paraphrased from *Defying Gravity (Wicked)*
by Stephen Schwartz

I wanted to make the premiere as special as possible and remembered how Tony Key hyped his 4R productions by booking the prestigious Lewisham Concert Hall.

I decided we should try to perform it as close to Graham and Marie's home as possible.

Guess what?

They lived very close to the Corbett Theatre, part of the prestigious E15 Acting School.

It seemed like a big ambition but it happened!

Fortunately Alison (Burkert) had links there, so I think she probably organised it (belated thanks). I have no memory of being involved in any negotiations. Not only that but we were provided with a student Stage Manager - Gus Shield.

All these things fell into our lap!

I had always wanted to emulate what I'd seen with Roy Nevitt's Stantonbury Campus Drama Group (documentary) performances where the real person in the play was in the audience watching the play.

Hawtin Munday (the World War 1 soldier) from **Days Of Pride** being in the audience had made an indelible impression on me.[23]

I wanted the kind of resonance Roy's theatre caused but there was so much to distract me from savouring the moment.

---

[23] I was talking to Johnny Carrington about this book just as I finished writing it and he said how influential **Missing Dan Nolan** had been on his practice. I asked if he would be prepared to write his thoughts down and he agreed. I have included it in the Appendix section of this book. It provides a beautiful bookend and shows how this wonderful way of approaching playwriting has served to inspire down the generational teacher/playwright line. Thank you again Roy and Peter before him.

VERBATIM - The Fun of Making Theatre Seriously by Mark Wheeller

- One of the cast didn't turn up to the dress rehearsal. Fortunately the second cast offered an instant resolution, and for once having two casts offered a distinct advantage.

- The guitarist suddenly informed me that he couldn't make any Saturdays... including the premiere!!! A replacement was found but added significantly to the pressure I was feeling.

- The adult Alison had roped in to head up our technical team revealed he wasn't available on the premiere date either! Would John (in the 3rd Year) be able to cope on his own? Was it fair to ask him? Was there any other option? If so, I was unaware of it.

- Word learning continued to be a worry.

- Benjy (playing little Graham) has lost one of the white sticks. We didn't have spares, they were expensive and very hard to get quickly.

I was worried! **WORRIED!**

I took it all personally and the problems punctured the fulfilment I felt should be getting from the project.

I was at the final hurdle but seemed to be unable to secure commitment from all of those around me.

I was fearful that this lack of commitment would be contagious.

I was VERY fearful about that. I was paranoid about it. I remember at 21 a girlfriend cheating on me. I was devastated. I remember thinking I can control my youth theatre work so I will focus on that rather than personal relationships (yes I actually did think that)... yet here I was losing control!

Aside from the line learning, the problems came from a tiny minority but I REALLY didn't want anyone to let Graham and Marie down. I couldn't imagine how awful that would be after all the trust they placed in me and my (blind?) faith in our young and inexperienced cast.

Putting on a show is an up and down experience!

I had made it far more labour intensive as, with two casts, everything had to be rehearsed twice. This added to our problems of being able to prepare efficiently.

VERBATIM - The Fun of Making Theatre Seriously by Mark Wheeller

10/05/1984

Today we enter the performance phase of the project. I woke at 5am very excited and in a dilemma about whether I should cut from Crystal Palace to Bulgaria. I have decided I need to and will edit it later today and rehearse it as early as possible tonight.

10/05/1984 (Late night)

We did this and poor Zara (Marie) didn't get through unscathed. She needed a prompt. Sad because it had been a good second half.

Nic (Harry) had problems with lines and the lights were abysmal. The adult who I had reservations about on the tech team, was unhappy by how I spoke to the cast and told me I shouldn't have 'torn into them'. I replied:

"They trust me to say what I feel."

Graham was magic just when needed, saying:

"Tell John I didn't notice the lights!"

Nor it seemed had the sighted members of the audience. Graham's sister, Junie, had been sobbing and that brought a lump to Graham's throat. I feared she was laughing from how banal it was, as from the top of the theatre all I could see was her head going up and down.

Matt and Julie (Maud) stood out as the stars. Robbie Currie, one of the supporting cast, was superb and said at the end: "I can't wait for the other performances!"

I hope, once the other cast has performed we can relax a bit and then it can really grow. I'm full of hope but don't yet think we've done ourselves full justice!

VERBATIM - The Fun of Making Theatre Seriously by Mark Wheeller

> It would be years later that I discovered the art of good stage craft. They didn't even teach that at Drama School. It was only with experience I picked it up and that journey began with this production. It really isn't that complicated. However, as a teenager, body awareness, vocal clarity and emotional integrity are things you're just beginning to work out for yourself.
> **Matt Allen**

> Corbett Theatre (E15) was daunting as it took *Race* from a school production to a professional level. I remember feeling very nervous and out of my depth.
>
> My friends and family thought it was a very modern play. They had only ever seen "traditionally" staged plays before with elaborate scenery and extravagant costumes. *Race* was none of that. I remember telling my mum... "It's the story that is important, not the scenery or costumes." She had asked if we didn't have costumes or scenery because we couldn't afford it!
> **Bernadette Cleere** (née **Chapman**). 😆 😆

ABBEY NATIONAL BUILDING SOCIETY
High Road, Loughton, Essex
Would like to wish every success to Epping Youth Theatre with their production of
"GRAHAM – A LIFE WORTH LIVING"
at the THE CORBETT THEATRE
Rectory Lane, Loughton
on MAY 12
Tickets available from Corbett Theatre Box Office
Tel. 01-508 5983
Get the Abbey Habit

We'd clearly not updated the Abbey National with our final title!

EPPING YOUTH THEATRE PRESENT
RACE TO BE SEEN
A DOCUMENTARY PLAY WITH MUSIC
PREMIER ON
SAT 12TH MAY/84
7.30PM
CORBETT THEATRE LOUGHTON
£3.00
000056

EMAS23 56
RACE TO BE SEEN
SAT 12TH MAY/84
£3.00
TO BE GIVEN UP

12/05/1984

Last night's performance was undoubtedly the happiest evening I've ever spent. Graham was overwhelmed.
Matt said his face was aching, he'd been smiling so much. Lisa (ensemble) was tearful as she hadn't managed the new lines... but Dawn stepped in to save the situation marvellously!
All the work has been worthwhile!

VERBATIM - The Fun of Making Theatre Seriously by Mark Wheeller

After the first preview Matt, Graham, and I went back to Graham's parents' house, elated. We were offered pizza and stayed there enthusing about it all til long after midnight.

We had lots of reviewers in (The Stage, TES, various disability interest magazines and the (national) Amateur Stage magazine) for the official premiere.

It was already gaining more interest than anything I'd ever done before... certainly more than my musicals.

Graham was particularly interested by a reporter from a magazine for the visually impaired, and he asked me:

'Is he blind?'

I replied, *'Does it matter?'* with a big grin on my face, which I knew Graham would be totally aware of.

'I think you should find out for yourself if it matters that much to you?'

And he did, by putting his hand out for the reviewer to shake. He shook it immediately and Graham sniggered.

'He can see.'

Clever!

The audience seemed impressed by our performance and Bernadette's voice was often mentioned, singing the songs throughout the play as a gentle Brechtian-style commentary. Bernadette was the gold plated icing on our tasty cake.

VERBATIM - The Fun of Making Theatre Seriously by Mark Wheeller

Our sponsors, Gilspur Bullens, said they would aim to boost our audiences with coach-loads of people from their companies!

Many of the cast made an effort to thank me personally, which was very rewarding.

The accolades I appreciated most came from Roy Nevitt, my former Head of Department at Stantonbury. He invited us to perform the production at the Campus and, apparently said:

'I fully expect to see Mark "in town" directing his plays!'

Not only that but... shortly afterwards, he contacted me to offer me a promotion where I would work with their Stantonbury Youth Theatre as part of the newly established Documentary Centre. I would also have a responsibility to establish a documentary input in the school curriculum. Wow! This boosted my confidence but, what I was doing here was my baby. I could never have that in Milton Keynes, despite how much I adored it. I thought about it very seriously but decided to turn the generous offer down.

The cast were particularly keen to be the chosen cast for the Stantonbury performance and I was getting requests from some asking to attend even if they weren't performing. This was the commitment I had always wanted. This heightened excitement was short-lived.

Race to be Seen was not the centre of everyone's world like it was mine. In school on Monday it was mentioned but with no real zeal.

People had enjoyed it but the reaction was somewhat lukewarm. Jenny Roe, one of the English teachers said:

'It was good for "our kids" but unimaginative and undisciplined.'

VERBATIM - The Fun of Making Theatre Seriously by Mark Wheeller

Looking back on the performances I realised our excitement afterwards might have exceeded the general reaction from the audience.

It was as if people were bottling up their emotions.

I was wanting a Cup Final atmosphere.

The following week the first reviews were released and I wrote in my diary:

> They should be more complimentary.

Typical me! Never satisfied! Worried it wasn't enough to keep the cast's momentum going.

The first review was the **Epping Forest Classified** (local free newspaper) who had seen the preview performance at our school on the 5th May. This is the earliest independent review of the production other than Ken Saunders'.

EPPING FOREST CLASSIFIED & NEWS

Mark Wheeller's direction of the production achieves such sympathy and understanding from the cast that their youth is totally belied. The task of portraying a life so charged with emotion as that of blind athlete Graham Salmon would tax any actor. These young people have an approach so fresh and utterly committed that the play keeps its audience spellbound to the very end.

Events are linked by the narration and singing of Bernadette Chapman. Her haunting songs, some of which were written by Graham, add musical emphasis to the emotions of each scene. ***Race To Be Seen*** is a play to suffer, to enjoy and to ponder.

Dave Stewart

VERBATIM - The Fun of Making Theatre Seriously by Mark Wheeller

Reading this now I think it's great... and my songs get a positive mention! Then the **Harlow Star** and **West Essex Gazette** released theirs. They had watched the first night at the Corbett Theatre, two nights before the official premiere and on the premiere respectively.

HARLOW AND EPPING Star VFD

A Moving Play About Graham - Blind Athlete.

Audiences nationwide will soon know the life story of blind athlete, Graham Salmon, thanks to committed young people in Epping Youth Theatre. Not least of them is Matthew Allen, who movingly depicts the remarkable runner. What a story! This documentary play with music, directed by Mark Wheeller may have lasting values. Short term, it has a dazzling year ahead after opening with Graham himself listening to his new friends telling his story.

Matthew put humour into his portrayal of the hero's life, a sure ingredient of Graham's will to win against "impossible" odds. Mark Wheeller's bold ploy to use track-suited players as scenery came off thanks to their tight discipline. Chairs, kitchen sinks, windows, swinging doors appeared effortlessly as required: seeming natural enough after players first sat down casually on the arch-backed schoolmates.

The music and lyrics are integral to the show, so is the powerful singing of soloist, Bernadette Chapman. Like Matthew and others in this rare team effort, she bids to be "discovered" during the tour which ends at the Edinburgh Fringe Festival. With subject matter of enormous value to the handicapped and their families, **Race To Be Seen** could, so easily, have slipped into mawkish sentimentality. Thanks to Graham Salmon's and Mark Wheeller's influence, it ended as a song of triumph. "Don't let your dreams slip away" sang the cast, to the blind runners own lyrics. Congratulations to all who have made this possible.

Ron Freeman

VERBATIM - The Fun of Making Theatre Seriously by Mark Wheeller

West Essex Gazette

A Rare Theatrical Event

A moving experience, presented with sincerity by a dedicated team of young actors. Matthew Allen, who had the task of portraying the determined and tenacious young man, made a remarkably good job. His similar build and good projection captivated the attention of all, as the story, quite harrowing at times, unfolded, all the more praiseworthy knowing the subject was in the audience.

Benjy Shepherd who played "little" Graham on the night I attended, endeared himself to all with his naturalness. Bernadette Chapman's sung narration linked the scenes together with clarity and attractive musical accomplishment to add to the flavour.

Phil Romerill.

The review I was really waiting for was the Times Educational Supplement. I was awaiting my national acclaim! It appeared unexpectedly as the second of two (unrelated) reviews in one and the reviewer loved the first play, **Something's Burning** by Peter Speyer. I'll include some quotes about that to give you a flavour of his delight regarding their production:

It's not what the Lyric Theatre do, it's the way that they do it which is so important. Leaving **Something's Burning** I was fired (as I was after their previous productions) with a new enthusiasm for young people's theatre... 14 young people being themselves, presenting stage personas with a practised polish (we could hear, we could see and no staginess anywhere) that would put a lot of the London Fringe to shame. Anthony Lennon stole the show every time he came on with his virtuoso demonstrations of body popping. The rest of the cast were equally good, strutting, rapping and sparring, just like young people in any city, any evening...

VERBATIM - The Fun of Making Theatre Seriously by Mark Wheeller

Then Hugh goes on to offer his thoughts on our effort. ☹

THE TIMES Educational Supplement

Away from the city in the small town Essex, the Epping Youth Theatre were also getting their own show together. **Race To Be Seen** was a documentary with music, researched and written around the life story of Graham Salmon, the record-breaking blind athlete. And, Chariots of Fire stuff it was too - though unfortunately without Vangelis' music or a script as solicitous as Colin Welland's screenplay.

Documentary drama is notoriously difficult to put together. Being true to the material, as the Epping group were to the 2000 pages of interviews they collected often means weakening the dramatic line and here, this was, unfortunately, the case. A lot of the dialogue in particular that given to Graham's parents, did sound like interview answers, and there was too much to-audience declamation for us to become really involved with the characters. What really kept us in our place however, firmly locked outside the drama, was the style of the production. Inspired by the SNAP theatre company to work entirely without props, EYT substituted crouching figures for real chairs and then sat on them when there wasn't really any need to sit in the first place. It was difficult to concentrate on what the consultant was saying when his office was full of such grotesque human furniture. Minor considerations, however - what is important is that the company have devised an impressive (and impressively well-documented) show that was socially valuable as well as entertaining. They have all had to think through what it means to be blind, and, as a result of the work over the past few months, have issued an open invitation to any young people who have a disability to join them.[24]

Hugh David

All I wanted (expected?) was for him to say this was the best theatre he'd ever seen anywhere in the world!

Anything else, especially putting the script so directly in the firing line, was 'not what the doctor ordered', as my mum would have said.

---

[24] See Chapter 9 for the details of Graham's legacy regarding my youth theatre work.

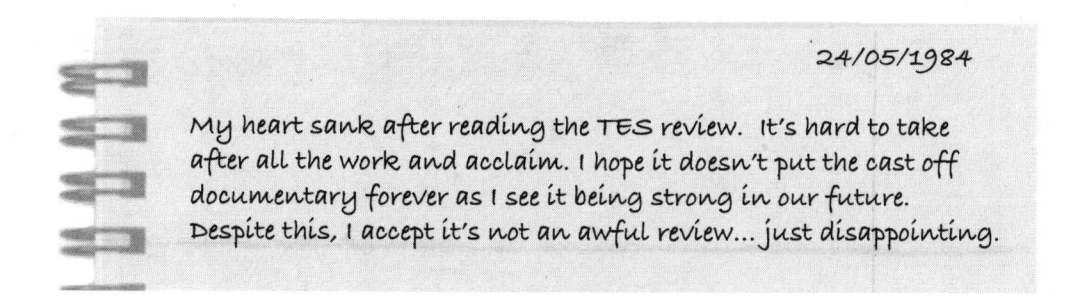

VERBATIM - The Fun of Making Theatre Seriously by Mark Wheeller

> 24/05/1984
>
> My heart sank after reading the TES review. It's hard to take after all the work and acclaim. I hope it doesn't put the cast off documentary forever as I see it being strong in our future. Despite this, I accept it's not an awful review... just disappointing.

I can see myself trying so hard to see the bright side of things...

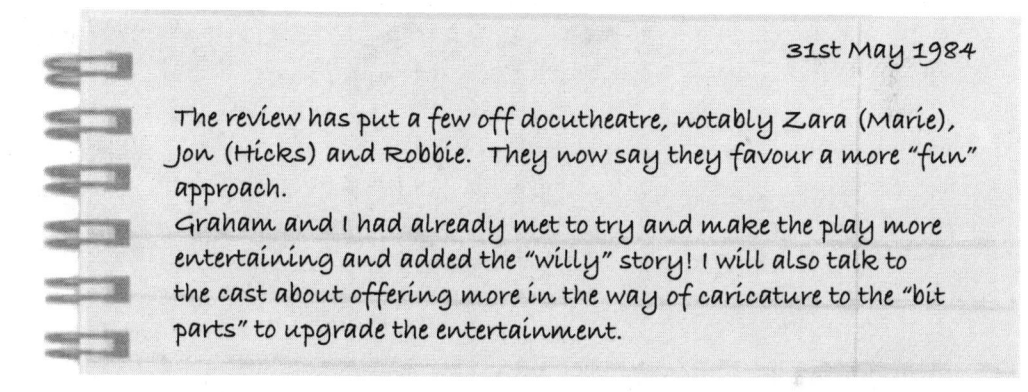

> 31st May 1984
>
> The review has put a few off docutheatre, notably Zara (Marie), Jon (Hicks) and Robbie. They now say they favour a more "fun" approach.
> Graham and I had already met to try and make the play more entertaining and added the "willy" story! I will also talk to the cast about offering more in the way of caricature to the "bit parts" to upgrade the entertainment.

These changes had an instant effect, which I reported in my diary after the following performance. Hooray!

Now... here's an interesting discovery...

The 'clever' ending in the published version of **Race To Be Seen** was not mine at all but was inspired by our Drama Advisor.

Roger Parsley, my Essex Drama Advisor, often visited my school to share planning or to model a teaching idea. He would always watch our productions and offer incredibly useful feedback without that feeling of 'judgement'. He was always supportive and nurturing.

This particular advice was offered through his review for the national Amateur Stage magazine. It is one of many examples as to how we used reviews/adjudications to sharpen our work.

VERBATIM - The Fun of Making Theatre Seriously by Mark Wheeller

amateur STAGE

NEW PLAY REVIEWS

The performance is simply presented with no props. The device of using actors the scenery was strikingly effective in some places, but less so in others where it appeared quirky and intrusive.

The songs, including some lyrics written by Graham Salmon were pleasantly sung by one girl at the side of the stage; however, they did not all add significantly to the piece. This is one of several areas where some judicious cutting might be done before this potentially very exciting and different work goes to the Edinburgh Fringe later in the year. The script abounds with humour and vitality and it is certainly a vehicle that other companies might like to use but the focus at the end needs some consideration. The plays climax is clearly Graham's personal success, and this tends to lessen the impact of the messages that emerged earlier and cried out for some final rounding off.

These points – that adversity can be overcome, and that integration of the people who have a disability within society still has a long path to tread, were lessened by the lyrical nature of the final song.

Perhaps Graham's personal difficulties in job-hunting presented earlier might be used more effectively at the end rather than where they occurred.

I hope amateur and young peoples theatre groups will explore this rewarding kind of theatre more often. In this respect **Race To Be Seen** is an inspiration.
Roger Parsley

VERBATIM - The Fun of Making Theatre Seriously by Mark Wheeller

From a conversation I had with him later on, I am aware that Roger was suggesting we use the prejudicial comments regarding his employability as Graham approached the end of the final race.

I decided this would mess up the pace and excitement of that race but...

... we could use the idea in the medal ceremony...

... and that's what I did.

It brought the play to a more thought-provoking end.

All praise the Drama Advisors of the '80s. Alistair Black, the Hampshire Drama Advisor, made a similar suggestion regarding the end of **Too Much Punch**. He suggested I reprise the Bob 'n' Nob scene (originally portrayed to be fun and laughter) with the audience having the benefit of hindsight. It proved a winning suggestion.

Roger's suggestion led to another significant milestone in my life.

I wrote the music for the title song with Graham who had written the lyrics.
It was, in my opinion, the best song in the production and Bernadette sang it magnificently.

Despite this, for the sake of the ending, I took the decision to cut it.

For the first time I placed greater importance on the narrative as opposed to my song getting an airing.

This was the start of my realisation that playwriting was more important to me than songwriting.

The other aspect Roger (and Hugh in the TES) encouraged us to explore was our use of body-props.

Perhaps we had overdone it?

We took opportunity to use them only where they were most effective.
Less is more as opposed to my assumption that more is MORE is **MORE!!!**

VERBATIM - The Fun of Making Theatre Seriously by Mark Wheeller

Bernadette, having just lost one of her standout moments, made another significant suggestion:

'Why don't we cut the interval? It will help with continuity.'

She was right.

Another change that would be a feature of nearly all of my plays in the future. I wanted the play to be worthwhile and I equated that with being a two-act play. We'd always had problems placing the interval... there was no natural break but we had never questioned having no interval.

This focused my mind on the idea that the play should be shorter. If it is a one act play, it's important we don't go on too long.

This helped me to edit further.

Would our audience mind?

We discovered they didn't and, as the play became tighter, our audiences enjoyed it more.

No one ever expressed concerned about it (or any of my plays[25]) being too short.

Impact was the crucial factor!

It was at this time that I experienced a brush (off) with fame.

EYT were invited for an interview on **Round Midnight** programme, a favourite of mine as it often had arts based interviews. This show was hosted by Radio 2 DJ Brian Matthew. I was particularly enamoured by him as he'd presented a documentary about Lionel Bart, writer/composer of **Oliver!** Suddenly, I was about to be interviewed by him on this high profile programme... except...

... except when we arrived he assumed Nicki Harris (one of our Maud's) was the organiser...

... my name was not on the list at reception, so they didn't want to let me in.

---

[25] This is not entirely true. Sometimes when theatre groups perform my plays, they choose to present two of them as a double bill. They work... but they work equally well as a single play in a shorter evening.

VERBATIM - The Fun of Making Theatre Seriously by Mark Wheeller

When I was finally allowed in Brian said he was only interviewing Nicki and Graham as they were the only ones listed. I guess there was a payment issue as I was also excited about being paid (£9) to do an interview... not only that...

... but where I was to wait?

I wasn't even able to hear the interview as there weren't any headphones.

My heart sank!

My ego imploded.

This must have been obvious to everyone because I was suddenly invited in, paid £9 and included in the interview.

Clearly I wasn't as important as I wanted to be. Not only that but...

... but Graham and Nicki both found it absolutely hilarious!!!

The three months leading to our much anticipated premiere at the Edinburgh Fringe offered us an opportunity to explore the play further as we embarked on a number of 'touring' performances.

We performed at Linden Lodge, Graham's old school. It went down well and I know Graham particularly enjoyed it. However, we were all disappointed the Head Teacher didn't stay and watch, which made it seem more duty than desire for them to be hosting the play.

These performances proved, for me, a roller-coaster of emotions.

It was the lure of success that kept me going. In my diary, I talk about winning a Fringe First (the prestigious **Scotsman** award) more than once. It wasn't a fait accompli but, was very much in my sights.

This self-imposed pressure kept me going but pressurised me and that pressurised my young cast.

At Linden Lodge, I was again disappointed by Matt's performance and wondered if the opportunity should be passed to John Rowley or Barrie Sapsford who were both, in football terms, in better form.

VERBATIM - The Fun of Making Theatre Seriously by Mark Wheeller

I report in my diary that Matt told me he had got to the point where, when he saw a **Race To Be Seen** poster, he felt embarrassed. We had a heart to heart where he said he was determined to improve his attitude.

One good thing is that I did challenge these things but, it must have been frustrating for the EYT members. It was probably perceived as picking at scabs by some. Fortunately, these were highly committed young people, most of whom who were willing to be challenged and didn't just walk off!

Things did get to such a point that I had a period of reflection, which I'm glad I recorded in my diary. This will be a familiar experience for those who have been in my productions. One of "those" discussions. Sigh.

> 15th June 84
>
> We started off with a comedy workshop which did raise spirits and allowed us to forget the tempting weather outside. Then I asked:
>
> > "Who feels they have got all they can ever get out of this play already?"
>
> No hands went up.
>
> Then:
>
> > "Who has got more out of it than they imagined they ever would?"
>
> Neil Chase, who was new to EYT and playing Harry - brilliantly, raised his hand confidently and explained, he knew nothing of the quality of the work we did as he had never seen our productions.
>
> I attempted, in four sentences, (and failed to be that brief) to explain that I felt we should be looking for a more football crowd like response than the church service response we actually seemed to be eliciting.
>
> To boost our confidence, I proposed that we needed a more lively response and we need to cue our audience to give us this rather than half attempt the "intellectual ending". People agreed this would affect their motivation.
>
> cont...

VERBATIM - The Fun of Making Theatre Seriously by Mark Wheeller

> ...cont
>
> I also discovered from Jeremy (Turner) that previous productions had been successful because of the enthusiasm I managed to engender from groups over a short period is self-generating. This wasn't being sustained over the long gaps where we don't perform. So, each person must discover a way of tricking their physiology into being excited to produce the adrenaline.
>
> We needed to commit to a faultlessly positive approach. Jeremy, John (Rowley) and Matt were particularly impressive tonight!

I mention in my diary walking out of a rehearsal because Dawn and Nicki were 'being negative'. I wrote but (fortunately) didn't say:

'Stuff your Youth Theatre! Maybe I'll leave, then you'll be sorry!'

I am sure I would have been regretting turning the Stantonbury job down at this point.

I drove home (not a long journey) but quickly reflected on my actions.

> 26th June 1984
>
> If someone walked out on me. I'd lose faith in them, not to mention it was my legal obligation to supervise the rehearsal so, I returned. I went back into the room, lay on the floor (not unusual) and said nothing as the cast continued a run through of whatever they were doing. When it came to the end Matthew came over and invited me back into the group.
>
> I admired his strength. It took some courage as perhaps not everyone would want this to happen or view him as "creeping" to me. John (Hicks) had already left the rehearsal and gone home and when I returned, Nicki decided to walk too. It was a real moment. What would happen if more went.
>
> In the end we actually did a lot of work. I find it strange that this EXCELLENT and special play should become the setting for traumas like this.

VERBATIM - The Fun of Making Theatre Seriously by Mark Wheeller

I mention this because it was challenging to do this new and untried work in this democratic way. I constantly questioned myself. I didn't have the 'authority' status to barge my way back into the group. I had to wait to be invited, just as any of the cast would have done.

None of us knew where we were going... just that we wanted to go!

There were also ups... moments of joy and exhilaration.

We performed another (even shorter) version, (losing ten minutes - some edited on the coach), at Stantonbury Campus and, it's interesting to hear that, although we performed at a number of venues, this was the performance the cast remember most clearly.

We had the longest ovation I can remember at the end and I remember it because Roy Nevitt came up to me afterwards and said:

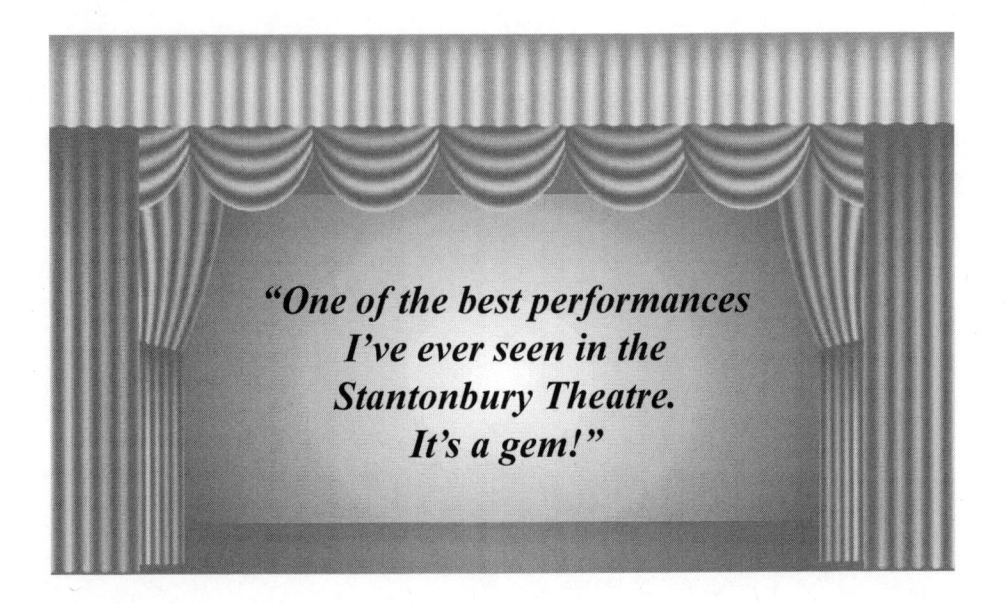

"One of the best performances I've ever seen in the Stantonbury Theatre. It's a gem!"

He suggested some additional cuts which I duly made for the following performance.

VERBATIM - The Fun of Making Theatre Seriously by Mark Wheeller

In the original version there were many more races. Some weren't staged, just described. So, if I edited some out, those that particularly mattered would immediately stand out more. This seriously assisted us to communicate the narrative. Thanks Roy!

One of my ex-Stantonbury YT members, Mark Eagle, said:

'It was the best piece of youth theatre I've ever seen.'

Unfortunately Graham wasn't able to see this performance. He was in America at the Paralympics. He won a bronze medal in the 400 metres and was no longer the world's fastest blind runner.

Amusingly, I took some photos of the Stantonbury performance... so that Graham could see them!!! **Doh!** (I can't find them now!)

The reviewer from **New Beacon** was in tears watching the play... what a shame no one seems to have a copy of that review either.

We were garnering incredibly positive coverage which was, in turn, doing my profile no harm.

- I wrote an academic article about our development of the play, published in the prestigious **National Association of Drama Teachers** (NATD) magazine.

- I delivered a lecture and workshop to the **National Association of Drama For The Visually Handicapped in Loughborough.**

- We were reviewed on BBC Radio 4's *In Touch* comparing us favourably with another play about visual impairment, **Crystal Clear** by Phil Young (praise we loved because that was a professional production)

- An 'unbelievable' review from audio magazine **National Sounds**, which sadly I have no copy of other than a brief quote we included in our publicity leaflet:

VERBATIM - The Fun of Making Theatre Seriously by Mark Wheeller

Our first touring date at the Chelmer Institute of Higher Education (where I was doing a Drama in Education Diploma) brought us back to earth with a bump.

Only 30 tickets had been sold.

In the early part of the performance one of the audience fainted and put everyone off their stride but the situation was sorted out and the person recovered fully.

The cast lifted things for the second act and we received a detailed review!

Brentwood Gazette and Mid-Essex Recorder

The 16 youngsters, under the capable and sensitive direction of Mark Wheeller, created a most moving performance which included mime, movement, song and dialogue, illustrated with slides from the athletes life.

Nicki Harris played the blind boys mother with warmth and poignancy and was ably supported by Neil Chase, whose portrayal of the father, combined determination, bewilderment and support for his family. Benjy Shepherd gained the sympathy of the audience and his cheeky determination around both the laughter and tears as the young Graham, while the self-assurance and athletic look of Matthew Allen brought to life the later scenes of Graham's amazing story. Graham's wife was played by Zara Chapman with maturity, warmth and charm.
All involved are to be congratulated for their skill and hard work. The cast of 16 were on stage all the time and created whatever scenery the action required with their bodies/movement. Crowds, train seats, even wardrobes, were created by these talented actors.

After the play, the audience were able to meet Graham Salmon and his wife, Marie. The company are performing it at the Edinburgh Festival Fringe. Don't miss it.
Mike Turner - Brentwood Gazette & Mid Essex Recorder.

VERBATIM - The Fun of Making Theatre Seriously by Mark Wheeller

Amazingly we also featured on **Sixty Minutes**, the BBC national news magazine program of the era.[26] I noted in my diary that the grumpy office lady at the school brought the television crew down to the studio 'resentfully'. There were a few who wanted to see me fail because my relationships were perceived as a challenge to the status quo. This unheard of TV publicity rubbed salt into that wound most effectively. My challenge was to charm her and by the end of my five years at Epping there was a much better understanding between us. I was not the threat I had once appeared to be.

It was fantastic to get feedback from the TV crew about our cast and they told me they were particularly impressed by Julie Knope who played Maud. You can see this clip on YouTube now and yes..., she was particularly impressive... and only 14 years old! All these positive reactions from people in the know really helped our confidence and feelings that we were onto a winner!

Our appearance on **Sixty Minutes** was transmitted prior to the second of our three 'sold out' Harlow Playhouse performances and really motivated the cast. We were now attracting an audience that was far in excess of being merely 'parents and friends' and offered me evidence that this was the way forward, rather than the normally accepted diet of pre-written musicals.

For our performance at the Harlow Playhouse Studio Theatre we had to re-stage the whole production to work on a thrust stage (audience on three sides). This was a further big pressure but, I felt it worked better. I mention in my diary that Robbie Currie's performance was the stand out. It's wonderful to see that each of the cast seemed to rise to the top at different times in the life of this production. Robbie wrote to me recently saying how his involvement in **Race** had been such a big part of his teenage years. This was so moving to read as I had no idea at the time, more particularly that this happened against the backdrop of a cultural atmosphere that led to Section 28, which prohibited the 'promotion of homosexuality' by local authorities.

---

[26] This can be watched along with all the coverage of the play on the Mark Wheeller YouTube Channel

VERBATIM - The Fun of Making Theatre Seriously by Mark Wheeller

> I have such fond memories of EYT, it saved me in my youth and gave me untold confidence to live life and be myself.
>
> I probably never mentioned but, about six/seven years after leaving Epping, on a Pride March someone stopped me. They knew me from EYT and said that I was an inspiration to them; being so visible and confident and "not giving a damn" I showed them how to be an out and confident young gay man. I was silenced and truly humbled. Of course, I rather hilariously thought I was in disguise in those days but of course, my disguise in plain sight was the freedom to be 'theatrical'! (I know, that itself is so wonderfully dated!) so much has changed since then.
>
> I am immensely grateful for the freedom you and EYT gave me. It really set me up for life. These strange times have allowed me to see some things more clearly and to reflect well on the good moments and influential people and times in my life. My time with EYT and you feature heavily. I have very clear memories of the way we worked with Graham - from running with him on a track, to feel the power and crucially the responsibility to 'hold' but not lead... these were profound, the empathy needed to faithfully portray this for Graham and for his running partners.
> **Robbie Currie**

I think it's important to say that at EYT in the mid-80's I didn't think we were doing anything unusual but clearly whatever it was made an impression on Robbie and that's truly rewarding. EYT was all about 'inclusivity' before that became a recognised term... and doing a play about Graham embodied this ideology. For me, like Geoff at Stantonbury, it was treating everyone as I'd like to be treated myself.

My feeling was, if people are willing to help me get my plays on I was indebted to them! We were all different... and I saw that as a positive!

The Harlow Playhouse performance led to me making a very cheeky move, to forward my own career and I did it totally spontaneously!

I had a rare, free afternoon at school and, unusually, nothing to do. I decided to make a phone call to the Harlow based educational publisher Longman, who published a well respected series of plays for schools.

I informed them that many other companies were chasing this script (they certainly weren't as I hadn't sent it out to any) but Graham and I wanted a local company to publish the play and for the announcement to be made prior to the Harlow performances.

Guess what?

They asked for a copy and sent a response to me in record time!

VERBATIM - The Fun of Making Theatre Seriously by Mark Wheeller

Longman

S/JW/BP   12th July, 1984

Longman Group Limited
Longman House
Burnt Mill
Harlow
Essex CM20 2JE

Telephone
Harlow (0279) 26721
Telex 81259

Cables/Telegrams
Longman Harlow

Mr Mark Wheeller,
St. John's School,
Tower Road,
Epping,
Essex.

Dear Mr Wheeller,

<u>Race to be Seen</u>

Following our telephone conversation, I wish to confirm our intention to publish your play. I am very pleased to be able to tell you this and to say that we have all enjoyed the play enormously. We are starting a new section of plays which fits this material splendidly.

We now need to decide how we plan to publish in terms what will work with it. In order to help this, I would now like you to send to me the play which you described to me by 'phone[27] I can then come back to you in order to discuss details and perhaps meet you at some point quite soon.

With best wishes.

Sincerely,

Joan Ward

Joan Ward,
English Publisher,
UK Secondary Schools.

* Now with us — thankyou.

---

[27] I can't imagine what this would have been, other than Blackout, as I hadn't written anything else!

VERBATIM - The Fun of Making Theatre Seriously by Mark Wheeller

Race To Be Seen was to become my first published script.

My mind instantly translated this to be a HUGE event. I remember imagining the kind of wealth leading me to purchase my parents a house in Barbados, despite them being quite happy in Tamworth! You can see how successful I thought this could be.

It wasn't.

I remember the first royalty slip arriving.

There was no cheque enclosed.

There was a letter accompanying the statement informing me that Longman don't pay royalties until the book earns over £5.00.

Aside from the poor sales (down to incredibly poor marketing in my humble opinion[28]), it was exciting to have a book out (the following year) and it did wonders for my credibility as both a writer and certainly opened doors for future scripts to be looked at seriously.

The publication of the play attracted stunning reviews. No wonder my hopes were so high!

> Effective plays for classroom use are thin on the ground, so, a cautious welcome to these which are better than most. **Race To Be Seen** is the best and is about Graham Salmon a blind athlete who won a gold medal at the European Championships in 1983. It's an "against all odds" drama but, that's what will hold the attention of the pupils. It is very readable and should prove popular in the classroom.
> **Phil Dawson** - English Magazine
>
> Snappy episodes which add up to the moving, eminently performable show. Get this book if you are looking for something with substance which can be done with a cast of about 20.
> **H Wright** - NATD Drama Broadsheet

---

[28] In the catalogue they sent to schools they offered one sentence to introduce teachers to this completely new play. That sentence was: "Race To Be Seen follows the life of Graham Salmon, the internationally famous blind athlete." That was it!!!

VERBATIM - The Fun of Making Theatre Seriously by Mark Wheeller

> **Race To Be Seen** is remarkable play… a story of great courage and dedication… entertaining with plenty of scope for imaginative direction. It can be performed with a large cast or, as EYT did, with only 15 players.
> **Charles Vance** - Amateur Stage

Sustaining the casts interest continued to be a challenge in the period leading to our Edinburgh performance.

They thought 'we've done it', yet we were still meeting for rehearsals to serve as a reminder and also to develop what we had.

I have never been a believer in warm-ups but, with the play rehearsed, I discovered improvisation exercises generated enjoyment and an energy to look at the performance with fresh eyes (or brain).

> 28th June 1984
>
> Tonight's was an inspired rehearsal. All four (2 from each cast) playing the roles of Graham's parents were struggling to add supporting gestures to their words, making their performance look two-dimensional. They were really struggling with it and then something remarkable happened.
>
> I asked Robbie to stand in front of the group and, using gesture, to tell us a true story with the intention of drawing us in. He told us the story of his sister collapsing that afternoon. It was obviously painful to him. He illustrated dramatic pause perfectly.
>
> Then, Alis, (14) - stepped up and selected a recent painful experience with her parents. I advised her to feel free to step down whenever she needed to.
>
> cont...

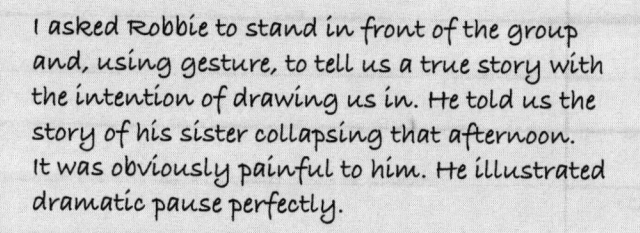

VERBATIM - The Fun of Making Theatre Seriously by Mark Wheeller

> ...cont
>
> Then came the inspiration, and it was my intuitive recognition of a dramatic frame that allowed us to make meaning from these exercises.
>
> Dawn and Siobhan playing Maud and Harry improvised their reactions to Graham becoming blind. It's incredible how little exploration we have done of the subject through improvisation.
>
> It clearly has a purpose and today deepened understanding. We were able to re-see Grahams parents as a vulnerable mother with her husband feeling unable to comfort her.
>
> Julie, reluctantly, and Neil willingly, attempted the "It was a Friday" scene using this alternative take on their relationship generated by the improv.
>
> It added more depth than I could have imagined. The cosy dad comforting mum that we had always had became too simplistic. I now understand the importance of psychological pressure on the audience. They want Harry to comfort Maud, the fact he doesn't, means they have to empathise with Maud's emotions.
>
> The improvisation opened up the script and made us aware there are more riveting possibilities.

This discovery led me to be more willing from this point on to use different 'ways in', when exploring scenes. It also helped us to escape a rough patch and an opportunity to halt the ever decreasing circles of frustration.

One of our best performances was the next one, at my dad's school, At this point he was a Deputy Head and had a wonderful Theatre in a new build school near Tamworth, Staffs.

Following that we performed at **The Cockpit Theatre** in London and were reviewed by a newspaper for the visually impaired.

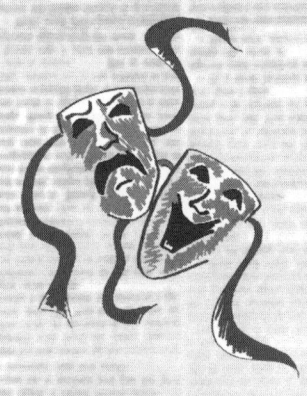

VERBATIM - The Fun of Making Theatre Seriously by Mark Wheeller

REVIEW

It was Rudolph Laban who claimed that "movement was a man's outward expression of living energy within", an apt description of a remarkable man who I had the pleasure of meeting recently. Even before had our first tentative introductory words, I knew this man intimately. I had empathised with his parents when they were brutally informed their only son, who was not yet a year old, would be blind for the rest of his life; I had delighted when he, as an inquisitive child, discovered that the magical thing called "light" was merely a hot bulb; I had sniggered at his dubious antics at Worcester College and cheered as he won the 400m Gold Medal at the third European Games. Yet we still hadn't said "hello".

Graham Salmon is an extraordinary man, not because he has achieved an international reputation as an athlete, but because he (and his family) have courageously exposed those long boarded up skeletons which have been sensitively shaped into a documentary play with music called **Race To Be Seen**... a 90 minutes uninterrupted excursion through the living photograph album of the Salmon family.

How could a youth theatre understand the real and very personal implications of blindness?

Was I going to witness another attempt to dramatise "real life" into a not too convincing theatrical experience?

I need not have worried. My return journey was peppered with very inferior renderings of the captivating title song **Race To Be Seen**, (Yes... I'd managed to put that song back in... but re-located it! Ed.) my mind excited by what I had seen and my emotions understanding more fully this man, Graham Salmon.

I found the simplicity of presentation a most refreshing experience and undoubtedly assisted the audience to comprehend the plays messages.

cont...

VERBATIM - The Fun of Making Theatre Seriously by Mark Wheeller

> *...cont*
>
> The problems and prejudices visually handicapped people encounter were there and pointed, but not overdone.
>
> The emphasis lay in understanding the man, not his handicap. Matt Allen, who plays the adult Graham Salmon obviously understood both. His portrayal of the character so far removed from himself was sheer magic and to be commended.
>
> The other person who literally captivated me was Bernadette Chapman as the Narrator. Her voice, frequently unaccompanied, was like a cool mountain stream. What a talent she has.
>
> By mentioning only these two players does not imply a lack of talent and empathy amongst the rest of the company. As with any production, it is the ensemble that has the power of success or failure hidden in its ranks and **Race To Be Seen** would not succeed so well without that power being harnessed, disciplined and directed so well by Mark Wheeller. I would have enjoyed a slightly less rushed ending and a little more ensemble singing to help the beginning overcome a somewhat slow start.
>
> I am sure we will hear much more of the life of Graham Salmon and his links with Epping Youth Theatre in one form or another for some time to come. I predict a successful run at the Edinburgh Festival.
> **David Mumford**

It's interesting, reading all these reviews together, how the iconic feature of our presentation style, the body scenery divided opinion. Hugh David from the TES, in particular had hated it... others had viewed it as a sign of our creativity. It goes to prove, 'you can't please all the people all the time' and you have to do what you feel is right... anything less and you lose your integrity.

... and so we come to Edinburgh.

Gus Shield, our Stage Manager from E15, had fallen in love with EYT and came to the Fringe as our Stage Manager/ Technician. What a boost for us!

VERBATIM - The Fun of Making Theatre Seriously by Mark Wheeller

Meanwhile, I was still tinkering with the script.

Knowing it so intimately, I spent parts of my school summer holidays listening to the interview tapes again and spotted lines the interviewees said that I'd missed first time round. These were really small alterations and must have been so hard for the cast to re-learn (apologies).

We were ready for our appearance at the Fringe.

I was ready to win a Fringe First!

We all sensed it was the start of something big...

I mentioned in my diary how this could be the first step to an Oscar!!!

Then...

Tragedy...

Down to earth with a bump.

Zara Chapman, who had played Marie so beautifully (I'm actually surprised she hasn't been mentioned more in this book so far, as I remember her being so central to the project and such an obvious choice for the caring role of Marie), was involved in a hit and run accident. She emerged from it with two broken legs.

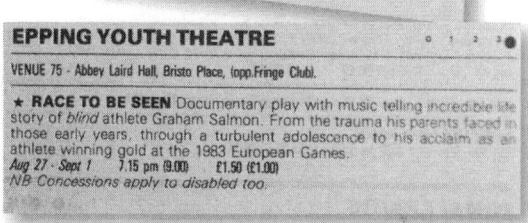

EPPING YOUTH THEATRE
VENUE 75 - Abbey Laird Hall, Bristo Place, (opp.Fringe Club).

★ **RACE TO BE SEEN** Documentary play with music telling incredible life story of *blind* athlete Graham Salmon. From the trauma his parents faced in those early years, through a turbulent adolescence to his acclaim as an athlete winning gold at the 1983 European Games.
Aug 27 - Sept 1   7.15 pm (9.00)   £1.50 (£1.00)
NB Concessions apply to disabled too.

VERBATIM - The Fun of Making Theatre Seriously by Mark Wheeller

She was confined to hospital for eight weeks.

We visited her in hospital but it was difficult.

Our lives were continuing but poor Zara's had been abruptly arrested.

Jan and Matt at Edinburgh

Some of the cast outside the Royal Edinburgh School for the Blind

Jan Farringdon, aged 14, was pleased to hear she would play Marie in all the performances in Edinburgh (though obviously was shocked to hear about Zara).

The second cast was now a positive benefit here as Jan had already performed the role multiple times so we didn't have to find and rehearse someone new.

In Edinburgh, we were staying in Bill (Graham's old PE teacher) Aitken's school. Bill was by this time a welcoming and inspiring Head Teacher at The Royal Edinburgh School for the blind.

Our adventure was in its next phase, albeit without Zara.

A small contingent of us went up in advance and to see how other groups managed the publicity... leafletting and street theatre.

VERBATIM - The Fun of Making Theatre Seriously by Mark Wheeller

Our venue, the Abbey Laird Hall looked great... better than I expected. It was actually a little church hall transformed into a magnificent studio theatre space.

The others arrived a week later and those of us who were there in advance were so excited to meet them at the station. I remember the exuberance... not to mention a little fear of the unknown rising up.

I wondered how many people would be in our audiences?

That year there were 843 performances competing for an audience.

Epping Youth Theatre, founded less than a year before, had six performances of **Race To Be Seen** at the Edinburgh Festival (Fringe).

This was about to become VERY real!

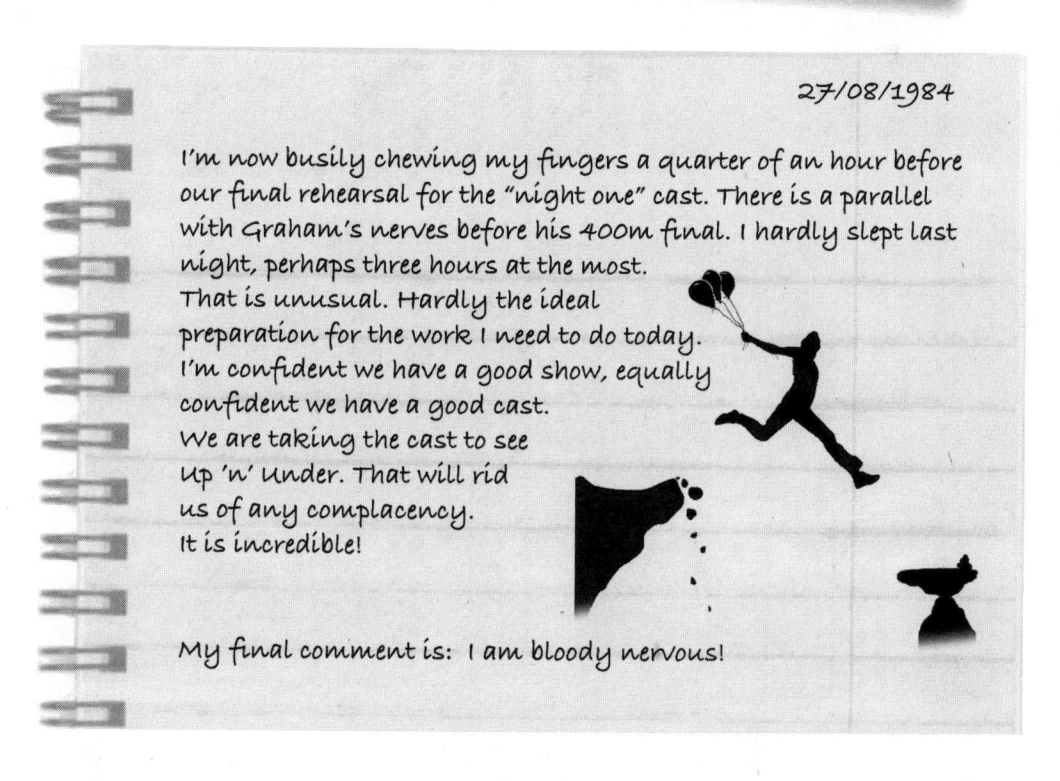

27/08/1984

I'm now busily chewing my fingers a quarter of an hour before our final rehearsal for the "night one" cast. There is a parallel with Graham's nerves before his 400m final. I hardly slept last night, perhaps three hours at the most.
That is unusual. Hardly the ideal preparation for the work I need to do today.
I'm confident we have a good show, equally confident we have a good cast.
We are taking the cast to see Up 'n' Under. That will rid us of any complacency.
It is incredible!

My final comment is: I am bloody nervous!

Chapter 7: EYT Race to the Fringe

Please let me claim fifteen minutes of fame
So that everyone, everywhere, remembers my name
I'd like taps shaped like me on everyone's bath
And have Huff made us happy for my epitaph
Such acclaim... for fifteen minutes of fame.
Mark Wheeller from the **Happy Soap** musical.

29th August 1984

Our first night was fraught with complications. John (Rowley) and Robbie were late... and unapologetic. The key to the door behind which our screen is kept was lost by the church hall. Fortunately, Gus found an imaginative way to successfully project onto the back curtain.

The Forth Radio reviewer was there and, I can now report, was impressed. My nerves before the performance spoilt it for me and the problems turned my frustration into anger!

The second night, with the very much younger cast, had to perform in front of the "important" critics (The Scotsman). Once again, technology let us down. The projector decided not to work at all! Julie Knope emerged as the star, giving the best performance I have ever seen in any Youth Theatre production.

Matthew was also stunning. He has throughout this diary come in for a lot of criticism but is now portraying Graham brilliantly. The performance was good and, if we get bad reviews, we have no excuse. As for a Fringe First? Well, I think it's well within the realms of possibility. If this doesn't get one I won't t ever win one. This is the best that I can ever do.

The other question is could we become Forth Radio's 'Pick of the Fringe'?

VERBATIM - The Fun of Making Theatre Seriously by Mark Wheeller

Bill Aitken was giving us an amazing time in Edinburgh and we were getting to know his students, doing drama workshops with them most mornings to pay our rent. They were also great fun AND we were truly integrating! Then we'd go off to the Royal Mile with our street theatre pieces and leaflet the crowds.

We seemed to generate some interest.

One highlight was the meeting between Graham and a mime artist. They attracted a big audience as they figured out how to communicate.

We attracted decent audiences and in a venue that could hold about 80 we had from 38 to 65 people each day. We had done well. The average audience for the Fringe that year was, apparently, 4.5 people.

Did we win a Fringe First?

Well…

Let's deal with the other reviews first.

Radio Forth invited Graham, Matthew and I in for an interview and made us one of their **Pick Of The Fringe**, saying:

> **RADIO FORTH   Pick Of The Fringe**
>
> This documentary play is well worth watching… pathos is mixed with hilarious anecdotes. Jason Lawrence as the young Salmon steals the show. Both he and Matthew Allen capture the sheer cocky spirit of the blind runner.
> ***GREAT!***

VERBATIM - The Fun of Making Theatre Seriously by Mark Wheeller

The *Scottish Evening News* DID include us in their *Best of the Fringe* list, a *Critic's Choice* saying:

> ## Scottish Evening News
>
> Out of sight out of mind sums up some attitudes to the disabled and this inspirational play from the Epping Youth Theatre smashes down these barriers.
>
> The young cast put on a convincing performance that belies their years. Any danger of the piece being swamped in sentimentality vanishes with the realistic touches in this documentary style production.
>
> Graham not only provided the theme for this moving theatrical event, he also co-wrote some of the beautifully sung some songs illuminating his story of true grit.

Once again my songs were being listened to and applauded but I have to confess by this point my focus was beginning to be on the play... my songs were starting to play second fiddle.

A significant shift!

... and so to the *Scotsman* and their review...

...the one to qualify us for a *Fringe First.*

Spoiler Alert... we DIDN'T get one.

'We was robbed!'

This was The Scotsman review...

... spe*LL*ing my name incorrectly!

146

VERBATIM - The Fun of Making Theatre Seriously by Mark Wheeller

THE SCOTSMAN

This play has been devised by Mr Salmon, the company, and the young director Mark Wheeler. It encompasses the athlete's birth, youth, schooling, period of "unemployability," marriage, and track successes, incorporating songs written by Salmon himself. It is at times bitter about a world which seems determined to frustrate and oppose, but, a philosophical humour always manages to come out on top.

Perhaps because the acting is intelligently underplayed, almost conversational, I sometimes have the odd sensation of eavesdropping on this man's brave and determined life. You never get the chance to distance yourself and attempt to generalise a "message" from what you were saying as more conventional theatre encourages you to do. The program describes the piece as a "documentary play," and normal aesthetic criteria are inapplicable, since this, whatever its dramatic structure, is how it was, it's true. The life is the message, and it's a refreshingly optimistic one.

As reviews go, this wasn't bad. It's probably the best I've received at the Fringe. It features a reservation that was to be repeated throughout my career. The nature of the documentary plays means "normal aesthetic criteria" are suspended. What rubbish! It's a cop out for the reviewers.[29]

We had an amazing time in Edinburgh. For the first time I'd seen a range of plays/productions. Amongst my highlights were **East** by Berkoff and a production of **The Odyssey** (by a university group - sorry I have no idea who it was) staged as a promenade production. I had never seen such a thing previously and it inspired the way I directed our next production, **The King of Elfland's Daughter** and then a few years later, **The Most Absurd Xmas Musical** and, finally in 2014, **Silas Marner**. Promenade remains my favourite way of staging plays.

I was gaining a useful theatrical palette that would continue to grow over the years.

---

[29] You can see my own detailed analysis of this performance in the Appendix section of this book.

VERBATIM - The Fun of Making Theatre Seriously by Mark Wheeller

The best on the Fringe that we saw was John Godber's ***Up 'n' Under*** and ***Woza Albert*** by the Market Theatre, Johannesburg both of which were being premiered.

What a stunning year for premieres!

Both plays wonderfully demonstrated how quality theatre could be developed on a low budget. I could relate to this in a way that wasn't possible with the big West End Musicals I was more familiar with. This discovery contributed to a confidence I was slowly developing about using zero budget as conscious force for creativity rather than an obstacle.

Up 'n' Under was also a lesson in how to stage seemingly 'impossible' scenes. Hull Truck staged, with a cast of only 7 (I think), a rugby match. The cast wore rugby shirts designed as one team when they faced forwards and the opposing team when facing backwards. The final rugby match scene was absolutely WOW!

There were moments when we, in the audience, were actually cheering on the team we were rooting for!

Amazing!

This was what I had wanted for Graham's 400 metre final.

I knew we'd failed to achieve this and watching John Godber's work confirmed that.

Hull Truck were so far in advance of what we had managed to do. It made me wonder if all the effort was worth while.

Should I give up?

Up 'n' Under not only won a Fringe First but also an **Olivier** for **Best Comedy**... underlining how far we had to go.

John Godber was also a teacher, recently an ex-teacher. His work impacted on schools across the country from this point onwards, more through **Bouncers** which we all went to see in London the following term... and we adored that too!

Woza Albert was another inspiration... and another deserving Fringe First winner that year.

VERBATIM - The Fun of Making Theatre Seriously by Mark Wheeller

Written by Percy Mtwa, Mbongeni Ngema and Barney Simon, its premise is the second coming of Jesus Christ to South Africa during Apartheid.

It was a 'workshop theatre performance with the two actors multi-roling'. The content was so thought provoking.

The style of presentation so, SO imaginative!

It showed that in the most humble of circumstances, unbelievably imaginative theatre can be produced.

Along with SNAP Theatre, both these productions, in their different ways, inspired all my future work which would always be low budget.

I was now determined to make that an advantage rather than a handicap... just like Graham had done with his personal disadvantage!

Prior to our final performance (literally a few minutes before) as we were heading to the venue, a small group of us saw a joke shop.

'There must be something in there we can get for Graham to thank him!'

Looking through the window I spotted something perfect and went round the corner to the door...

... but...

... disaster!

The joke shop was closed.

'Bugger'!!

We hammered on the door.

We were desperate.

A shopkeeper emerged inside the shop.

We explained our predicament loudly through the glass door and the magic of Graham Salmon worked again.

VERBATIM - The Fun of Making Theatre Seriously by Mark Wheeller

The proprietor opened the shop and sold us this utterly perfect gift.

We were beyond delighted!

When we gave the little present to him in front of the whole cast, I said:

'We've found a very silly present for someone we've learnt can be a very silly man. I will take your glasses away so that there can be no peeping before you open it ...'

Graham fumbled around with the small package and, to cover the embarrassment, said:

'I'm not very good at opening presents.'

He opened it and as people saw the box containing the gift they laughed.

Graham put his hands inside to pull out a joke pair of glasses with eyes on springs.

He put them on and absolutely creased up…

…and so did Marie!

He always brought these glasses out at the end of his after dinner speeches when he talked about **Race To Be Seen**, and he told me:

'They always get a great reaction.'

They symbolise our wonderful relationship.

Just before we said goodbye to our hosts at The Royal Blind School, a group of the older ones and I were chatting about something quite serious, and I recorded in my diary a brief exchange with John Fradd, our 15-year-old technician, which tickled me.

VERBATIM - The Fun of Making Theatre Seriously by Mark Wheeller

> *John:* The trouble with you intellectuals is that you need to talk or else you get pissed off!
>
> *Matt:* Thanks for that John... are you saying you don't fit in?
>
> *John:* Not at all. Joining EYT has been the best thing I've done in my life!
>
> *Me:* Seriously? Why's that?
>
> *John:* Well, before I was just a wanker!

He's a 'wanker' I've remained in regular contact with since that time and I enjoy his company as much as I did back then. It's strange as originally he was put into my tutor group as a last ditch attempt to stop him from being expelled. Somehow, despite being very different we just clicked. We've never had a cross word in over 30 years.

After the festival, in my diary, I referred again to the Fringe First...

... it remained an important target.

I felt I needed one to get the recognition I needed to make any progress as a...

... yes... as a writer/director...

I was beginning to see that I may actually be able to write...

... my next project would give me the opportunity to flex those muscles.

I was planning to adapt a book, using the techniques I had used with all the words from these transcripts.

The King Of Elfland's Daughter
(by Lord Dunsany), using the wonderful songs from a concept album by Bob Johnson and Pete Knight of Steeleye Span.

VERBATIM - The Fun of Making Theatre Seriously by Mark Wheeller

> 03/09/1984
>
> The festival is over.
>
> We did everything except win a Fringe First. I am surprised rather than disappointed that we didn't manage this but, it makes the challenge for it in future years that little bit keener.[30] We have to go all out to amaze, impress and thrill. It has to be a world beater.
>
> Graham has been on the phone to me for ages tonight and said: "When you phoned to suggest writing a play about my life I had my doubts. You have all become my friends. This may be the end of the tour but it has left me with something deeper and longer lasting than that. Thank you."

At that time I thought I was saying goodbye to **Race** but I knew Graham and Marie would remain friends. They both continued to play an in increasingly important part in all my life... and, more surprisingly... so did **Race To Be Seen**!

---

[30] A Fringe First still eludes me or one of my plays!

VERBATIM - The Fun of Making Theatre Seriously by Mark Wheeller

Despite the positive reviews for the Longman script, **Race To Be Seen** didn't sell.

A review is only any good if it is seen. The reviews of the script clearly weren't being read and I had no way of 'pushing' them out there, as is now easier via the internet.

Where it was performed, it created enormous interest.

I remember Northwood School in Hillingdon inviting me in as they were using their performance of the play as the centrepiece to a progressive Integrated Day.

Nick Baker of the **Times Educational Supplement** ran an incredibly complimentary double page spread about it. Everyone loved the play.

There were a handful of other performances but it didn't set the school performance world on fire. I was disappointed, but not desolate.

BBC Schools programmes expressed interest in me adapting it for TV but it came to nothing.

I had brought it to the attention of drama in education guru Dorothy Heathcote who a few weeks later sent me a handwritten letter congratulating me. This was, to me, like getting a letter from David Bowie. She sent the letter to my school as she didn't know my address... incredibly thoughtful:

> Mark,
>
> Excuse my paper. I'm listening to the tape of your songs as I read the script.
>
> This whole area of documentary/Youth Theatre genre is so exciting and I consider it to be one of the most interesting developments at this time.
>
> I do hope that you can share some of the experiences of making such material transformed into theatre so that others may develop it forward. It is so right for its age.
>
> Go Well in 1986.
>
> Dorothy

VERBATIM - The Fun of Making Theatre Seriously by Mark Wheeller

Graham became an integral part of EYT, playing guitar in our amazing large cast promenade, musical production of ***The King of Elfland's Daughter*** as he had done in ***Joseph*** and indeed the ***Race To Be Seen*** cassette tape we recorded.

He closely followed our success with ***Quenchers*** and ***Too Much Punch For Judy*** and we all (Marie, Graham and I) became very close. We went on to have an important lifelong relationship with each other.

My break from any involvement with ***Race To Be Seen*** lasted until 1987 when I was offered a fantastic new job at Oaklands Community School. I was appointed to be part teacher and part youth theatre director, an amazing opportunity in a school where the leadership team believed in the arts and were keen for me to come in and 'do my thing'.

At this point my diary writing stopped so, the rest of this book will be the result of my own (and, in places, others') memories, together with the record of VHS and DVD (when they were invented) recordings of our productions.

For my move to this dream job, as I saw it, I needed a production I could totally trust to introduce me to my new Oaklands Youth Theatre group.

I never had any doubt... ***Race To Be Seen*** was the obvious choice... and so the story continued.

VERBATIM - The Fun of Making Theatre Seriously by Mark Wheeller

Chapter 8: Race at Oaklands

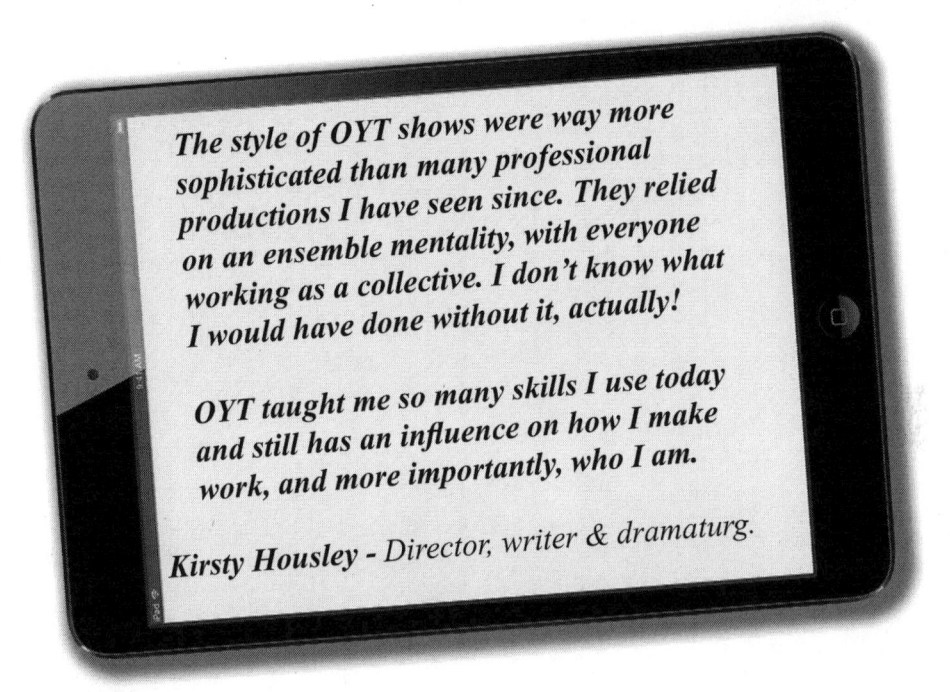

The style of OYT shows were way more sophisticated than many professional productions I have seen since. They relied on an ensemble mentality, with everyone working as a collective. I don't know what I would have done without it, actually!

OYT taught me so many skills I use today and still has an influence on how I make work, and more importantly, who I am.

Kirsty Housley - *Director, writer & dramaturg.*

Oaklands Youth Theatre, the new Southampton-based group I was working with were mostly under 15 as Oaklands was a 12-16 school.

The older ones had moved on to sixth form colleges, dismayed that their old, more experienced, teacher had left. This young upstart doing his unknown productions didn't interest them.

So, for this production, I would miss the older, more experienced people I had been used to working with at Epping. Many, like John Rowley had ended up working with me for the whole of my five years there.

VERBATIM - The Fun of Making Theatre Seriously by Mark Wheeller

This lack of experience was a rude awakening and led me to regret more than once my move, despite better pay and a much better (fully equipped) Theatre in our new purpose-built school.

Nevertheless, I was determined to crack the 400 metres final scene in **Race**. By this time I'd seen a professional director's work on the accident scene in Touchstone Theatre Company's production of **Too Much Punch For Judy**. This and increased visits to the theatre over the years (Cheek by Jowl were a new favourite, making Shakespeare accessible even to me!) began to offer me a larger toolbox of possibilities which I was keen to use and extend the range of techniques in my productions even further.

I shall describe the staging of the 400 metres scene in OYT's production in detail because it represents a moment of solid progression for myself as a director/curator.

My approach began by thinking back to the rehearsal where John Rowley (EYT) had run on the spot in front of us and we had all begun to change our breathing to involuntarily match his. I remember replicating this for my new OYT cast and, they were stunned by it. I remember saying:

"We need to find a way of making the audience experience this when we present this scene."

So, given the inexperience of the cast, I was delighted when a 4th Year (year 10 in new money), Richard Brown (who would come to be an integral part of my **Hard to Swallow** development team), piped up:

'We could do step-ups.'

I had no idea what a 'step-up' was.

Richard demonstrated.

I could see the potential instantly and one idea followed another until we generated a far more impressive scene.[31]

---

[31] You can see this on my (Mark Wheeller) YouTube Channel.

VERBATIM - The Fun of Making Theatre Seriously by Mark Wheeller

We had Graham and Roger, his guide runner, positioned centrally on a 2m square rostrum, standing half a metre high and positioned diagonally on stage right.

Positioned around the front part of the rostrum were six of the ensemble, representing Graham's competitors.

When the gun is fired to indicate the start of the race, the ensemble counted (out loud) from 1-55. 55.5 seconds is Graham's time for this race... and the world record.

Others, plus Marie, cheered people on... mostly Graham haha.

With a cast of 40 this was noisy and generated an exciting atmosphere.

Simultaneously, all those positioned around the rostrum did step-ups as fast as they could, gradually tiring themselves out over the 55 second count.

Note: In a rehearsal I asked the six step up volunteers to do a test see who was able to keep going the longest. This gave us the order in which I asked them to drop out and sit on the rostra, actually somewhat out of breath.

They were given a pre-determined number of seconds to signify the point at which they dropped out of the scene (gradually from about 25 seconds and up to 54 seconds).

They remained, breathing heavily, sitting on the rostra trying recover their breath.

Meanwhile Graham and Roger, in the middle of the rostrum facing front, performed a slow motion running action (linked by a short length of rope as in real life) until the count of 55.

VERBATIM - The Fun of Making Theatre Seriously by Mark Wheeller

At that moment, as he won, everyone shouted **'Yeah!'**

Graham and Roger offered a celebratory victory salute image, which they held until Marie approached excitedly, asking if Graham had won!

Everyone stopped and looked towards the victors but remained silent, allowing Graham and Roger's (now heavy) breathing to be heard under the continuing dialogue as it recommenced.

The scene, as we performed it each night, was greeted by spontaneous applause.

After one of the performances, I was thrilled to hear from Roger Black (then Olympic champion and local celebrity) that he had inadvertently dug Graham in the ribs during the scene (they were sitting next to one another) because Roger's arms had started to do a running action involuntarily!

We (a 'mere' Youth Theatre) had achieved what I had so admired in John Godber's **Up 'n' Under** only four years previously. Hull Truck's inspiration had moved us forward and I had real evidence of genuine progress in my work!

All this... with a new and inexperienced Youth Theatre group!

There was hope.

I didn't need to return to Epping!

VERBATIM - The Fun of Making Theatre Seriously by Mark Wheeller

Developing the existing production

My way of working was never to regurgitate what I'd done previously; in this instance, the original EYT performance. I don't do well at simply telling people, in a didactic manner, what they should do. I need my casts to invest in projects, working organically and collaboratively with me to develop how a scene should look.

I think one reason why my plays are popular with students might be that the scripts purposely lack stage directions and thus open up opportunities for cast members to have a unique and important input, offering them a strong sense of ownership over the resultant work.

Also, unlike scenes where people only talk to each other on stage, there is no obvious way of staging my more narrative plays. This forces creativity.

The professional theatre companies who tour my plays have also felt a sense of release from the straitjackets they tell me they have often had to work within.

I arrive at a rehearsal having done little (probably nothing) in the way of preparation, although having put this production on previously I did arrive with some stimulus ideas (such as the starter for the 400 metres race scene); but I still need cast input.

This caused anxiety as some of the cast and staff who had offered to help saw my approach as disorganised. It was hard to allay their fears but I was more confident at this point because I had done this production before and so had something to fall back on.

I was keen to show off and use the freshly published text so was not interested in refining the script, which I felt was now sacrosanct!

One big difference was the size of the cast. In Epping it was 15. Here is was around 40. This OYT production would be a very different production.

VERBATIM - The Fun of Making Theatre Seriously by Mark Wheeller

I found myself part of a supportive team of adults rather than alone, struggling to deal with everything, alongside a few willing late teens filling in the gaps.

I had a choreographer (a proper dance teacher!) and someone who acted as a publicity officer.

Central to the support I benefitted from was Brian Price.

Brian was the Music Teacher at Oaklands. He wasn't just a music teacher. He was more like a pop star in a school and many of the students (certainly the ones involved in the production) like his fans!

It was exciting to invite this energy into what I had imagined was 'my' project.

Now, I had to share it. **Eek!**

I was excited to work with him but it demanded a sacrifice for me, which a few years previously would have been a few staircases too far.

To involve Brian, I had to drop the very thing that had instigated this play.

I had to drop all of my songs.

A huge sacrifice.

HUGE!

That said, when I heard Brian's songs, I realised they were in a different class to mine; the kind I would like to have written but never could.

Brians songs sounded modern; good enough to be on the radio. His singers, Loretta Power and Min Rodriguez, were what I'd describe as undiscovered star singers... icing on what was already an incredibly tasty cake!

I remember the excitement, at his house, as he played early versions of his (music and lyrics) songs.

VERBATIM - The Fun of Making Theatre Seriously by Mark Wheeller

They were to lift the production and make it more exuberant.

I remember the pride I felt having these songs, sung so perfectly, as part of my play.

Although Brian and I worked as a natural partnership, he would express fears about my ability to deliver the production on time. I worked slowly and, to an observer, it must have seemed like we were getting nowhere fast. It didn't help that I was openly operating without any form of a map!

However, Brian trusted that I'd done the production before and, once we put it in front of an audience and he saw the reaction, his fears subsided.

I don't think anyone failed to see the impact it had on the cast from a very early point in rehearsals.

One of the few exceptions to the fact that all the over-16 year olds had deserted this new drama teacher was Jason Eames, who I cast to play Graham. Little did I know how valuable he would be as a support to me in rehearsals. He was only one person but he made a valiant effort to fill the boots of the many over-16s I had in Epping Youth Theatre... and he proved to be an exceptional performer.

I lost contact with Jason following the production but, while writing this book, I was put in touch with him. He generously offered his memories to further emphasise the power of this work with real people, telling their stories.

> I remember, with a smile, thinking: you had arrived from London with your bag of plays and experience and thinking you must have thought we were a bunch of carrot crunchers!!! You were self-assured and could have been perceived as a little arrogant. Having said that, I did all I could to balance those who viewed you with suspicion and get people on board with what I felt would be a very positive end result. I believed in you from early on, driven by a sense that you knew your trade... and could prove it! Your drive and focus was truly your strength and although you could be strict, you did listen and let things develop in a natural way which I appreciated. That gave me the confidence to perform in a way I hadn't previously.
> I had been a member of the Oaklands Community Theatre (the company that preceded OYT) for 4 years before *Race* and had the lead role in my first production. I'd also managed to gain a place at the National Youth Theatre the year or two before *Race*.
> I remember the elation of getting the role of Graham but also, and probably more importantly, the feeling of a real responsibility to the subject, especially as at this point I'd not met Graham. I remember when I did meet him I was in awe of him and what he'd achieved. Seeing him and Marie in their own environment, and understanding the total love and understanding they had for each other, their challenges and their successes in life, was fascinating.
> *cont..*

VERBATIM - The Fun of Making Theatre Seriously by Mark Wheeller

> *...cont*
> I count myself very lucky for that opportunity and insight.
> I spent hours blindfolded at home. I often recall trying to make a cup of tea and the challenges of that! It's surprising how that engages the way people then understand the challenges the visually impaired have.
> Spending time with Graham was invaluable, especially the first time we went for a walk at his local park where he showed me how he could 'hear trees, lamp posts, etc.'! i.e. the bouncing sound-shadows. Hugely important for my performance was understanding the way he looked almost 6 inches above where he believes the sound was coming… and that appears to be the same for many visually impaired people. Then the hand movements and even the differences in his walking.
> Staging the play was different for me as we were using an adaptable space without props and scenery which we'd always had in previous productions, so being descriptive with words and actions to paint the scene and bring it to life was essential. We also had to pinpoint when taking our positions on stage. The whole production offered a great learning curve and I preferred this way of working and the outcomes to how we had before.
> **Jason Eames** *(aged 16 when he played Graham in this production)*

We previewed the performance on a Wednesday.

Graham and Marie arrived the next day to see the following three performances.

Their lunch-time arrival is etched into my memory.

We had a Community Lounge (with a bar, which was closed during the school day!) outside the purpose built theatre.

The cast (most of whom were at the school) had time off lessons to meet them and sat on either side of the central walkway.

I brought them up from the car park and, as we walked into the Community Lounge, the cast greeted them with a spontaneous, loud and long lasting standing ovation.

I was honoured to introduce these very special people to my cast.

Graham and Marie Salmon were real and the experience for OYT was so different to how it was for EYT. It offered a unique climax for our production week to meet those whose story we were telling.

That night they'd be in the audience watching the play.

VERBATIM - The Fun of Making Theatre Seriously by Mark Wheeller

It mattered.

It really mattered.

There followed a period of non-stop conversation and, as always when Graham was around, lots of laughter!

Myself, Marie, Graham and Lisa who played Graham's sister in the OYT production.

We had coverage from the local news programme, **South Today** and, the following morning, further publicity on Radio Solent.

Graham always attracted media interest.

VERBATIM - The Fun of Making Theatre Seriously by Mark Wheeller

We went to one of our feeder schools and Graham did a 100-metres run on their sports ground.

There was such a buzz around him and Marie everywhere they went.

The run was already sold out.

Marie and Graham being with us made the production week all the more special.

The performances were electric.

The reaction thrilling.

The standing ovation at the end went on and on and on!

> The performances were full of intensity and pressure. The audience expectation was very high and I remember the silences. They were always so strong! My friends and/or family were fascinated about the story and how we'd put it on stage. I think they were very proud but I never really asked them!
> One thing I will forever be very proud of was that someone from the audience in the interval approached either you or Graham? (can't remember) and asked how long the guy playing Graham had been blind for? I loved that.
> The pleasure of knowing Graham and playing him did involve pressure and responsibility but the learning curves I went through, and the outcome, will always be one of my top 5 life moments. My whole experience was sealed when Graham said he couldn't have played himself any better... I shall always remember that.
> **Jason Eames**

VERBATIM - The Fun of Making Theatre Seriously by Mark Wheeller

As I watched the VHS of this production for the first time in more than 30 years (and a poorly filmed version of the play can not be compared to the real thing) I realised, somewhat belatedly, this production was <u>very</u> special. I should have remembered, particularly as Graham wrote this in his letter to the cast following the performances.

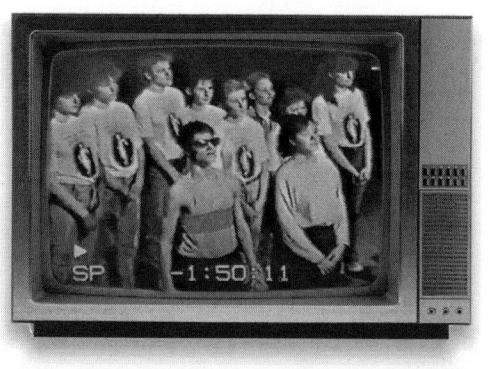

> Dear Friends
>
> The quality which makes a great champion stand out above the rest is the ability to produce something extra special on the big occasion and you did just that on Saturday night. It was the 27th performance of "Race To Be Seen" that I have been to and, honestly, it was the very best. Thank you for making it such a memorable occasion; you are forever my champions.

I don't think I appreciated it at the time but Brian's songs (and his incredible arrangement of Graham's Worcester College song) lifted the play to help make it the uplifting piece I had always wanted **Race To Be Seen** to be!

As I had enjoyed the video of the production so much, I decided to write a **Director's Commentary** on this version which you can read in the Appendix of this book. It also inspired a commentary on each of the performances recorded in this book. They offer clear insights as to how we staged these 'difficult' verbatim plays in a surprisingly visual manner. That focus on the visual is of supreme importance and is not obvious from a simple reading of the written script.

I have limited records of reactions to the play but these two will give a flavour...

> *Dear Mark,*
> *I wanted to tell you how much I enjoyed Race To Be Seen last night. It was excellent! A tremendous story, and I loved the inventiveness with which it was told. A fantastic ensemble group effort - concentration and enthusiasm were superb. It made it a very special evening. It deserves to be seen by a great deal more people! I loved every minute. Well done!*
> *Yours,*

Richard Martin Headteacher of Priestlands Shool

165

VERBATIM - The Fun of Making Theatre Seriously by Mark Wheeller

DIRECTOR OF LEISURE, TOURISM AND AMENITIES
JOHN BULLOCK F.I.L.A.M.(Dip), F.T.S.
Civic Centre, Southampton SO9 4XF
Telephone 0703 223855

Please ask for: Mr M Fuller
Direct phone: 832456
Our ref: MAF/JA
Your ref:

SOUTHAMPTON CITY

15 December 1987

Mark Wheeler
Head of Drama
Oaklands Community School
Fairisle Road
Lordshill
Southampton

Dear Mark

I am writing to say how much I and my family enjoyed your production last Friday. It was a gripping story and well put together. You were helped enormously by Brian Price and his musical arrangements. Your actors were a great credit especially your leads.

I thought that the direction of all the actors was entirely in keeping with the theatre space and its open stage. The lighting was also effective in its simplicity with the useful addition of the slides.

My children know what they like and will let me know fairly soon if a play is not keeping their interest. 'Race to be Seen' gripped them from the beginning with its direct style and enjoyable music. I must say that my wife Lesley and I found the play a 'good night out'. You must be very pleased with your team's efforts. Congratulations with your first production.

Best wishes

Michael.

Michael Fuller
Arts & Entertainments Officer

Leisure for you

Telex No. 477142 Fax No. 832424

VERBATIM - The Fun of Making Theatre Seriously by Mark Wheeller

The highlight of all the reactions I have came from Graham himself who, in addition to writing to the cast, typed a letter to me and signed it.

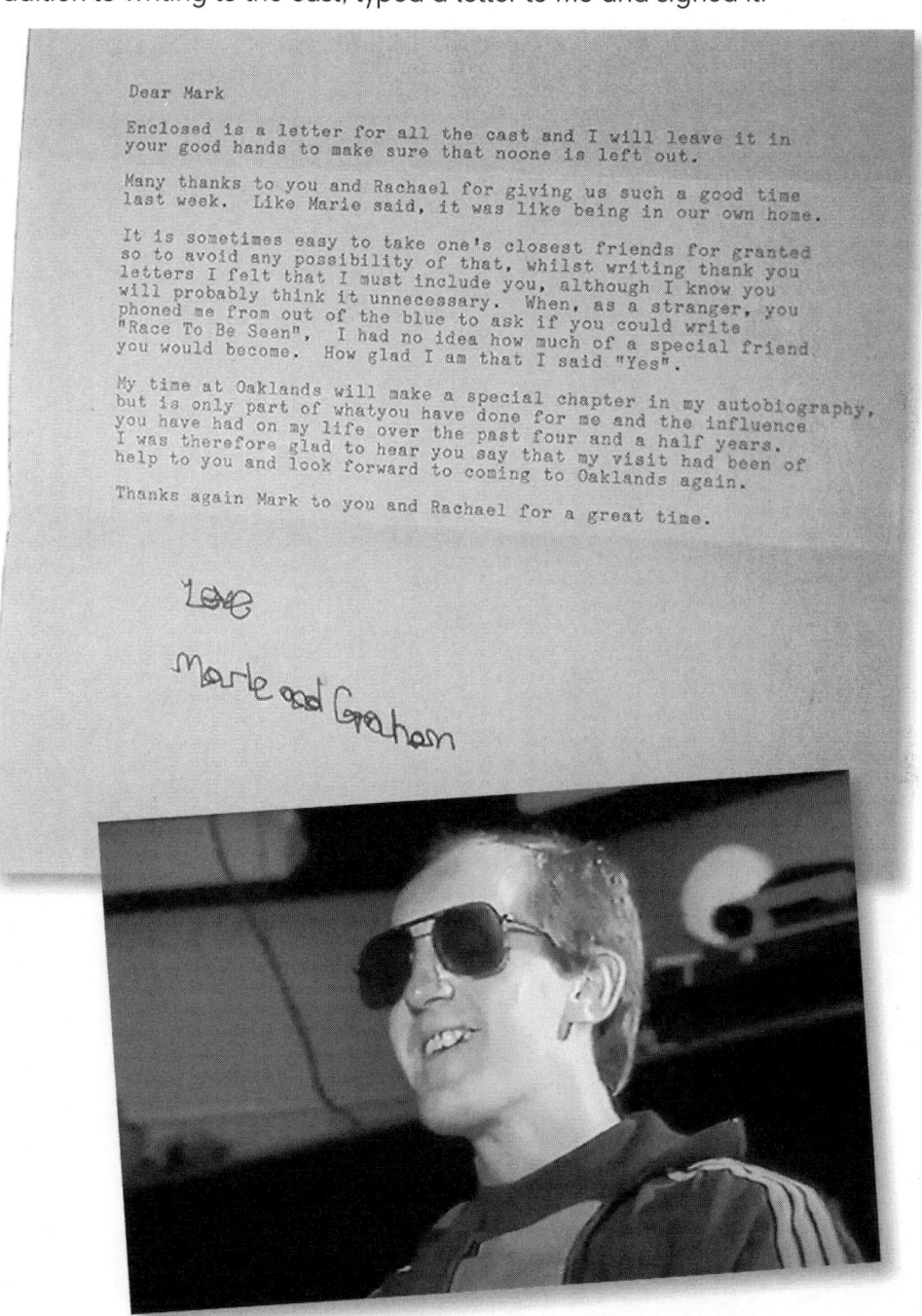

> Dear Mark
>
> Enclosed is a letter for all the cast and I will leave it in your good hands to make sure that noone is left out.
>
> Many thanks to you and Rachael for giving us such a good time last week. Like Marie said, it was like being in our own home.
>
> It is sometimes easy to take one's closest friends for granted so to avoid any possibility of that, whilst writing thank you letters I felt that I must include you, although I know you will probably think it unnecessary. When, as a stranger, you phoned me from out of the blue to ask if you could write "Race To Be Seen", I had no idea how much of a special friend you would become. How glad I am that I said "Yes".
>
> My time at Oaklands will make a special chapter in my autobiography, but is only part of what you have done for me and the influence you have had on my life over the past four and a half years. I was therefore glad to hear you say that my visit had been of help to you and look forward to coming to Oaklands again.
>
> Thanks again Mark to you and Rachael for a great time.
>
> Love
> Mark and Graham

VERBATIM - The Fun of Making Theatre Seriously by Mark Wheeller

Jason told me he remained in contact with Graham and this is a supremely important feature of my verbatim plays… the friendships they generate.
I am astounded by the loyalty of the young people who have made up the membership of my YTs over the years. At every production, we had people from previous productions or versions of them attending… and this was no exception. There was a large contingent from EYT, 'the originals' as they were referred to, in the audience… and of course at the after-show party!

> I have always been very proud of *Race* and my association and friendship with both you and Graham. I kept in contact with Graham for a time afterwards and used to go to the Arsenal with him, even a Cup Final at Wembley! Unfortunately, life and me moving around the country and abroad led our friendship to drift but I will always be extremely thankful for meeting both yourself and Graham and the opportunity that you both gave me. It has always stayed with me and been a part of me.
> **Jason Eames**

I will close this chapter with Graham's words on *Race* (sadly to be his final words about the play) in a letter he wrote to Jason following the 1987 performance. It clearly made a deep impression on him. One of the great pleasures of writing this book was reading this, which I didn't even know existed!

The Grahams

VERBATIM - The Fun of Making Theatre Seriously by Mark Wheeller

15 Kenilworth Gardens
Loughton
Essex
IG10 3AG

Tel: 01 508 7623

15th December 1987.

Dear Jason

I have already written to all the cast and, no doubt, you have by now read that letter. However, I wanted to write a few additional lines of thanks to you personally for the hard work and effort you put into "Race To Be Seen" and for the support you gave Mark during the preparation and performance of the play.

As you know I am a very proud person and the way in which I am portrayed on stage is very important to me. That is one of the reasons why I was a little uncertain whether to agree to the play being written in the first place. I was delighted with the way in which you put my character across, particularly on Saturday evening when your performance was outstanding, the best anyone has played me. There is no doubt that you lifted the entire cast to make the evening the best performance ever in the history of "Race" and an occasion Marie and I will never forget. Indeed, we will treasure our memories from Oaklands for the rest of our lives. You really seem to have understood the way things are with me and, perhaps the biggest compliment I can pay you is to say that I could not have played me better. Thanks Jason.

I am glad that you enjoyed "Race To Be Seen" so much and thank you for taking the trouble to write. Your letter means a lot and is one which I will always keep. I am currently writing my autobiography and last week will make an unexpected extra chapter which I will greatly enjoy writing.

I will keep in touch Jason. It is great to know you and I hope it won't be too long before we meet again. Come and see us some time; you will always be welcome here.

Lots of Love

Graham and Marie

Chapter 9: The Graham/Race Legacy

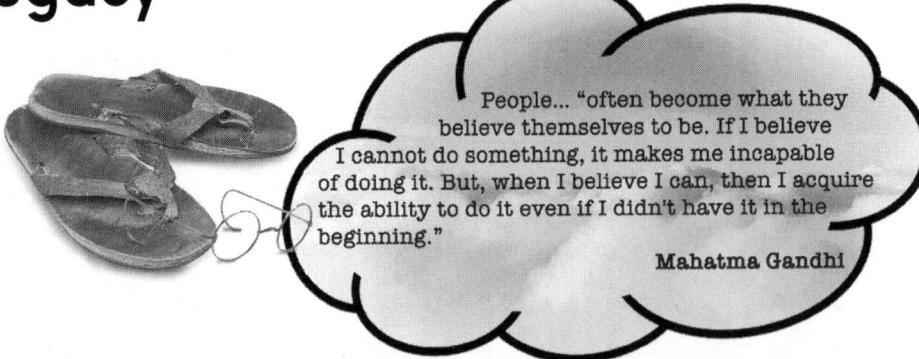

> People... "often become what they believe themselves to be. If I believe I cannot do something, it makes me incapable of doing it. But, when I believe I can, then I acquire the ability to do it even if I didn't have it in the beginning."
>
> Mahatma Gandhi

After the OYT production, I imagined I would end my direct involvement in **Race To Be Seen** and move forward to other projects. **Race** continued to have a deep impact on my extra-curricular (Youth Theatre) work and also, important ones on my curriculum work. As I write this, I realise I failed to highlight these to Graham. I don't regret many things but I do regret this.

Extra-Curriculum Legacy - A Writer (Slowly) Develops

The documentary approach I used for **Race** offered me my first taste of success.

- **Race** was a published play (but wasn't selling).

- **Too Much Punch For Judy** (1987) was selling. It had a limited (3,000) print run and sold out in a couple of years. Inexplicably, IAS (Institute of Alcohol Studies) chose not to reprint it and, while it remained 'known', it remained unpublished for a further ten years. It toured into schools and attracted attention because it was good theatre. Drama teachers seemed to love it.[32]

In the spring of 1988, Frank Nunnelly, a Road Safety Officer who had seen the original EYT production of **Punch**, contacted me to book six weeks (60 performances) in Hertfordshire for Autumn 1988.

---

[32] PSHE (Personal, Social and Health Education) teachers often booked the touring performances for their lessons and so drama teachers sometimes didn't get to see it... but I am assured they still heard about it from students.

VERBATIM - The Fun of Making Theatre Seriously by Mark Wheeller

Touchstone Theatre Company, who had toured the play successfully throughout Essex and Scotland, said they wanted to 'move into new areas' and turned the offer down. This seemed odd because this RSA was keen to sink substantial amounts of money into the touring. I suspected (correctly) this might be replicated across the country.

I was a full time teacher and couldn't make time to mount a professional term time production and didn't have the know-how to do so. I wasn't sure how I would find anyone to do it. SNAP Theatre Company sprang to mind but I wasn't confident they'd be interested. Andy Graham (director) hadn't liked its didactic approach.

I clutched at a straw.

Matt Allen, who played Graham in EYT's **Race To Be Seen**, was now in his final year at the Guilford School of Acting.

I wondered: might he be prepared to form a company and tour **Too Much Punch**?

It was a long shot... a really long shot, but I knew I could work with Matt and he'd be sympathetic to the documentary approach which had been a bit of an issue with Touchstone.

I phoned him.

Things moved very fast!

Graham and Matt

VERBATIM - The Fun of Making Theatre Seriously by Mark Wheeller

> At GSA my special project was on Community Theatre. I explained how at EYT we found stories from our community, which that same community would be interested in watching - such a great starting point. I knew the strength of *Punch* and I had used it as an example.
> I called Fay Davies (who had played Judy in the EYT production) from my parent's house in Epping and asked her to recite Judy's speeches over the phone while I wrote them out.
> I edited them into one monologue, to tell the complete story. For my final second year project to the GSA first year students, I performed that monologue.
> Towards the end of my third year Mark approached me saying Frank Nunnelly from Hertfordshire wanted to book a professional touring production.
> I had no idea of costs but printed up some Ape Theatre Company Ltd notepaper and cobbled together a budget with everything I could think of. I arrived at Frank's office full of confidence but no idea of what I was doing.
> "Yes," I lied to Frank happily, "we've already produced lots of plays."
> I knew he wasn't buying it but he didn't let on; well, not until later when we'd become friends. The meeting went well and Frank said he might book the show.
> "Might book it?" I said, "Hmm, what would swing it to WILL book it?"
> "Get Fay Davies to play Judy and you have a deal."
> Fay was 18 and about to leave college.
> She had raw talent oozing out of her.
> I had to move fast. I called her that evening and the deal was done.
> **Matt Allen** - (Ape Theatre Company)

Matt hired me to direct the production.

It toured from 1988 until 2014 and was performed over 6,000 times here and abroad. On some days there were 8 performances in the UK, 4 in New Zealand and the odd school production on top.

You'd imagine, that by this point, I would have considered myself a "proper writer". I didn't.

From my perspective, everything was effectively an extension of my small scale youth theatre work, led by myself and a few ex-youth theatre members. No major theatre company had come in and taken on my work. In retrospect, there were positives in that I didn't lose my works to a faceless organisation and maintained close control over them. However, it left me feeling I was still not a 'proper writer'... whatever that is!

When I did try to get interest from outside organisations, I received polite rejections.

VERBATIM - The Fun of Making Theatre Seriously by Mark Wheeller

Too Much Punch was turned down by all the major (and not so major) publishers. These two offered reasons for their decision... most didn't.

> I know this will disappoint and annoy you, but our decision not to publish is based on two principal issues.
>
> - Firstly, it is strongly orientated towards a TIE format rather than a conventional play.
>
> - Secondly, it has already been published and we cannot risk investment in a play, which may have run a substantial part of its print life.
>
> This may not be the case and I am aware that you are often approached for direction to copies. Unfortunately, that is often the experience of many of our writers and the eventual production in covers too often doesn't bear witness to the interest that was believed to be around previously. Cogently, the investment is probably too uncertain for a series that operates on slim profit margins.
> **Peter Rowlands – Series Editor CUP Act Now Series.**[33]

> I submitted the play to Andy Kempe, the series editor of our Dramascripts series for review. I am afraid that he does not consider it suitable for the series. We are looking for scripts that are longer and offer greater depth of characterisation and narrative. However, Andy intends to contact you in the near future to discuss other work you have, which may prove suitable for inclusion in the series.
> **Lisa Thomas – Nelson Thornes, Commissioning Editor – Humanities.**[34]

---

[33] Cambridge University Press went on to have considerable success when, instigated by Peter Rowlands, they published **Hard to Swallow** (which became their second best seller in the series, the first being **Gregory's Girl**). Both **Punch** and **Swallow** are now published by Salamander Street.

[34] Andy did contact me and we worked together on **Arson About** which Nelson Thornes published. It has now been rebranded by Oxford University Press as **Butcher Butcher Burning Bright**. You can find it in all good bookshops!

VERBATIM - The Fun of Making Theatre Seriously by Mark Wheeller

My message to wannabe writers here is:
Get your work performed and use that to inform your final draft.
Submit your play to publishers who publish the kind of play you are offering. Your play may not be accepted but be prepared to follow up with something else.

If you never submit your plays they can never be accepted. If you do there is a chance they might be. Always submit with evidence (reviews) that your play worked as a performance.

Those 'in the know' did not consider my plays worthwhile despite all the above. I continued to believe… because… because I did believe!

The reaction to Ape's touring performances were consistently fantastic and they garnered a wonderful reputation… but I wasn't benefitting from any of this! No one was aware of Mark Wheeller. ☹

I remember cheekily inserting my name into the final monologue of **Punch**. Judy had actually said this in a TVAM interview so it was ethically sound.

Do you know... I hadn't talked to anyone about the accident before Mark... like, Mark Wheeller interviewed me for this play three years after it happened? Chris Caten had said it might do some good... so that's why I did it. Without this I'd've probably never talked about it.

VERBATIM - The Fun of Making Theatre Seriously by Mark Wheeller

I was determined to get some recognition! My dreams of celebrity were about as realistic as me becoming a pixie.

I was also bothered by the feelings I had of being a fraud. It was, to continue the pixie analogy, like I was trying on these pixie clothes but they so clearly didn't fit and bits of me were bulging out all over. Embarrassing.

To be a "writer" I need to "write"!

The plays I was writing weren't 'written' at all. I was using other people's words. I knew of no-one, other than Roy, at Stantonbury, developing plays in this manner. Perhaps I was cheating and might explain why I wasn't being taken seriously by those who mattered?

To be a 'writer' I need to write!

Hard To Swallow was my next project after the OYT performance of **Race**. This was an adaptation of Maureen Dunbar's book **Catherine**. I took the opportunity to 'write' within the framework of a story whose narrative was pre-set.

My writing for **Hard To Swallow** emerged in two distinctly different approaches.

1. The 'two word', or '**Two Touch/Précis**' technique, was a stylised approach derived from the work of two St John's School, Epping students (Tony Holland and Barrie Sapsford) who had précis'd an over-long scene for a performance exam. The technique they used highlighted the essence of the scene in quick fire (one or two word) narration. I linked this with the Berkoff (**East**) exchanges I'd seen at the Edinburgh Festival and witnessed the Ape actors who had helped develop the earliest version of Bob 'n' Nob scene in **Punch**. These scenes also (like the narrative sections in my verbatim plays) forced more imaginative staging. The meal-time scene in **Hard To Swallow** offers a good example of this.

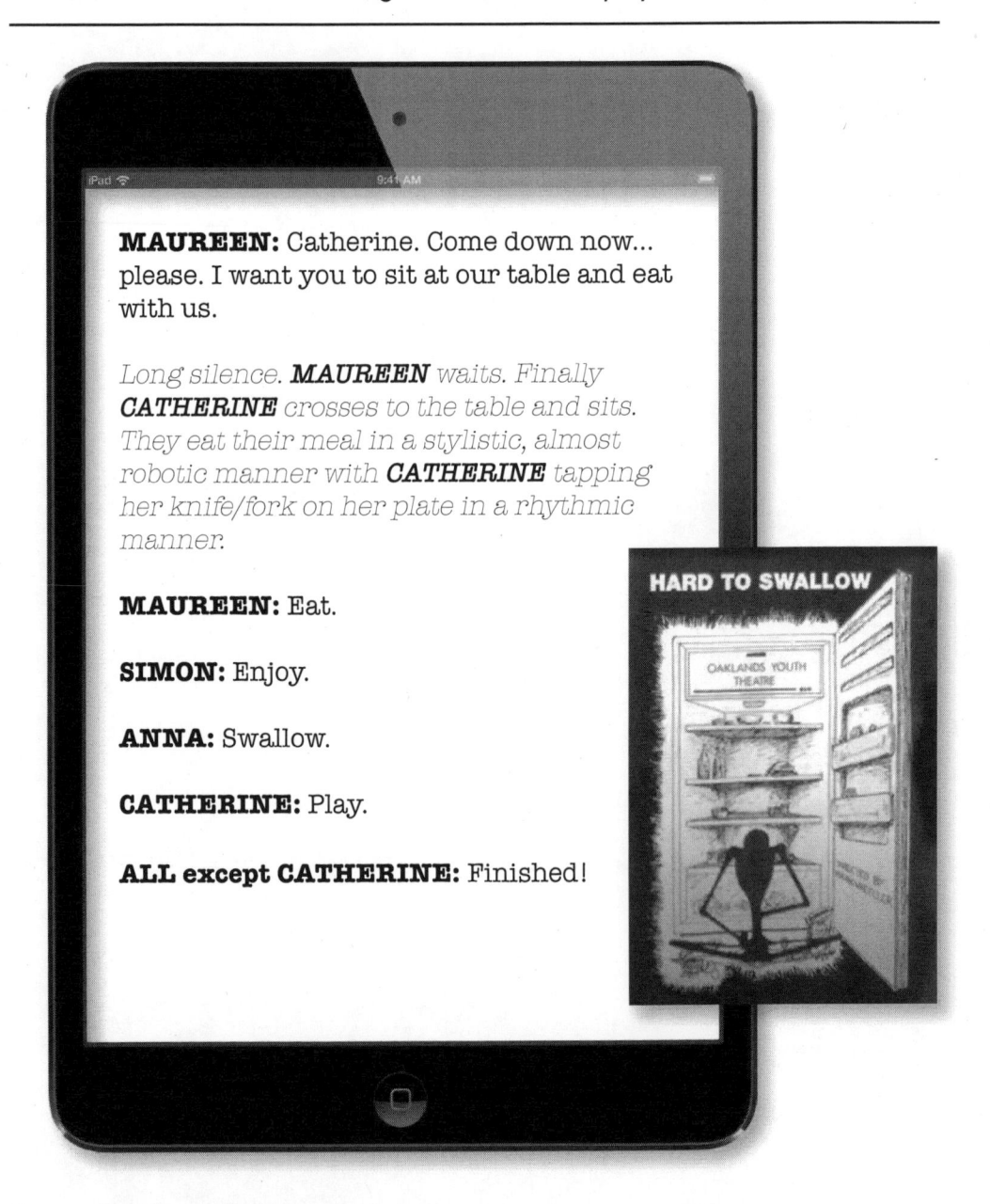

> **MAUREEN:** Catherine. Come down now... please. I want you to sit at our table and eat with us.
>
> *Long silence.* ***MAUREEN*** *waits. Finally* ***CATHERINE*** *crosses to the table and sits. They eat their meal in a stylistic, almost robotic manner with* ***CATHERINE*** *tapping her knife/fork on her plate in a rhythmic manner.*
>
> **MAUREEN:** Eat.
>
> **SIMON:** Enjoy.
>
> **ANNA:** Swallow.
>
> **CATHERINE:** Play.
>
> **ALL except CATHERINE:** Finished!

2. Simple dialogue writing.
In Maureen's book a situation was outlined and I filled the gaps with invented dialogue. An example of this is the scene where Anna hides Catherine's scales, originally described in narrative form by Anna and her mother. Presenting this in dialogue showed the dramatic nature of the impact on Anna.

CATHERINE: (*Musical box music.*)

26 February 1983:

Without Mummy I am totally unable to cope. I dread and fear Daddy's reaction, his fury, frustration and anger because of my inability to be away from Mummy. Anna is being a little hard on me. If only she could understand. Where are my scales? I am sure that Anna has taken them. (*She approaches ANNA who is asleep and jogs her aggressively.*)

CATHERINE: Anna! Anna, wake up!

ANNA: What do you want?

CATHERINE: I want to know where you have put my scales.

ANNA: I haven't touched your stupid scales. What would I want with them?

CATHERINE: I need to know where my scales are. I know you hid them!

ANNA: Okay, so I did!

CATHERINE: You wouldn't dare do this if Mummy and Daddy were here. You've no right to touch them.

ANNA: You've no right to be in my room!

CATHERINE: Tell me where they are Anna! (*Grabbing her violently.*) I need to see how much I weigh!

ANNA: You know how much you bloody weigh! Your obsession is ruining all our lives! And what's more, I know that you've begun hoarding tablets again. What are you trying to do? You've got enough to kill you four times over.

CATHERINE: I don't know what you're talking about.

ANNA: Alright, if you won't admit it, I'll show you! (*She runs to CATHERINE's room.*)

CATHERINE: (*Running to the case and clutching it.*) You don't understand. They are helping me to get better. You don't want me to go on like this forever, do you?

ANNA: Won't you ever face up to the truth!

CATHERINE: Go away! Leave me in peace. I know what I am doing.

ANNA: So that's why they had to put you in a psychiatric hospital, isn't it? (*Fighting to get the case.*) Give it to me! (*In the struggle the case is opened and a vast number of medical bottles fall out.*)

CATHERINE: Get out! (*Pushes **ANNA** away with great strength.*)

ANNA: I can't stand you when you're like this! I hate being your sister!

CATHERINE: You'll regret saying that, Anna... you'll regret it.

VERBATIM - The Fun of Making Theatre Seriously by Mark Wheeller

I remain happy with my writing of this scene.

Verbatim/documentary playwriting was slowly scaffolding me into becoming a proper writer.

Hard To Swallow confirmed my feeling of doing well as a director when it was selected to be performed at the Royal National Theatre as part of the Lloyds Bank National Theatre Challenge.[35] It was published by Cambridge University Press, a mainstream publisher, and I credited that to the fact it had originated as a book and successful ITV film rather than anything I had added to the adaptation.

Following this, I tried to write a hit musical using predominantly, but not exclusively, the verbatim approach.

Sarah Stanbury (Sedge) was in my 4th year (Year 10) drama class. She wanted to be a footballer. I saw her story as a potential **Zigger Zagger** for girls (and boys).

Brian Price (who wrote the songs for OYT's **Race**) collaborated with me on a fabulous show which proved a minor hit at the Edinburgh Fringe.

> **THE TIMES Educational Supplement**
>
> The ensemble work by the Southampton-based company was immaculate and the way music, dance, mime and acting were brought together in the production was stunning.
> **John Hart** - Times Educational Supplemen

I discovered major publishers don't tend to pick up on non-West-End musicals. **Lethal In The Box**[36] was published by a small-scale schools publisher. It barely made it out of their stock cupboard. (There are plans for Salamander Street to publish a re-visited version of this musical.)

---

[35] **The Lloyds Bank National Theatre Challenge** became the **National Theatre Connections** where ten new plays are commissioned for young people and performed by schools around the country. Some are selected to be showcased regionally and then nationally. I have never (as far as I am aware) been considered to write for this but would jump at the chance... it would provide a neat bookend for my work.

[36] **Lethal** was published under the uninspiring title, **No Place For A Girl** (my choice so no blame attached) and then as a play, **Sweet FA**.

VERBATIM - The Fun of Making Theatre Seriously by Mark Wheeller

Far from becoming my hit musical, it was licensed only 49 times, aside from OYT's performances. ☹[37]

Lethal included a good dose of my writing and this monologue I still rate as one of my most imaginative, despite it being 'cod-Berkoff'.[38]

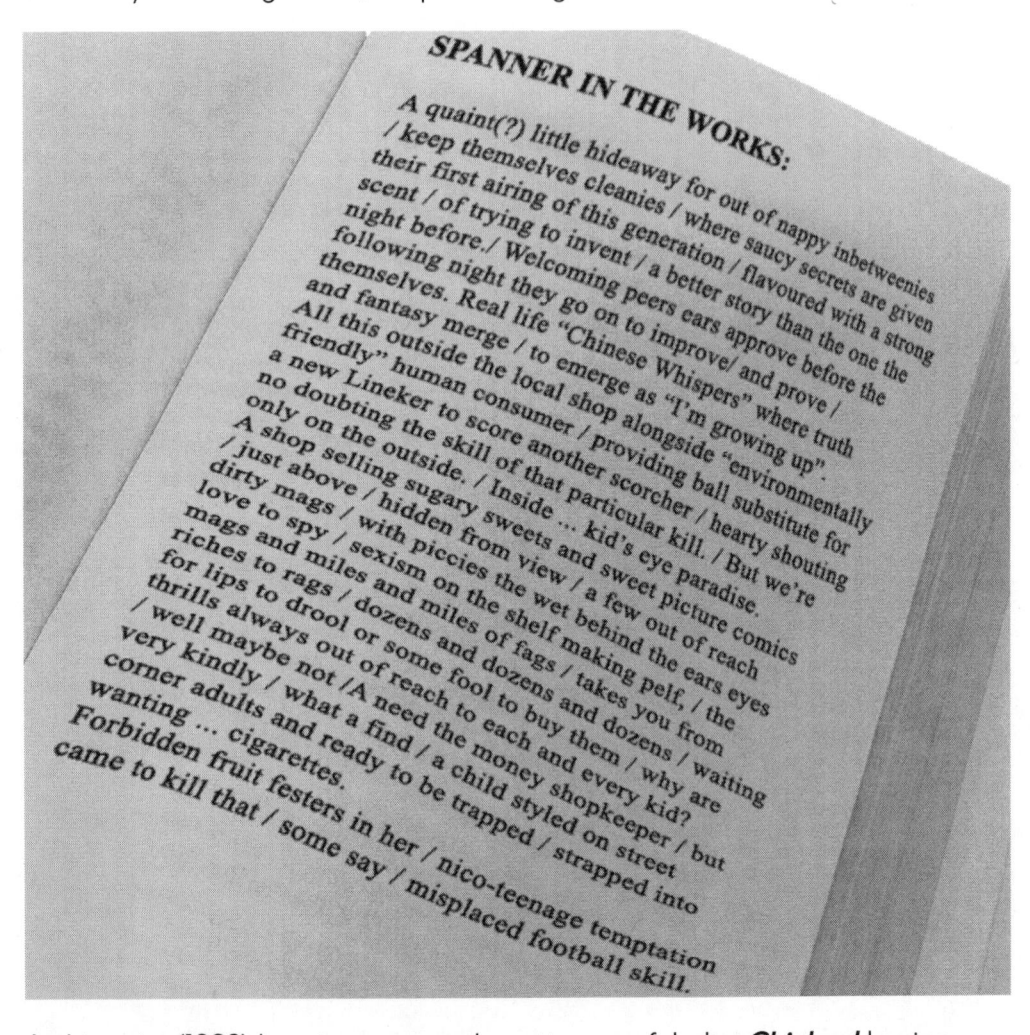

SPANNER IN THE WORKS:

A quaint(?) little hideaway for out of nappy inbetweenies / keep themselves cleanies / where saucy secrets are given their first airing of this generation / flavoured with a strong scent / of trying to invent / a better story than the one the night before./ Welcoming peers ears approve before the following night they go on to improve/ and prove / themselves. Real life "Chinese Whispers" where truth and fantasy merge / to emerge as "I'm growing up". All this outside the local shop alongside "environmentally friendly" human consumer / providing ball substitute for a new Lineker to score another scorcher / hearty shouting no doubting the skill of that particular kill. / But we're only on the outside. / Inside ... kid's eye paradise. A shop selling sugary sweets and sweet picture comics / just above / hidden from view / a few out of reach dirty mags / with piccies the wet behind the ears eyes love to spy / sexism on the shelf making pelf, / the mags and miles and miles of fags / takes you from riches to rags / dozens and dozens and dozens / waiting for lips to drool or some fool to buy them / why are thrills always out of reach to each and every kid? / well maybe not /A need the money shopkeeper / but very kindly / what a find / a child styled on street corner adults and ready to be trapped / strapped into wanting ... cigarettes. Forbidden fruit festers in her / nico-teenage temptation came to kill that / some say / misplaced football skill.

At this point (1992) I wrote my second most successful play **Chicken!** having now been licensed nearly 6,000 times.

I had originally planned to develop this from cast improvisations (as per **Blackout**) but we ran out of time and I was forced to write it myself.

---

[37] I plan to develop **Lethal In The Box** by adding a commentary, Gogglebox style, from contemporary Saints footballer, Shelly Provan.

[38] This features in my **Act Normal** collection of Wheellerplays monologues published by Salamander Street.

VERBATIM - The Fun of Making Theatre Seriously by Mark Wheeller

Chicken! combined my two styles of writing, Two Touch and naturalistic dialogue. I added rhyming couplets to my writer's toolbox and also invented the story off the back of some simple research in local Junior Schools.

Chicken! toured successfully in England, being performed more often than ***Too Much Punch*** from 1992 to the present day. Like ***Punch***, it was funded by Road Safety Departments across different counties, was published and, significantly, the script was distributed free to schools by Dawn Boyfield Design Associates (dbda)... and had my name on it! It has been updated frequently, most recently in 2020 when it was published by Salamander Street.

After ***Chicken!*** I collaborated with Graham Cole, a colleague at school who had disliked my documentary work. I wanted to work with someone who believed in a more traditional form of playwriting and, as he was a Modern Languages teacher, we created a bi-lingual teenage pregnancy story. It was a great discipline for me to write naturalistic scenes although I did include a few stylistic sections and some great monologues in my cod-Berkoff style.

Chunnel of Love was successful in a way none of my other plays have been. It was selected for the prestigious ***National Student Drama Festival*** where, on a personal level, for the first time I benefitted from playwriting tutorials from Tim Fountain (***Sex Addict/ Tchaikovsky In The Park***) and Stephen Jeffreys (***Valued Friends***).

Then... out of the blue...

Commissions!

At this point I started to acknowledge myself as a 'writer', albeit one at the bottom rung of a ropey old ladder. I thought of myself as stepping, somewhat tentatively, onto that first rickety rung because the commissions were from road safety organisations rather than 'proper' literary/theatrical ones. This pixie was finally dressed in clothes that were just about 'acceptable'!

VERBATIM - The Fun of Making Theatre Seriously by Mark Wheeller

My wife (Rachel) and I were also commissioned (by RoSPA) to write 12 **Tufty** [39] stories for a children's book. They had to be completed in a month. One 350-word story every three days. It was paid... money... a new great way of motivating me to write as it seemed a cheeky way of earning money! I was inventing stuff! The pixie was out and dancing!

Frustratingly, writing **Tufty** coincided with OYT's final preparations for **Chunnel** at the NSDF a week after our deadline. Rachel and I collaborated on some of the stories and did others separately. It was an incredibly busy time with successive late nights. We had a four-and a two-year-old (Ollie and Charlie) who became a useful source of inspiration. Many of the stories in that book were based on our experiences with them. We completed it on time and it was published very fast.

We were then commissioned to write one story a month for a comic which ran for a further year! We didn't see the final art work until we dashed over to Sainsbury's on the release date, having set the illustrators gentle challenges, such as casting the crossing patrol man (a hedgehog!) as a genie in the Xmas edition!

The following year, Oxfordshire County Council Road Safety Department, seeing the huge success of **Chicken!** (and to a lesser extent **Punch**), commissioned me to write a play about the dangers of driving too fast.

I used a verbatim account of a road traffic accident described by a convicted driver, framed within a love triangle story I invented.

The verbatim account was compelling. 'Andy' had been driving at nearly twice the legal speed limit and killed a moped rider as she pulled out of a garage... but...

... he was furious. He complained vociferously to me that it was the fault of the motorcyclist (whom I named Kelly) who, he claimed, had not looked before pulling out!

---

[39] **Tufty Fluffytail** was RoSPA's iconic red squirrel who was instrumental in helping millions of children to learn about road safety from the 1950s-1990s. The character was created in 1953 by Elsie Mills MBE, who worked on child safety initiatives at RoSPA. **Tufty** helped communicate simple safety messages to children across the UK. The 1993 **Tufty's Adventures** book rebooted the Tufty brand and was written by Rachel and myself.

VERBATIM - The Fun of Making Theatre Seriously by Mark Wheeller

I remembered Tim Fountain's tutorial at NSDF saying words to this effect:

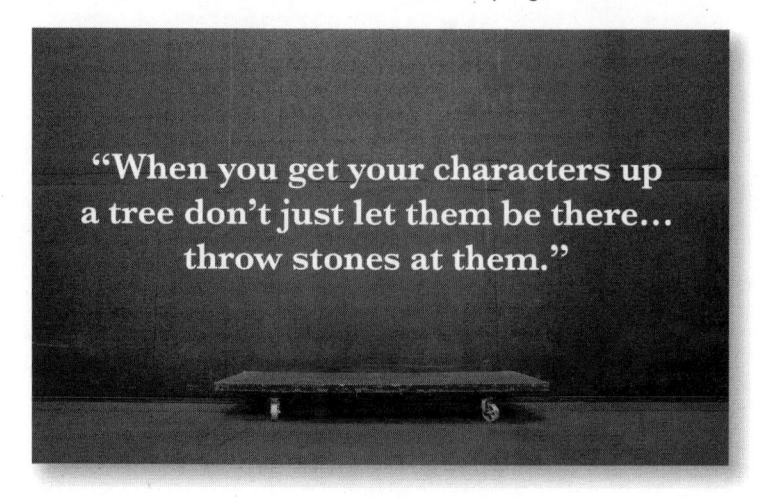

> "When you get your characters up a tree don't just let them be there... throw stones at them."

With that in mind, I did this to Andy following his RTA.

- Andy visits Jazz in her university hall of residence.

- Jazz plans to finish their relationship during his visit. She has two-timed him.

- Andy plans to to reveal the details of his role in the death of Kelly. Kelly happens to be one of Jazz's best friends back at home.

- As he reveals this appalling news, Kelly's parents phone to inform Jazz of Kelly's death.

- Before Jazz has revealed her news Matt, her new boyfriend, knocks on her door and interrupts Jazz trying to comfort a very upset Andy.

This set up a wonderfully dramatic situation for me to exercise my creative writing muscles.

The pixie was sweating in the fitness studio!

Legal Weapon went on to be performed over 2,500 times and was, in my opinion, the best of my 90s touring productions.

VERBATIM - The Fun of Making Theatre Seriously by Mark Wheeller

Matt's thriving Ape Theatre Company took a brief stage-direction suggesting the use of vocal sound effects in the opening scene and used them throughout the whole play. They amplified these vocal sound effects using microphones generating memorable comic AND dramatic moments. I was nothing to do with the direction of this but it remains one of my proudest stage achievements.[40]

There was no argument... my only association with this production was as the writer.

That said, I also remember deciding to read a book which had been suggested to me as the top book on playwriting. The reviews describe **Timebends** by Arthur Miller as a 'masterpiece'. I'm sad to say I struggled. I found it laborious and it served to confirm my view that, although I had written some plays, I would never be a proper playwright. Despite my self-doubt, I ploughed on. Whatever it was I was doing, I was enjoying my little venture into the world of making theatre (which is probably a better description as my role was generally more holistic than merely writing) and, importantly, it was very much being appreciated by those around me and a few further afield.

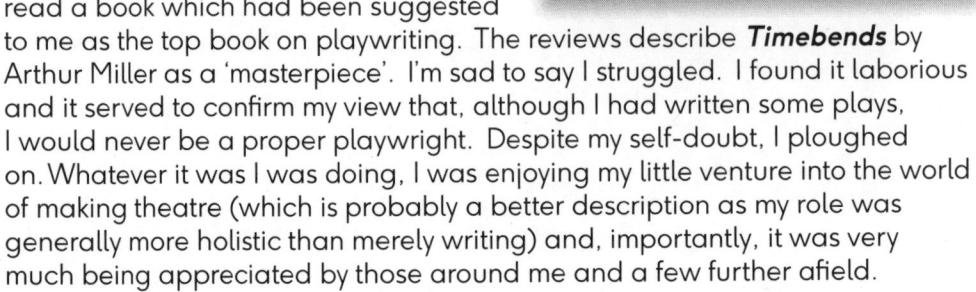

As the century drew to its close I wrote **Birth Mother** for OYT, using the model of **Legal Weapon**, i.e. part fiction, part verbatim and a sticking closely to a story structure introduced to me by Tim Fountain. It was about a subject that had long since fascinated me. I set it at the time of the 1990 World Cup Finals (Gazza's tears).

---

[40] I should also credit Tony Audenshaw and Andrew Mulquin who worked alongside Matt in directing the Ape productions.

VERBATIM - The Fun of Making Theatre Seriously by Mark Wheeller

It won multiple awards at our local Totton Drama Festival and was 'Highly Commended' for 'ambition' by the NSDF. It remains my only play not to have been published. The reason: I didn't have the confidence to submit it.[41]

In 1997 I made my second attempt to write a hit musical.

All schools need a 'go to' Xmas musical so, I decided plug this gap with a promenade production and gave it the magnificent title *The Most Absurd Xmas Musical In The World... Ever!*

I invited a group of able students (Linzi Adams, Stuart White and Michael Johnston) to bring added wackiness/humour to the table.

James Holmes wrote a magical musical score to my (mostly) lyrics. These songs are on my Xmas playlist every year but I am probably on my own in this respect.

I revisited it in 2005 and loved it all over again. A review compared it favourably with the local professional Xmas offering.

---

[41] Writing this paragraph led me submit this *Birth Mother* to Maverick Musicals and Plays who have now announced they are to publish it along with *The Most Absurd Xmas Musical*.

VERBATIM - The Fun of Making Theatre Seriously by Mark Wheeller

Towards the end of the 1990's dbda (Dawn Boyfield Design Associates) who had published **Chicken!**, flushed with its success, published more of my plays.

Some were touring schools so there was a demand, and a publisher who was not really a publisher found themselves with a hit catalogue. They exploited this wonderfully in those pre-internet days, with some brilliant direct marketing.

As a writer who was not really a writer, I had to admit... perhaps I was finally a writer.

Soon my plays started to become choices for school exam performances and then this happened... which I have now adapted into a little story for your entertainment!

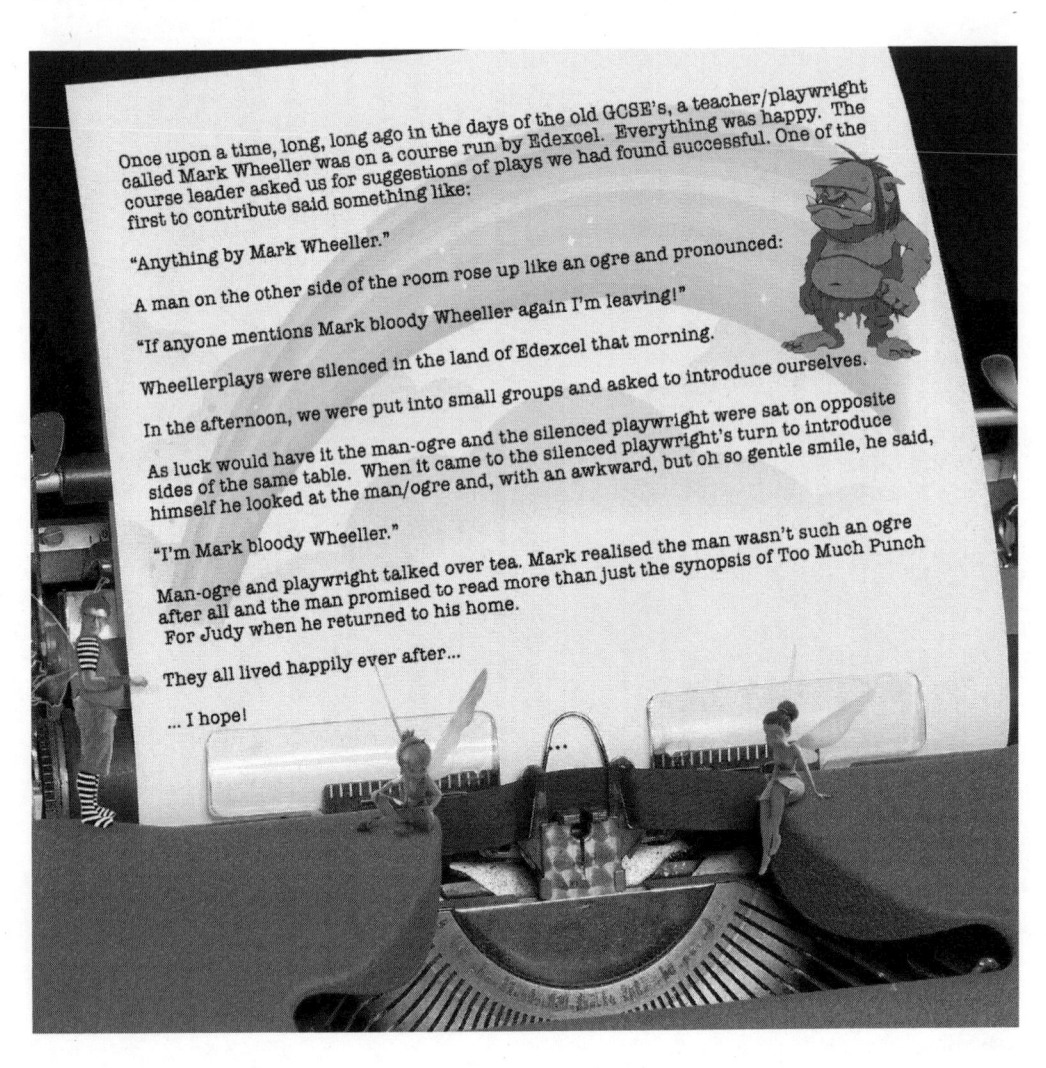

Once upon a time, long, long ago in the days of the old GCSE's, a teacher/playwright called Mark Wheeller was on a course run by Edexcel. Everything was happy. The course leader asked us for suggestions of plays we had found successful. One of the first to contribute said something like:

"Anything by Mark Wheeller."

A man on the other side of the room rose up like an ogre and pronounced:

"If anyone mentions Mark bloody Wheeller again I'm leaving!"

Wheellerplays were silenced in the land of Edexcel that morning.

In the afternoon, we were put into small groups and asked to introduce ourselves. As luck would have it the man-ogre and the silenced playwright were sat on opposite sides of the same table. When it came to the silenced playwright's turn to introduce himself he looked at the man/ogre and, with an awkward, but oh so gentle smile, he said,

"I'm Mark bloody Wheeller."

Man-ogre and playwright talked over tea. Mark realised the man wasn't such an ogre after all and the man promised to read more than just the synopsis of Too Much Punch For Judy when he returned to his home.

They all lived happily ever after...

... I hope!

VERBATIM - The Fun of Making Theatre Seriously by Mark Wheeller

It was with this growing confidence and beginning to see myself as a writer that I embarked on a new version of **Race To Be Seen**.

Before I tell that story, I want to explain the other more altruistic wonderful legacy my involvement with Graham Salmon led to.

Curriculum Legacy

You may remember in the original Hugh David TES review of **Race To Be Seen** by EYT, he said:

> ... *the company have devised an impressive (and impressively well-documented) show that was socially valuable as well as entertaining. They have all had to think through what it means to be blind, and, as a result of the work over the past few months, have issued an open invitation to any young people who have a disability to join them.*

This had never happened in Epping.

We didn't try that hard but had put some unsuccessful feelers out.

In Southampton, I became aware of a nearby Special School, The Cedar School, and remembering my invitation I made a move to work with them in 1990.

I ran a few sessions there using my students as mentors (and supporters to me!) working in role (Dorothy Heathcote style). The sessions were successful and they led to a few students from Cedar becoming involved in OYT.

Jimmy Hume was a particularly talented Cedar School student and gained the lead role in an early version of **Happy Soap**. The local paper described him as 'exuberant' in their review of the play, which went on to win Best Youth Production at the Totton Drama Festival.

Jimmy was one of three Cedar students in the production. We proved integration could work but I wanted it to impact on more than already confident people like Jimmy, Michelle and Pauline.

187

VERBATIM - The Fun of Making Theatre Seriously by Mark Wheeller

I wanted more Cedar students to access our drama curriculum but this was a far bigger idea and needed a major commitment from Cedar. That was out of my control.

Ali Garner, a key link worker from Cedar, along with Paul England, a Cedar student from that era, tell the story.

> It began in 1990 when I started work as a special school assistant in the Secondary department at Cedar School for physically disabled pupils. During my second term there, I was asked if I would support one of the pupils in his GCSE drama lessons at Oaklands.
>
> I had always loved drama, being a keen member of Fareham Drama Centre Youth Theatre in my teens and taking O' level Drama at school. I had also recently taken a group of our pupils to watch OYT perform *Lethal In The Box* and been blown away by their performance: the theme (having played football) the physical theatre, the catchy songs and the lyrics. So I snapped up the opportunity.
> **Ali Garner**

OAKLANDS YOUTH THEATRE PRESENTS
LETHAL IN THE BOX
DIRECTED BY MARK WHEELLER

> It was just another Thursday at school, swimming in the afternoon, but something different in the evening. Rather than the journey home on the bus, we had a trip to see a play at the local big school, Oaklands.
> I remember the school bus parking on a hill next to a big door. That big door was opened by Mark. That big door was my window into a whole new world. I had no idea what was about to happen next. I remember this as the moment that completely changed the course of my life. I saw *Lethal In The Box*, a musical theatre show that blew my 12-year-old mind! I loved every minute, the songs, the staging, the lighting, the atmosphere – everything!
> It left me with questions:
> Are all "normal" schools like this?
> Do all "normal" schools have facilities like this?
> Could I do this?
> If I did would the walking kids like me?
> The world was hugely different back then. People with disabilities didn't attend mainstream schools.
> **Paul England**

VERBATIM - The Fun of Making Theatre Seriously by Mark Wheeller

It was only a 5-minute drive away but it felt like a very different world, a large busy mainstream secondary school, compared to our very small special school. At first, I felt nervous and tended to work with the Cedar pupils within their groups, as they relied on me to help them join in or to give ideas.

As time went on, I felt my presence made the Oaklands students reluctant to welcome our pupils into their group. They seemed uncomfortable and inhibited by having an adult close by, especially a teacher they didn't know well.

Eventually, I decided to distance myself and only support the Cedar pupil if they requested help. This allowed space for Mark to teach them and encouraged my students to be more independent and experience normal mainstream behaviour which didn't happen when I was close by. They enjoyed the Oaklands banter and a sense of freedom. So my integration in the class aided that of the Cedar pupils.

Due to the success of the link, the numbers attending Drama classes grew so much that my working week was split equally between Oaklands and Cedar. I loved this, despite going backwards and forwards in a minibus between the schools so often. I fully integrated into Oaklands, eating my lunch in the staff room, attending end of term staff celebrations and playing in the staff v ex-pupils football matches. Oaklands felt like my school too.

Although our pupils were fully integrated in the drama classes they were still the minority. Mark wanted the Cedar/Oaklands ratio to be equal. And so, in 1995, it happened: a GCSE class made up of 10 Oaklands and 10 Cedar pupils with varying physical disabilities and learning needs.

The diversity of the group encouraged creativity. The class was fun to be in. There were special moments and stunning performances. Students flourished and the GCSE grades were impressive from both schools, A*s included.
Ali Garner

When I was asked if I would like to go to Oaklands to take Drama I was nervous but jumped at the chance. Ten went from Cedar School to be joined by ten, with legs, from Oaklands. It must have been scary for us all. There was no need for apprehension. We worked together, learned together, adapted together, and asked questions of each other in a safe environment for everyone led by Mark and Ali.

Whether it was introductory games or turning stage boxes into an imaginary car, sitting room or a Jerry Springer set, our imaginations and confidence grew. As time passed, we learnt that the other kids were just kids like us, minus wheelchairs or walking sticks. Of course, the Oaklands kids realised the same about us. What was weird very quickly became the norm, and we were not looking at what couldn't be done but what we could do together.
Paul England

VERBATIM - The Fun of Making Theatre Seriously by Mark Wheeller

> The drama link was so successful that Cedar students began attending other curriculum subjects, Science, Maths and joint Art projects. Cedar pupils were increasingly becoming a part of Oaklands school life, attending Year 11 Proms, school trips and Award Evenings.
>
> Our two schools teamed up to participate in events promoting integration, including the FieldFare Trust *Kielder Challenge* and the TV Show *Beat That*.
> **Ali Garner**

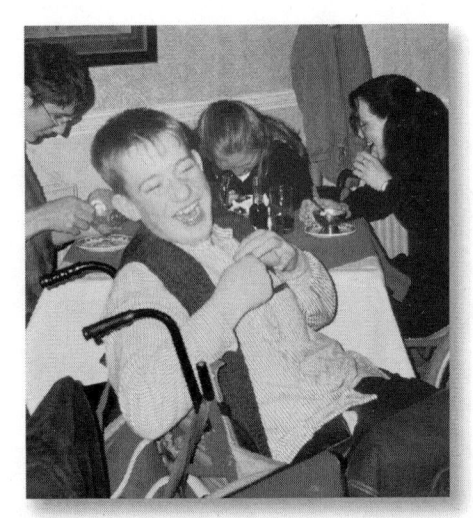

Paul enjoying a celebration meal with us in a local Chinese restaurant... we did a lot of these!

> Creativity and Performing Arts was a massive part of my life. I remember seeing the GCSE Drama course as a huge test of my ability to be good at something. Deep down I knew I was but would I have the confidence to push myself forward?
>
> The GCSE Drama journey was full of ups and downs... thankfully more ups than downs. In the month before my final exam Rob Reeve, my exam partner, died. Although Rob was physically less able than me, with his looks and comic timing he could hold an audience and command a stage with his presence. Luckily Danny Bond agreed to come in at short notice to support me. Then Danny was taken poorly two days before the final exam. Mark arranged for an Oaklands student who was not in our class to read the lines while I did my bit. It was a really stressful but rewarding time. I was beside myself with nerves, something that I still struggle with to this day.
>
> Coincidently, this was 1996, the year the Disability Discrimination Act was made law! The year when I was awarded an A* in Drama. The year I was offered and took a Stage Technician's apprenticeship at a local repertory theatre, but turned down a scholarship at the Liverpool Institute of Performing Arts (LIPA). It was a good year!
> **Paul England**

VERBATIM - The Fun of Making Theatre Seriously by Mark Wheeller

Paul received the Oaklands Drama Award, a very proud moment for Cedar.
Pupils from both schools gained and learnt from each other. Oaklands thrived and grew in confidence when working alongside our pupils, picking up on their positivity and acceptance of who they were.

Oaklands students became creative in overcoming physical barriers and their attitudes towards disability changed. Cedar pupils benefitted from attending two schools where their needs were met in different ways. Some who were deemed unable to attend mainstream school proved otherwise. They became more confident and assertive and relished the opportunity to socialise and perform with their peers as equals.

Two Cedar pupils who excelled in their drama classes and discovered their love for the performing arts went on to to achieve great things in theatre. Paul England served a Stage Technician Apprenticeship with the Arts Council of Great Britain. Martin Vaughan received an NSDF actors award and was selected for the NSDF touring production.

Many friendships were formed between Cedar and Oaklands pupils and a few romances too! While the pupils flourished, so did I. I loved and looked forward to Drama lessons. I learnt so much from Mark, not only his drama techniques but his relaxed, friendly and honest teaching style and his ability to engage those hard-to-reach pupils who in other lessons proved challenging or isolated. Best of all, we became good friends.
Ali Garner

During this time Ali and Di set up Branch Out Youth Theatre to encourage integration between my peers, siblings and others. I could write for hours about the benefits and opportunities this gave me. It was so exciting.

Not only was I performing for my school and Oaklands, I was performing to other schools and participating in local and national drama festivals. I was being recognised, and winning awards alongside the people I was performing with. This was happening because I was Paul, and not Paul with the wheelchair.
Paul England

Paul England (above Ali centre front) in Scarborough at the NSDF with OYT.

Cedar and Oaklands at NSDF

VERBATIM - The Fun of Making Theatre Seriously by Mark Wheeller

> Mark's plays and OYT productions inspired myself and Di Mahoney (Cedar Deputy Head) to set up Branch Out. We devised and wrote our own plays, often using Mark's techniques, although we decided not to focus on verbatim plays but develop our own style.
> **Ali Garner**

Di Mahoney - Goes Without Saying

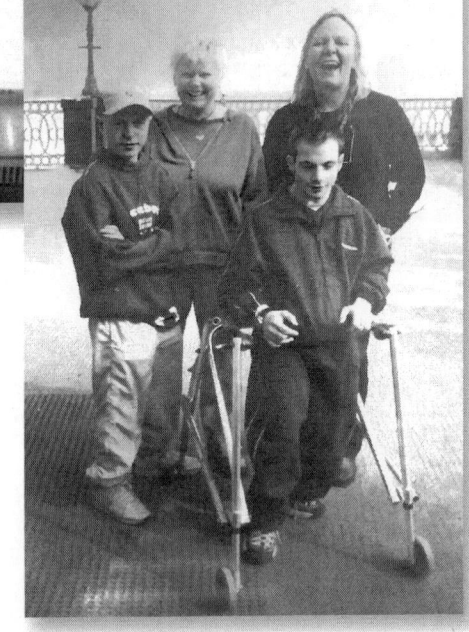

Errol, Ali, Di and Martin, Goes Without Saying

> Branch Out ran for many years and was very successful. Initially our productions explored disability issues but as time went on we moved away from this. We didn't want audiences to think this was the only topic our young actors could approach.
>
> We performed at local drama festivals and toured local schools. Mark invited us to join OYT on their trip to the NSDF in Scarborough, our first joint residential venture. True to form, the Oaklands and Branch Out Youth Theatre members integrated fully, enjoying each other's company. It was a wonderful week away.
>
> The following year we entered our play, *Goes Without Saying*, and were one of thirteen plays selected out of hundreds to perform at the NSDF. We also won two awards.
> **Ali Garner**

VERBATIM - The Fun of Making Theatre Seriously by Mark Wheeller

Martin and Errol were both important members of our drama department at Oaklands and were both superb comedians. I am sad to say that Errol passed away soon after this performance. We will always remember him for his cheeky smile, his incredible zest for life and his determination to make the most of every opportunity.
3.2.85 - 12.3.07.

Branch Out was a small youth theatre so, when the opportunity arose for us to be a part of The Performing Arts Children's Charity *Interact*, we took it; and this led to much needed funds and the security of being part of a larger organisation. The charity was passionate about integration, providing workshops for young people including those with additional needs. Eleven years later I am still the workshop leader of the Eastleigh group.
I fondly remember my Oaklands/Cedar days as very special times.
Ali Garner

Errol and Ali - Goes Without Saying

Errol and Di (Above) - Goes Without Saying

193

VERBATIM - The Fun of Making Theatre Seriously by Mark Wheeller

> To this point I've been fortunate. I've always worked. I live a normal(ish) life. I have no doubt that my experiences in formative years, especially with Drama and Performing Arts being my "North Star", enabled this.
>
> Looking back, I regret not taking the LIPA scholarship and I wonder what might have been. As Mark recently said to me, "Its never too late".
> **Paul England**

Reading these accounts told me so much I had either forgotten or overlooked. It was, like so much of what happened at Oaklands, just what we did.
No great plan... just lots of passion.

Oaklands soon integrated a wider range of students as standard practice, as other schools did across the country. I can't say we made this happen as no one knew what was happening down in Southampton but young people in our area had the opportunity to integrate into a mainstream school environment earlier than in most areas.

These achievements were kicked off as a direct result of my meeting and working with Graham. I mention this as the content of our verbatim plays were absorbed and became a part of who we were and how we conducted our lives.

This is a huge legacy that, sadly, I don't think Graham was ever aware of. I regret not telling him.

Thank you Graham... belatedly... always an inspiration.

VERBATIM - The Fun of Making Theatre Seriously by Mark Wheeller

Chapter 10: Special Friends

'The era of Britain winning gold medals in the Paralympic Games began with Graham Salmon in Bulgaria. He's an inspiration to everyone. Britain should be proud of him.'
John Anderson[42]

Graham and Marie remained a central part of my personal life. In 1987 they had met my then new girlfriend Rachel but, by the end of the year, there was a feeling that I should get on with asking her to marry me. I wanted to but I couldn't figure out when it would be possible to clear a date for our wedding. Christmas was the obvious time but, as an only child, I felt bad leaving my parents alone at that time of year.

I remember Marie, in July, saying I needed to get my skates on and propose, otherwise it might never happen. She said my parents would be fine about a home alone Christmas because the excitement of a wedding would more than make up for it.

She was right. I proposed soon after that. Rachel said yes and…

… I asked Graham to be my Best Man!

Our Christmas Eve's Eve wedding was amazing. I was so proud to be marrying Rachel (who was literally the girl of my dreams) and having Graham as my Best Man.

We had a Barn Dance at the reception and Graham said afterwards how good that was for him because he was able to "meet" so many guests during the dances where you're forever changing partners.

---

[42] John was not only one of Graham's coaches but was the national coach for the Amateur Athletics Association of England and the first full-time national coach in Scotland. Coach to an Olympian at every Olympics (1964 - 2000). Coached 6 world record holders (including Graham) and an estimated 170 GB internationals in every track and field event. He also was the head official on TV show **Gladiators** (1992-2000).

VERBATIM - The Fun of Making Theatre Seriously by Mark Wheeller

Just as I took a break in the **Race** play to say how Marie didn't like to do interviews, and went on to say my piece about her, I should also say how Rachel shuns publicity but I do need to say something... and I promise I shall be brief. Rachel has been the most incredible wife who has facilitated my focus (probably obsession) on my work.

She has run our household and made our family a loving home with a feeling of deep security to go out and do what we do. It's impossible to quantify this and any attempt to do so would both embarrass her and break my assurance that I would be brief. Suffice to say, as with Graham, there was a "good woman" behind him; the same is true of me... an incredibly good and caring woman.

My charmed life excelled itself in finding Rachel as a soulmate and partner.

Wobbly-bodies bring us back to 1988...

As Rachel and I left for our honeymoon (skiing at Mayrhofen, generously gifted to us by my lovely parents), Marie invited us to what she said was a "special New Year party" to be held at their house on the day we were due to return.

I thought nothing of it but on the plane home Rachel suddenly said:

'You know this party?'

'Yes.'

'I have a feeling Graham might have won an award.'

'What do you mean?'

'The New Years Honours list.'

'Really?'

As we left Heathrow I bought a newspaper and, sure enough, Graham had been awarded the MBE.

He was finally receiving proper recognition.

VERBATIM - The Fun of Making Theatre Seriously by Mark Wheeller

The following summer, the four of us went on a memorable camping holiday to the south of France.

Graham and Marie continued to be even more important in our family as they became godparents to our children.

They were active in this role and their visits were much looked forward to. They were both fun. They had a video camera and some of the earliest footage we have of our children was taken by Marie.

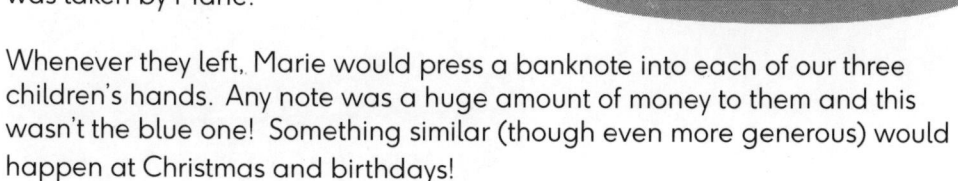

Whenever they left, Marie would press a banknote into each of our three children's hands. Any note was a huge amount of money to them and this wasn't the blue one! Something similar (though even more generous) would happen at Christmas and birthdays!

VERBATIM - The Fun of Making Theatre Seriously by Mark Wheeller

Graham being blind and the way he dealt with it was constantly fascinating.

Watch where you're going! Are you blind or something?

We have wonderful memories of Graham driving dodgem cars. Whichever of our family accompanied him adopted a self-imposed rule of not touching the steering wheel. Instead they madly shouted instructions as to which way he should steer!

The fairground workers loved seeing us all laughing and the other dodgem riders soon realised the situation and he was allowed us to break the one way system regulation. Everyone laughed and people often came over to chat our 'celebrity' friend!

One day, Ollie, aged about six, asked Graham what his eye socket looked like. Graham wasn't phased and invited him to go into the bathroom where he took his eye out and showed Ollie his empty eye socket. I asked Ollie what it looked like and he said:

'Like the inside of your mouth really.'

Graham normalised what was unusual to us and we were able to talk and laugh about it with ease.

We loved it whenever Graham's achievements reached TV. He remained our sole link with celebrity.

VERBATIM - The Fun of Making Theatre Seriously by Mark Wheeller

On 7th July 1995 Graham hit a hole in one at the Blind Open Golf Championship at the 124 yard seventh hole at a course in Fareham. There is a plaque to celebrate the achievement but, more impressive to me, was his interview on Channel 4's popular *The Big Breakfast*.

We were all so proud to know Graham even our little toddler Daisy, who would later go on to play his sister in a future production of my play.

A very personal legacy Graham left for me is his love of high end hi-fi. I remember taking some of my records to his house to hear them on his incredible system with the famous Linn Soldek LP12 turntable, matched by quality amps and impressively weighty speakers.

I couldn't understand how, on his system, I could hear details missing from mine, which had always been the pride of my front room and often admired by my visitors. Graham's system was in a different league. He said there was no other option than to build up a system of my own... but it would be expensive so, would have to be done gradually.

I was all for cheating and remember, when SACD was invented, I believed I could jump a few steps in one swoop! I visited our local high end hi-fi store (Audio T) and asked them to demonstrate an SACD player. They asked me what I wanted to achieve. When I explained they said SACD wouldn't do that but showed me a Naim system that would... and if I wanted even more from it it was upgradable. I was hooked.

VERBATIM - The Fun of Making Theatre Seriously by Mark Wheeller

I am now the proud owner of a hi-fi system Graham would approve of and I can hear each note played, separated into the air space of our front room. Every time I use it I think of Graham and my introduction to high end sound! My family aren't so grateful to him for the consequent hole in our finances!

I'd like something a little more modern!

I wish I could say that hole was filled by the income from the **Race To Be Seen** script and performance royalties flowing in. I can't. It came to the point where Longman contacted me to say they were discontinuing it. They gave me 50 complimentary copies (most of which I still have) and that was the end of that! My first foray as a professional playwright was over... it seemed.

I continued to feel this play deserved more but I had no idea how to make that happen.

Graham talked about writing his autobiography. I saw various chapters he had written as it was coming together but his plans to complete it were rudely interrupted by health issues.

He was diagnosed with Hairy Cell Leukaemia.

He underwent a gruelling chemotherapy treatment which he approached with typical Graham stoicism. Its life threatening nature was nipped in the bud. He continued to work at the Abbey National, in London, throughout this period.

We didn't manage to meet up as much but kept in regular contact.

Late in the 1990s I had the dreadful news that makes up the opening scene of the post-2000 editions of the play.

Following some pain in his leg, doctors discovered a tumour in his thigh muscle.

VERBATIM - The Fun of Making Theatre Seriously by Mark Wheeller

The only course of action was to remove his leg. A hind-quarters amputation. There's no pussyfooting around how horrendous this was.

I remember his phone call to me vividly. It must have been one of many calls he made that evening.

His use of the word 'grave', when describing the news, stunned me into an unusual silence. He lightened the load by saying one of the first things he would do when the operation was complete was to pop to the bookies to place a bet on him becoming the first blind amputee to hit a hole in one!
Typical Graham!

The hideous operation happened.

He and Marie visited us. The early signs seemed hopeful. He was in surprisingly high spirits and, with a big grin, revealed the title for his proposed autobiography: *Wide Eyed and Legless!*

I remember my Charlie, then aged 6, enjoying rides in his wheelchair as Graham was determined to make use of his crutches.

It was wonderful to see my two boys teaching him to play FIFA on their playstation with intense instructions being shouted about which button Graham should press to 'shoot', 'pass' or 'tackle'![43]

Then... a tumour was discovered in his other leg.

I decided to visit him at their home with Ollie (8) and Charlie (6). Rachel stayed at home with Daisy (4).

Given all that Graham had managed to overcome in his life, I couldn't accept he was on the final bend, so to speak.

When we arrived, Marie prepared us for the fact that Graham's physical appearance had changed. He was bloated from the painkilling drugs he had been prescribed.

---

[43] You can see a little home move of this on YouTube on my Mark Wheeller channel in the *Race To Be Seen* playlist.

VERBATIM - The Fun of Making Theatre Seriously by Mark Wheeller

He told us of a phantom pain in the leg that had been removed.

Other than that, he was in every way his normal self.

The doorbell rang as we were chatting. Marie answered it. Unbelievably, it was one of the cast (Nicky, who had played Maud) from EYT, who had randomly popped in to say hello. Marie had to explain the whole situation before she entered to surprise us all!

Soon, Charlie began to get itchy feet and asked Graham if he would go out to play football with him. I think Ollie probably kicked him. I remember feeling so embarrassed but Graham diffused the situation and went out into the back garden on his crutches where he and Ollie took shots at Charlie.

As he became tired, he sat in his wheelchair and my boys threw the ball at him to do headers. They were using a plastic football containing small lead (fishing) pellets in it so he could 'see' (hear) where it was.

These have become my final memories of Graham. This game exemplified his determined outlook, and an ability not to complain about his situation.

On a purely selfish level, I'm glad this was my final memory because it encapsulated Graham perfectly. That said, I regret not seeing him in hospital. Things weren't going well but it seemed impossible to make the time 'right' and I just imagined he would somehow pull through.

Suddenly there was no more time.

I was devastated. I had never experienced anyone I knew well passing away.

I felt awful for Marie. How must she be coping?

It was unreal and, it seems obvious to say this but... very final.

I sat in my room at home to compose a letter to Marie expressing my heartfelt love of Graham with the various **Race To Be Seen** soundtracks playing in the background as I typed through my tears.

Nothing I could say would make anything better... but it would show I cared and made me feel as though I had (belatedly) done something.

VERBATIM - The Fun of Making Theatre Seriously by Mark Wheeller

At Graham's funeral, Marie had a lot of family including Graham's wonderful parents and siblings around her. She seemed so detemined… just like Graham.

I remember at one point the vicar saying he was passing Graham's body into 'God's care', and I spontaneously whispered to Rachel: 'God's got a hell of a job to match the care Marie has given him.'

Marie gave us Graham's football containing lead pellets. Graham expressly wanted it to be passed onto Charlie and Ollie to mark his final game of football. It was used in a later production featuring Charlie and provides a wonderful source of stories for us all about the world's fastest blind runner, footballer, high-jumper, golfer and friend.

I felt more strongly than ever that Graham's story needed to go beyond our family and, realising **Race To Be Seen** had failed to do much for Graham's legacy, I vowed to review it and incorporate more of Graham, not only as a sportsman, but a fully rounded man.

Graham Salmon, my storybook man, my friend and my hero.

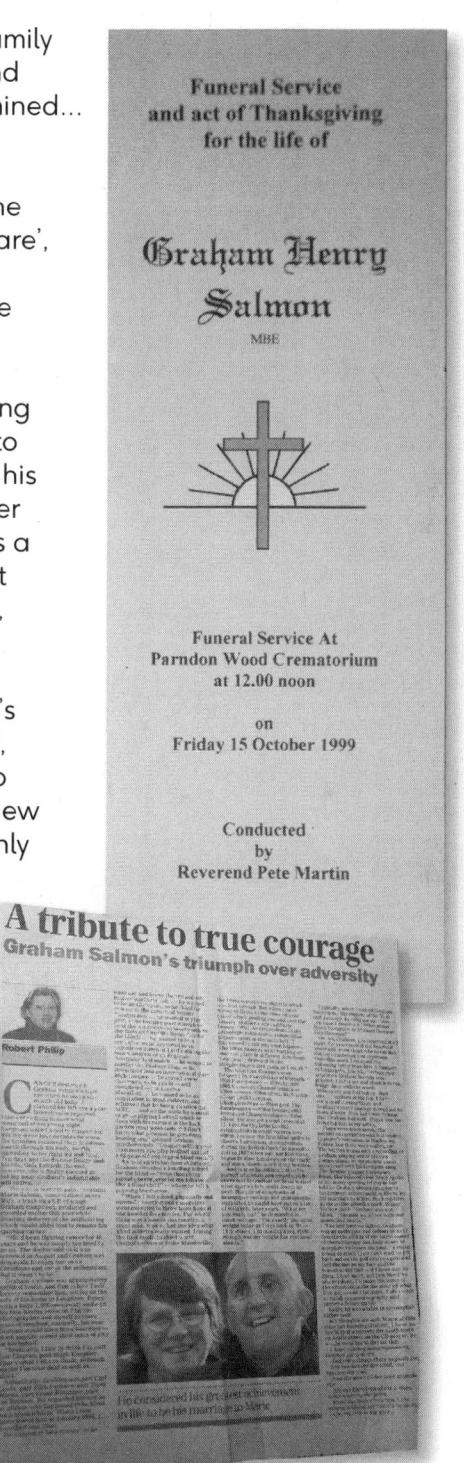

203

VERBATIM - The Fun of Making Theatre Seriously by Mark Wheeller

Chapter 11: A New Millennium - A New Play

"Graham Salmon has not only been an inspiration to blind athletes but also to those who are fully sighted. His outstanding achievements have been written about in great detail, but less well-known is the fact that he has led the way for full integration between the sighted and the blind, and for this alone he deserves recognition. I am not the least bit surprised that books and plays have now been written about him. I am very proud to have known him."

Ron Pickering O.B.E. Athletics coach and BBC sports commentator.

Marie had said to me how much Graham had wanted to see in the millennium. Sadly his body couldn't manage it. He died three months before 2000.

There were some wonderful tributes made in the wake of his death, none more openly complimentary than this, from Robert Philip, Sports Editor of the Sunday Telegraph in 1999.

> "**Graham Salmon** is the most inspiring athlete I have ever met; I say that without a moments hesitation, though I have enjoyed the rare privilege of sharing the company of Mohammad Ali, Pele, Sir Gary Sobers, Martina Navratilova, Nadia Comaneci, John McEnroe, Arnold Palmer and countless others in the course of my job."

I was determined Graham Salmon's story would feature in this new millennium and I set about working on a new, updated version of the play.

I wanted to narrate the story but felt too embarrassed, with me as a 'character'

VERBATIM - The Fun of Making Theatre Seriously by Mark Wheeller

[Newspaper clipping: "Salmon rising over adversity" by Robert Philip, Talking Points, featuring photographs of Graham Salmon running and with Marie Salmon. Caption: "Any tears shed are those of laughter at Marie and Graham Salmon's house"]

to put this play on with my own Youth Theatre. I needed someone else to do it for me.

I had, by this point, seen productions of my plays that brought something fresh to them.

One of these had been mounted by a new, local director Tim Ford, who viewed me first and foremost as a writer. His impressive production of **Hard To Swallow** a few years before led me to ask if he'd consider premiering my proposed new version of **Race**. He was keen.

He directed it... and that's it really... oh, and then he took it to the Edinburgh Fringe 2001.

Tim's version worked.

I wanted this play to get 'out there' so, so much!

I was disappointed that Tim decided to present this premiere in a small hut, normally used for rehearsals. I had anticipated it being performed at the more prestigious Point Theatre in Eastleigh, where Tim's Eastleigh Borough Youth Theatre productions were normally presented with fulsome media coverage. There was no big fanfare and only a few people saw the production.

VERBATIM - The Fun of Making Theatre Seriously by Mark Wheeller

A few more saw it in Edinburgh and loved it which made its underwhelming billing even more frustrating.

There were few reviews so Tim's production didn't broadcast knowledge of the play to schools or amateur theatre groups and inspire them to adopt the text for study or performance.[44]

One review I was aware of was written following the very early performances, as the group prepared for their showcase in Edinburgh.

> *It is rare to see even professional actors handling such a serious, emotional piece. EBYT delivered it with utter conviction and sincerity. They deserve the greatest respect.*
> **Andrew White** – *Daily Echo.*

The production of my new version of the play proved beyond doubt it had potential. My problem was how to communicate this to anyone else!

Dbda, who I now considered to be 'my publisher', took the risk of publishing it under a new and more direct title:

Graham - World's Fastest Blind Runner.

This did set the ball rolling...

---

[44] You can see my detailed notes on this performance in the Appendix section of this book.

VERBATIM - The Fun of Making Theatre Seriously by Mark Wheeller

Chapter 12: Therfield School - Where The Stars Aligned!

"You can't stay in your corner of the forest waiting for others to come to you. You have to go to them sometimes."
A. A. Milne - Winnie the Pooh

Between 2000 and 2007 dbda (who later became Zinc Publishing) published more of my back catalogue, so knowledge of my plays in UK schools was on the increase. They were being used more often in GCSE exams and school productions.

It came to the point where I was prevented from being a GCSE Drama examiner because the exam board was fearful I would have a vested interest to deal with when examining my own plays.

Up until this point at Oaklands we had taken the 'devising' option for exams, seeing how other schools were achieving results with my plays, Johnny Carrington my second in department said we were missing a trick and should use them.

I brushed my modesty aside and we did.

VERBATIM - The Fun of Making Theatre Seriously by Mark Wheeller

In 2007, one of my most wonderful GCSE students, Simon Froud, spied an unused copy of **Graham - World's Fastest Blind Runner** on the department bookshelf and, keen not to do a well-known play, decided he and his group would perform extracts from this.

I was delighted! Simon wanted to play me and I remember saying that may not get him the grade he wanted because 'I' was a glorified narrator. If he were to do it, he'd need to find imaginative ways of bringing 'me' to life.

He took that on as a challenge.

His performance (A*) was stunning and I overcame my embarrassment of being in the play and decided it should be our next OYT production... with Simon playing me.

2008 was to be significant year for OYT for two important reasons.

- It was 21 years since I had directed my first OYT production, **Race To Be Seen.**

- Oaklands was to close and merge with a local 'failing' school in September 2008... and (horror!) be Academised!

OYT's very existence came into question.

It seemed entirely appropriate to bookend my OYT output with this production.

Randomly, just before Simon's exam performance, I received an invitation from Cathy Hudson, then Head of Drama at Therfield School (Leatherhead), to see her production of **Graham–World's Fastest Blind Runner** being performed in The Leatherhead Drama Festival.

I was unable to make the performance but I had asked her to keep me in touch with the play's progress in the National Drama Festivals Association (NDFA).

When they won the local Festival, I remember kicking myself for not going to see it... particularly now we were planning to put it on.

However, in June, Cathy informed me they had qualified for the NDFA, England Winners Festival.

VERBATIM - The Fun of Making Theatre Seriously by Mark Wheeller

Wow!

Among those in the audience would be Sir Michael Caine.

Interesting!

It would be interesting to see another interpretation, particularly one that had achieved some, albeit limited, critical acclaim.

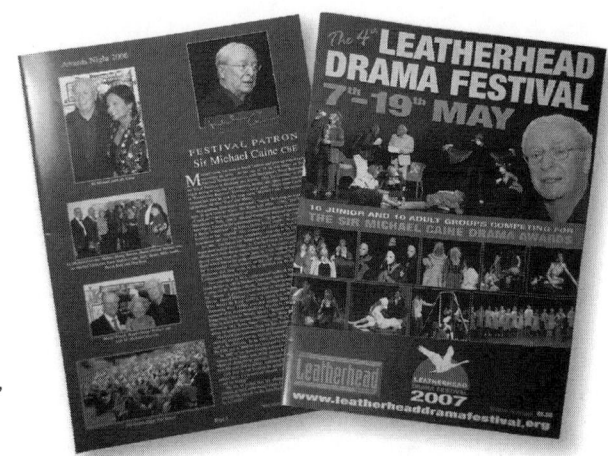

Rachel, Daisy, (my daughter) and I went to watch and were introduced to Sir Michael Caine.

Daisy, myself and Cathy meeting Sir Michael Caine.

I remember Michael Caine saying to me in his oh so recognisable voice:

"Should we know you?"

'Probably not,' I replied…
… and that was it! he was onto the next in the queue of people lined up to meet him!

It was original and differently staged to anything I would have conceived. It had a clear directorial 'vision', with the large cast costumed in black with white gloves apart from Graham, dressed in white with black gloves.

Each performer had a white cane they used in different, imaginative ways throughout the play.

They also had specially commissioned music… modern music where, during the transitions, the cast were wonderfully choreographed.

They had (with my permission) edited the production to 45-50 minutes from 80 to comply with the NDFA rules.

209

VERBATIM - The Fun of Making Theatre Seriously by Mark Wheeller

The play was tighter, more focused and... well... just better!

I was knocked out by its vision and, in a way that no other performance of one of my plays had ever managed, it altered my approach to directing my plays.

It received a standing ovation, led by Sir Michael Caine, and duly won the All Winners Festival. They went on to represent England in the NDFA British Final.

I'd never had that accolade attached to one of my plays.

Unlike the Therfield production, mine, prior to this, tended to use small casts (2m 2f). I did this partly to road test them for professional use. I felt, with these small casts, we could match the quality of the TIE Companies out on tour.

We had been very successful with *Missing Dan Nolan*, which also saw me decide on a positive return to writing verbatim plays.

I was originally planning something similar for **Graham.**

The Therfield production changed that plan because they used their onstage ensemble so imaginatively.

This was something no small-scale professional theatre company could ever match, as it would be too expensive to employ the performers!

I realised our production could achieve something they never could!

It flipped my perspective!

I decided to use Cathy's ideas as a starting point for our OYT production of **Graham**.

It became a bigger success than I could ever have hoped.

VERBATIM - The Fun of Making Theatre Seriously by Mark Wheeller

Chapter 13: OYT 2008 Graham Production

Like the runners, we're all part of a race
Some days you win some days you fall
But if you never help yourself then you'll never win at all
If you spend your life just dreaming, success won't come to you
Race to be seen and show the world what you can do!

Graham Salmon - Race To Be Seen (1983) - Music by Mark Wheeller

I had not made notes at the Therfield production but the way they edited it (I trusted it would be ok so didn't ever ask to see it) gave me a general direction as to how to edit the play successfully. Over the summer holidays I felt I had done just that!

It was 20 years since I had arrived at Oaklands and assembled a cast to rehearse this as my first OYT production in 1987.

20 years' stability in a Youth Theatre group can not be bought.

In the intervening years we had developed a clear 'house style' and I was working with experienced and committed members.

> I started OYT two or three years before *Graham*. I had a cherished, albeit small role, in *Sequinned Suits and Platform Boots* and, despite the role's size, I established myself within the company unknowingly... I was just having fun with friends.
> I was also involved in an original production at Oaklands run by Johnny Carrington and Danny Sturrock. I highlight *Sequinned Suits* and *Bang Out of Order* as they enabled my performing skills to grow but also underlined the trust required for an ensemble piece.
> **Michael Mears**

We had achieved much as a youth theatre and entered the autumn term of 2007 with high hopes of what we might achieve with **Graham**. We were entering it for the All England Theatre (One Act Play) Festival (AETF).

However...

...we were by no means over-confident.

VERBATIM - The Fun of Making Theatre Seriously by Mark Wheeller

My productions had never won through to the subsequent rounds of this Festival.

Our highest marks (for one of my productions) had been awarded to us way back in 1989 with **Hard To Swallow** when youth productions were forbidden to progress into the later rounds of the AETF due to some archaic rule which had since been overturned.

The adjudicators didn't seem to trust our style of performance. They seemed to favour more traditional box set plays.

That was our take on the situation. In retrospect, it was probably only part of the truth.

Nothing we had done could break through that barrier… and we certainly tried hard.

I say nothing…

…that's not quite true.

Two members of OYT, Rachael Dennett and Arjun Malhotra had, under the OYT - 006 banner[45] two members of OYT, Rachael Dennett and Arjun Malhotra, had devised a production called *Entropy* in March 2004.

This had won through to the Western Area Finals.

Entropy was by no means a traditional play. It was way more experimental than anything I had entered for the festival.

> It was an experimental piece of theatre (inspired by Artaud from our college work) which ultimately didn't mean too much to us, just a bit of fun. Arjun and I were compelled to do *Entropy*, not because we didn't enjoy your style of working but because Artaud's style was like nothing else we'd come across before and, as we both work practically with movement/dance, we were interested to experiment with different avenues to explore a storyline!
> **Rachael Dennett**

I remember feeling somewhat peeved about them achieving more than my own productions. I was delighted for them… but selfishly, I felt my own productions deserved more.

---

[45] OYT 006 encouraged OYT members to mount their own, independent productions without adult interference but with support. They were called OYT 006 because there were 6 people in the founding production.

VERBATIM - The Fun of Making Theatre Seriously by Mark Wheeller

Before this book was completed I admitted this and offered an apology to both Raechel and Arjun.

I was jealous. (Apologies Rachael and Arjun)

I would never have let on. It was totally unfair to feel that.

They had both done fantastically with literally no input from me.

I was delighted for them... but...

... selfishly, I felt my own productions deserved more.

> Awww, this is kind of you to admit. If it's any consolation, this is not new news to us. It was pretty obvious at the time how you were feeling and I guess we didn't have the words/knowledge of how to approach this with an adult.
> We also felt awkward about getting through. Your performances did deserve more but, I guess, this is just the way it goes sometimes. I'll definitely pass this onto Arj has we often joke about him being 'dead to you' because of this performance. 😊
>
> He'll be pleased to know that he wasn't ever 'dead to you' at all! You should put all of that in the published book. 😜
>
> Thank you for getting this off your chest! And yes, you're totally easy to read! 😄
> **Rachael Dennett**

The casting of Graham was to be impacted again by the success of OYT - 006.

Another big 006 successes had been Danny Sturrock's work.

In 2002 he had put on a production, his first one-act play **Gagging For It**.

This would have won through to the second round of the AETF had it not suffered a penalty for over running by five minutes.

I loved Danny's work.[46]

In 2007, Danny had a new play.

It was something incredibly special.

Danny Sturrock whose contribution is incalculable for both OYT and my plays

---

[46] Danny and I went on to collaborate on a couple of commissions: **Driven to Distraction**, which was toured professionally around London by StopWatch Theatre Company and **The Kids Who Look Out Of Windows**, which is now published by Maverick Plays and Musicals

VERBATIM - The Fun of Making Theatre Seriously by Mark Wheeller

Suicide Dot Com [47]

Suicide Dot Com told the true story of 18-year-old Simon Kelly who had used the internet to obtain detailed information on suicide methods and used suicide chat rooms to take his own life in 2001. He launched a website to act as his suicide note only minutes before he died.
Danny used the testimony of his family and also from Simon's own online conversations leading to the moment when he killed himself.

It was incredible. To this day it remains one of my favourite plays.

Simon's parents were quoted later, saying this about Danny's play:

> "In tackling topics such as suicide there is always the risk of over-dramatisation and glorification of the individuals concerned, which could lead other vulnerable youngsters to follow suit. We thank Danny for the sensitive and compassionate way he researched this play; he consistently responded to our concerns to avoid unnecessary detail, whilst at the same time achieving a play with remarkable dramatic impact."
> **Paul and Hilary Kelly**

There was no argument; Danny's production needed the most experienced members of OYT in its cast.

Graham needed an ensemble.

The cast I assembled was from less experienced OYT members. The oldest was 17, but, it was by no means a group of 'cast offs'.

> Along the back wall of Oaklands Theatre were framed posters of productions. I always wanted to be in one.
> I couldn't think of a better production to leave a legacy; my mark on a Mark Wheeller play! What an opportunity! I knew those performances could become legend, intrinsically connected with the piece itself.
> Alex Chalk in *Missing Dan Nolan*,
> Charlie Wheeller as the Blockbuster in *Sequinned*,
> Gemma Aked Priestley in *Bang Out*,
> Mike Mears as Graham in *Graham - World's Fastest Blind Runner*.
> That's what I wanted.
> **Michael Mears**

---

[47] This was later published by dbda/Zinc as **Surfing on Suicide**

VERBATIM - The Fun of Making Theatre Seriously by Mark Wheeller

The cast was headed up by Simon as me (Mark) and the equally committed Michael Mears as Graham.

> I remember arriving home and explaining to my mother that I'd been selected to play the lead in Mark's new play. I'll never forget what she said:
> 'Michael, you're not blind, how the bloody hell are you going to pull that off?'
> She doesn't get "acting" and, from that moment on the daunting prospect of developing a blind character would become one hell of a creative endeavour.
> **Michael Mears**

My son, Charlie, and daughter, Daisy were both in the ensemble, which was fantastic for me too.

As a direct result of Danny using all our older performers we had no over-18s, which qualified us to enter the AETF as a 'Youth' Company.

Danny's OYT 006 had a few over-18s so they became, for the purposes of the Festival, an 'adult' company.

So, within the local Totton Drama Festival we weren't directly competing.

However...

... if we progressed to the second round we would be. Only one group could progress into the second round of the AETF.

Danny was so generous. Despite directing **Suicide**, he also took on the responsibility for our lighting and multi-media.

Not only that but he also created the pre-recorded musical soundtrack using samples from Graham's radio interviews and my original EYT songs over his modern beat/sound/music.

Both plays often rehearsed on the same night. At the end of the evening, we showed each other what we had been rehearsing.

We became aware that we were both developing something quite special.

Michael was proving to be an incredible and committed Graham.

He undertook much work instigated by himself with the odd suggestion from me, such as 'try to do mundane activities at home wearing a blindfold'.

VERBATIM - The Fun of Making Theatre Seriously by Mark Wheeller

There's a line in the play, "Imagine what your knee sees?"
Just think about that.
I needed to draw on holistic experiences. I undertook numerous tasks to help build my understanding of having the sense of sight stripped away. I remember playing with characterisation early on in the process, using big gestures, seemingly always off balance, arms outstretched. I was playing into stereotypical imagery pulled from caricatures or my own imagination. I was wrong in my initial approach and that became apparent rather abruptly when I started wearing a blindfold.
I started with big bold statements of intent, commuting to school blindfolded and spending weekends and evenings blindfolded too. These early experiences were helpful, but ultimately I believe a character is best built through finding nuance: making sandwiches, walking up and down the stairs, washing, going to the toilet, brushing my teeth, tying shoe laces or buttoning a shirt. These smaller tasks presented a unique challenge but, as I overcame them, my confidence grew and those overblown gestures decreased.
Meanwhile, in our workshop/rehearsals, we played blind football and I would spend the majority of early blocking rehearsals blindfolded.
Mark works with an honesty which I'm grateful to have experienced. If he didn't like it, he would say but, more importantly, he'd usually have a plan to fix a scene.
For example, if a scene wasn't coming together, he might introduce someone not in the scene to direct or to offer ideas. He might split the cast up into groups to work on specific problems or he might simply rewrite it.
Change through challenge was a good thing and solutions through failures happened almost every rehearsal.
He allowed us players to play.
Michael Mears

Mike Mears as Graham in OYT

VERBATIM - The Fun of Making Theatre Seriously by Mark Wheeller

We loved every scene we saw of **Suicide Dot Com** in rehearsal.

Danny's groundbreaking use of multi-media in this production was awe-inspiring.

His cast were also open in their enthusiasm about our emerging **Graham** production.

It was difficult to tell if they were just being supportive but I guess they might have felt this about our reaction to their play. One of the **Suicide** cast, Georgina, had been in Simon's GCSE group, also achieving an A*, so she was particularly keen to help and encourage us all.

As I had the younger cast we felt, in the natural order of things, it was they who would progress into the AETF, if either did.

I remember thinking how unfortunate it was that **Graham** had ended up in competition with something we could all see was so extraordinary, so right for its time and derived from our own OYT stable!

Both groups had a secret weapon.

We hoped, for one of us, this would be the silver bullet.

It was something we had learnt a few years previously when presenting **Missing Dan Nolan** at the Totton Drama Festival.

We were so confident with our production after generating huge media interest in it that we entered the festival with <u>very</u> high hopes.

We were placed last but one.

VERBATIM - The Fun of Making Theatre Seriously by Mark Wheeller

Looking at the mark allocation, it is clear to see where our problem was.

13/15 for Presentation

30/35 for Production

8/10 for Endeavour, originality and achievement (I think we deserved more!)

... and...

28/40 for Acting

In Peter English's (**GODA**) adjudication, all was explained.

> The director needs to constantly check and to insist on clear enunciation at all times. The movement and stage positioning was often excellent. The whole effect was spoilt by the tendency to rush words and, made them difficult to hear and understand. The words in this piece have a deep importance being those of the real people themselves. Pace is important, but not at the expense of clarity.

This 'diction' issue had been an ongoing criticism of our work and I/we had always roundly ignored it. I passed it over, thinking we weren't drama trained and didn't want those 'drama school' affectations. We were being 'natural'... I wanted my performers to "be themselves".

Suddenly this comment spoke to me... and the cast... **L O U D L Y !**

At our next rehearsal we all said we HAD to address this... and we did. I remember saying:

"To do this successfully you will have to enunciate in your everyday life as well as on stage. It needs to be natural and not forced"

Bless them, they did too! It caused much talk around our school and I know felt very strange to them all... but... it had instant results.

We entered pretty much the same version of that production, with this one alteration, into a much bigger Festival (Woking Drama Festival) and won the Award for Best Youth Production.

VERBATIM - The Fun of Making Theatre Seriously by Mark Wheeller

Rachael Dennett, who was in **Missing Dan Nolan**, was one of the two people in **Entropy**, the first OYT play to progress into the AETF semi-final. Could clear diction really be the silver bullet?

If so... it was a silver bullet for both us and the older group. Many of them had been involved in productions following this change and it had become part of our practice (belatedly) in curriculum drama lessons.

We had everyone enunciating.

It improved our exam results too!

Looking back now, it's so obvious. If the audience can't hear the words, how can they possibly understand or enjoy the play?

I can't believe how arrogant I had been to dismiss this criticism, made so often in the past.

When we came to perform in our school Theatre, we felt ready.

OYT and 006 performed our productions separately and both won plaudits from the Southern Evening Echo. What an incredible year!

Suicide Dot Com was premiered in January 2008 and had its first review a couple of months before us.

> *Danny Sturrock has fashioned a drama which is honest, humane, humorous, informative and emotional without being emotive... fast paced and pitched perfectly... a mature, sensitive and beautifully acted piece. Theatre at its best.*
> **Karen Robson – *Southern Daily Echo* (review of *Suicide Dot Com*).**

We didn't know it at the time, but **Suicide** was to be nominated for the Production of the Year in the south of England by Karen, the reviewer. That had only happened once before with our musical **Happy Soap**.

It was such a strong production. The image I hold in my mind is the slight figure of the lad committing suicide dwarfed by the enormous screen behind him as he typed his life away.

VERBATIM - The Fun of Making Theatre Seriously by Mark Wheeller

George Mattack, Anthony Jennings, Sean Gradidge, Charli Wells - from the original cast of Suicide Dot Com

I remember thinking, despite Danny never having met Roy Nevitt from Stantonbury, this had all the hallmarks of Roy's best documentary plays that inspired me back in the '80s. Roy's work had been syphoned through mine into Danny's output. Roy deserves grandfather rights over this wonderful play.

Like my own verbatim plays, this garnered significant media interest including a feature on Radio 4's **Today** programme.

In March it was our turn to show our play to an audience.

> I remember how hard we worked. The performances required such focus and energy, and knowing we had to "bring it" every showing was exhilarating.
> My family loved it! To this day I have people recalling *Graham* as a piece of theatre they remember. An extended family member was so impressed by the work they saw OYT produce that, when their growing son was old enough, they encouraged him to join a youth theatre, citing OYT as the reason.
> Last summer at Kathryn Wiltshire's wedding (she was one of the cast, I was a brides-man) this lad, who I don't know well, approached me and praised the production and specifically my performance.
> He informed me that his choice to study theatre and pursue acting came from seeing *Graham*. My mother still insists that *Graham* was by far the best production we'd ever put on.
> **Michael Mears**

We couldn't have been happier with the reviews.

VERBATIM - The Fun of Making Theatre Seriously by Mark Wheeller

SOUTHERN EVENING ECHO

Author[48] and director Mark Wheeller has every reason to be proud of this final production under the Oaklands Youth Theatre name after 21 years at the helm of this company of talented actors.

The symbolism in the imaginative use of white sticks for the inspirational story of Graham Salmon, blind from birth yet who achieved so much, added to the poignancy of the story.

The multimedia work of Danny Sturrock, aided by the technical expertise of the backstage team, made this an event to remember.

Michael Mears (Graham) skilfully took us from Graham as a baby through the various stages of his life.

As a narrator, Simon Froud (Mark Wheeller), expressed a range of emotions commensurate with the different phases of Graham's life.

The play gave all eleven cast members an opportunity to excel in a variety of situations which they did most successfully.

Jim Rumsey - *Southern Evening Echo*

noda TODAY

Oaklands Youth Theatre's production of GRAHAM was full of emotion, which was communicated to the audience very well. You could hear a pin drop in the full theatre. With the costumes and set being minimal and the fantastic use of sticks portrayed the ever changing settings. The emotion of the script came through unimpeded. The back projection added to the production.

Barbara Fairclough NODA

---

[48] See... I was now perceived as an author!

Graham became the production that initiated an era where schools (initially local, further away in the coming years) started to treat OYT performances as opportunities for their students to see 'professional' theatre and review it as part of their GCSE/A'level courses. Quite an accolade for our humble city comprehensive school.

The first to take this up was The Westgate School in Winchester. Their Drama teacher, who I had come to know from a Drama workshop I'd led (after which, he directed the school premiere of ***Arson About***), wrote a beautiful 1600 word review for us.

I have edited it for the purpose of this book but it gives a clear impression of the kind of features that made our plays popular with Drama teachers.

> ## Blind Athlete Blasts through the Ignorance Barrier!
> 'Graham: World's Fastest Blind Man!'
> Oaklands Youth Theatre, Friday 7th March 2008
>
> When he originally set his sights on researching the achievements of blind athlete Graham Salmon, back in the early 80s, Mark could never have predicted how phenomenal Graham's achievements would be… or how deeply he would himself become a part of the life he sought to dramatise.
> Mark's plays can disarm you with their sparkling theatricality and cheeky comic licence. They have the power to sweep away an audience's feelings of distance through intimate monologues and direct narrative. Graham was like a "gospel" in the way it documented and celebrated his charmed life.
> Mark became a narrator (his voice given to a younger incarnation). He told of the miracles of Graham Salmon. Mark wrote himself into the story because, in the process of researching and devising the original play **Race To Be Seen**, he became a dear friend of Graham; someone who Graham would phone with the most intimate news of his battle with cancer.
> Graham and Mark's narratives run parallel to each other, if at different speeds! Graham is shown as a delightfully funny and phenomenally driven "ordinary" bloke. Mark was, by contrast, portrayed as an honest, open and at times, rather naff figure. His goal: to finish writing a play for the Epping Youth Theatre! Mark's triumphant air punch at meeting this challenge is seen as a comic "icing on the cake", following the moment that Graham Salmon, Mark's 'storybook-man', achieves immortality and a gold medal.

VERBATIM - The Fun of Making Theatre Seriously by Mark Wheeller

The cast created a rich stage poetry that was as near to magical illusion as is possible without the help of smoke and mirrors.
The razor-sharp cast was the key to making all this stage trickery come to life. In lane one was Michael Mears (Graham) who radiated optimism and innocence, with Graham's trademark "megawatt smile" and athleticism that was, in itself, impressive.
By his side, and guiding Graham on every bit as much as Graham's sighted shadow runner did on the track, was Louise Costin (Marie Salmon). Louise's warmth was equally radiant and her performance was full of tender looks and gentle smiles.
Simon Froud spent an hour camping up his old teacher's achievements in front of a paying audience and it was clearly enjoyable for him. Simon also made a genuine connection with Mark's gripping story.
Gemma Priestly, despite being younger than Michael, grounded the story through her charming portrayal of Graham's mum, Maud. You can see clearly from her bickering and chirping how Graham got his confidence and humour but she also portrayed the sadness of a mother who lives through a traumatic operation on her infant child and delivers her lines with such immediacy and warmth.
Mark's children, Charlie and Daisy, who will no doubt have grown up going to the OYT 'church', were core members of this memorial drama. Daisy Wheeller's unaccompanied solo was one of the most precious moments of the play. In contrast, Charlie took the award for comedy and slapstick - especially when playing the unfortunate under-dog in the park. If any moment could illustrate the benefits of being blind, Graham's standing calmly by, while his dog is, well, erm… "dogging" another owner's dog, has to take the Gold, Silver and Bronze for comedy! Playing the enthusiastic Top Dog in all this was Matt Griffiths. Well done for being game for a laugh Matt – how pleasant to see an OYT old-hand passing his skills down to the new recruits!
The production is due to be released on DVD and I hope that, with the popularity of Mark's plays, his own innovative direction will be valued as a means of demonstrating how physical theatre can open up a narrative.
As the laughter spills over, it is this sound that provides a lovely ending to such a touching and funny play.
Full of tenderness and humour, **Graham** was consummate narrative[49] theatre capturing the inspirational life of a lovely, funny man. Oaklands School – home of Oaklands Youth Theatre - is due to be taken over later this year and merged with another local School. For that reason, **Graham** felt very much like a "Last Supper" for Mark Wheeller and his

---

[49] You can see this production streaming at SalamanderStreet.com

VERBATIM - The Fun of Making Theatre Seriously by Mark Wheeller

> OYT disciples. I hope they are able to borrow some of Graham Salmon's magic and turn every obstacle into a bar to be leapt over!
> **Paul Mills** - Head of Drama - The Westgate School, Winchester.

Finally, I had an unexpected email from Tracy, Graham's niece. The cast loved hearing this!

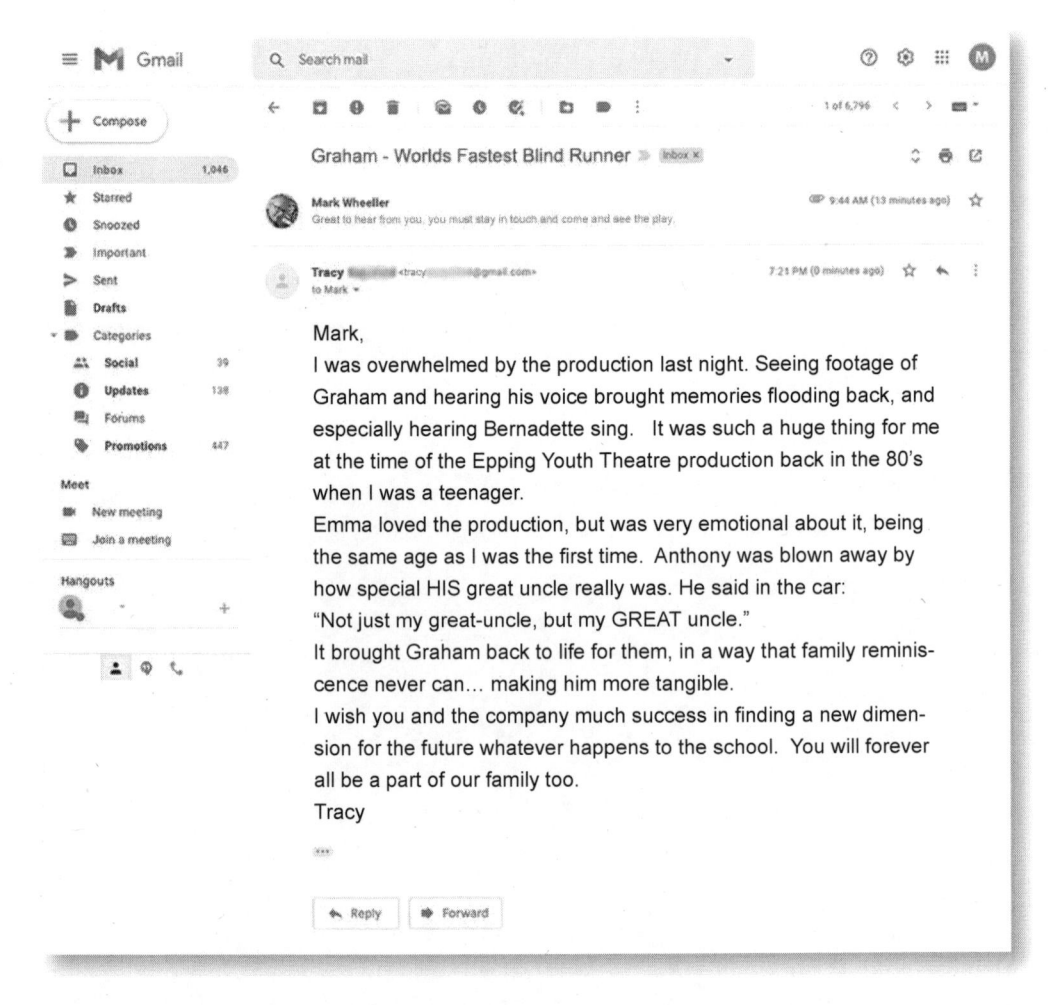

> Mark,
> I was overwhelmed by the production last night. Seeing footage of Graham and hearing his voice brought memories flooding back, and especially hearing Bernadette sing. It was such a huge thing for me at the time of the Epping Youth Theatre production back in the 80's when I was a teenager.
> Emma loved the production, but was very emotional about it, being the same age as I was the first time. Anthony was blown away by how special HIS great uncle really was. He said in the car:
> "Not just my great-uncle, but my GREAT uncle."
> It brought Graham back to life for them, in a way that family reminiscence never can... making him more tangible.
> I wish you and the company much success in finding a new dimension for the future whatever happens to the school. You will forever all be a part of our family too.
> Tracy

So, performances of both *Suicide Dot Com* and *Graham - World's Fastest Blind Runner* in our own theatre were complete.

Both casts had special plays.

We were ready, set and go for the competitive festival performances.

Chapter 14: OYT 2008 Competitive Festival Performances

> My home life as a child was complicated, raised on a council estate by young parents with virtually no money. Education wasn't an important factor to them. I was bullied at school and hung around on the street with people who were older than me. The odds were stacked against me achieving anything in life. What made the difference? I was fortunate enough to be at a school that had youth theatre and allowed us to develop our own work, which made us feel valued. Drama festivals allowed us to show our work to a wider audience. Opening our productions up for review taught us to value constructive criticism and respect other people's opinions. We saw work other groups were producing, and could take away ideas/inspiration to enrich our own productions. It didn't hurt to win a few awards and become ambassadors for our school! Festivals opened us up to a world outside of Lordshill, and was key in my ability as an adult to feel comfortable in a strange place or situation.
> **Samantha Silver (née Phillips)**

Suicide Dot Com was first to perform at the Totton Drama Festival on Thursday 13th March (unlucky for some). It doubled up as the qualifying round for the AETF.

I don't have the adjudication but the adjudicator liked it so much, they won all these awards!
- Danny Sturrock - Best Director (jointly)
- Danny Sturrock - Technical Achievement
- Suicide Dot Com - Adjudicators Award
- Anthony Jennings - Best Adult Actor (aged only 18)

They received a few other nominations too!

Suicide Dot Com marks at the Totton Drama Festival.
- Presentation **14/15**
- Production **30/35**
- Acting **31/35**
- Originality, endeavour and achievement **9/10**
- Total marks: **84/100**
- **Deducted 3 points** for over-running by 3 minutes.
- New Final Mark: **81/100**

The cast were gutted by the deduction (as happened with ***Gagging For It*** before).

VERBATIM - The Fun of Making Theatre Seriously by Mark Wheeller

They were fearful this might prove crucial.

Over the next three days the other companies performed and received their marks.

Maskers Theatre Company: **Harlequinade** by Terence Rattigan. **74**/100
C.A.T.S YT: **It Snows** by Bryony Lavery & Frantic Assembly **75**/100
Bench Theatre Company: **Stand and Delivery** by Mark Wakeman **72**/100
Bursledon Players: **And The Winner Is**... by Stephen Humphreys **60**/100

Suicide Dot Com were, despite their deduction, in the lead by 6 clear points.

When we performed **Graham**, we had no idea what scores had been awarded but, of course, the adjudicator would have known.

We were the last to perform... on Saturday the 15th March.

I remember when we finished, we walked up into the audience of predominantly our competitors and, as we did, they stood up and gave us an ovation.

We sat down for the adjudication... and this is (extracts from) what we heard. You can imagine us hearing these comments and turning to each other to react, then turning back to watch/listen, so we didn't miss the next comment.

> *This play is full of lively humour!*
> *The poignant use of the white sticks, making them into the shapes of the action really worked well with this talented cast.*
> *The start was fantastic, giving it the energy it needed.*
> *I especially liked the a-cappella singing, and the use of projection really enhanced it.*
> *The changing stage pictures throughout the production enhanced this play enormously.*
> *The physicality of the riding of the bikes was great. You certainly have faith in your cast to pull this off.*
> *It was good to see you use the whole area, especially in the swimming scene.*
> *The dog-shagging scene was cleverly done and not at all smutty!*
> *The play came to a beautiful ending which left a tear in our eyes.*
> *cont...*

VERBATIM - The Fun of Making Theatre Seriously by Mark Wheeller

> *...cont*
>
> **Graham** (played by Michael Mears)
> *You looked great as Graham. You had a tenderness in your speech which I was looking for. You delivered your lines with conviction and honesty.*
> *A very intelligent performance. I actually believed you were blind.*
> **Mark** (played by Simon Froud)
> *You are a wonderful actor! Your storytelling skills are good and sincere in the delivery of your lines. You gave a very good last speech about Marie.*
> **Marie** (played by Louise Costin)
> *Lovely interpretation of the part, sincere and truthful. I loved the way you looked at Graham, and how you helped him through his life.*
> **Maud** (played by Gemma Aked-Priestley)
> *Wonderful, tender performance, as was that of Caidyn White playing your husband* **Harry** *and Daisy Wheeller playing* **Junie**. *There was a nice touch with the doll and your reactions to Graham getting all the attention. You delivered your lines really well.*
> *In summary, this was an intelligent interpretation of the script, making this a wonderful piece of theatre.*
> *There were a few times when the pace dipped in the middle of the play, which is hard to sustain. Well done for bringing this thought-provoking production to the festival.*
> **John Scowen. (GODA)**[50]

John also awarded us both of the Youth Performing Awards which is unusual: Gemma for her portrayal of Maud and Mike for his, as Graham. Mike had now achieved that legendary status he had so much wanted and duly went on to appear in a huge framed photo at the entrance to the Oaklands Theatre.

I was awarded **Best Director** jointly with Danny.

The cast were lovely and clapped like mad for me but I was embarrassed. My way of working meant the cast had done more than me in making it as imaginative as it was. I accepted the award with due humility and then made sure I thanked them... a lot!

---

[50] I am sad to report that John passed away in 2014 following a brave battle with motor neurone disease. I remember John's enthusiasm after the production for our play. His effervescence with the cast and his special love of the "dog-shagging" scene, as he called it, remains in my memory for all time!

VERBATIM - The Fun of Making Theatre Seriously by Mark Wheeller

Finally... the marks...

... remember, Suicide was leading the field with **81** points.

So...

... drumroll...

- Presentation... **14**/15 (the same as Suicide)
- Production... **31**/35 (We were one point ahead)

Then, the category where we had previously fallen down badly with our poor enunciation. Danny and I were both delighted that lack of clarity of speech had not been mentioned in either adjudication.

Had we found our silver bullet?

- Acting... **33**/40 (We were now 3 points ahead of Suicide... and surprised!)
- Originality, Endeavour and Achievement **9**/10 (Same as Suicide)

We hadn't overrun so there were no penalty points...

... and that meant...

We had a total score of 87!

We had won!

I had been entering this festival for 20 years.

This was a first!

I was delighted.

We were delighted.

Graham would have been so proud.

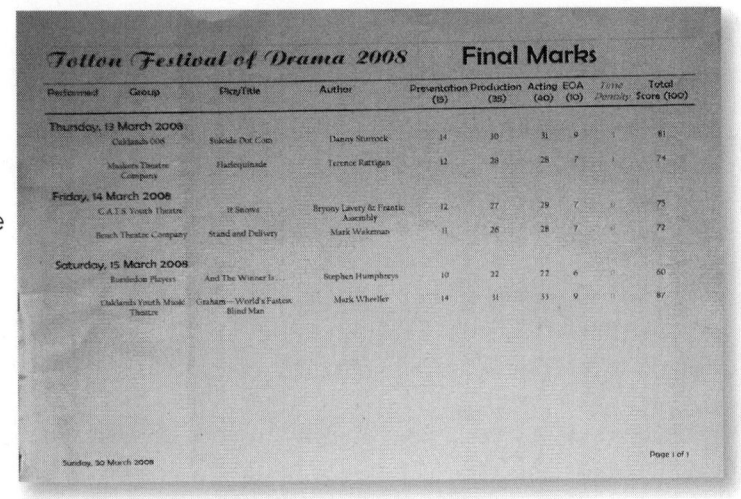

VERBATIM - The Fun of Making Theatre Seriously by Mark Wheeller

We would now be included on the list of 'previous winners' on all future editions of the TDF programme just in the nick of time as Oaklands (and maybe OYT) ceased to exist.

I felt dreadful for Danny and the cast of **Suicide**.

They were very sweet about it... especially Danny.

Georgina, who had been in Simon's GCSE performance, took the time to write me a beautiful card... and encapsulated how they all felt about it.

> *Dear Mark,*
>
> *CONGRATULATIONS! (Even if your play is 'shit'.[51] LOL) I have to admit, even though I'm gutted "Suicide" didn't make it, I'm glad you did. I know how much "Graham" means to you. Like me, you must be so proud! I want to say that, behind the jokes, I am so happy for you and hope you and "Graham" continue to kick-ass! Well done, you deserve it!*
>
> *Loads of love*
>
> *George*

We had qualified for the Western Area Final.

If we won that, we'd be in the English Final.

I mustn't get ahead of myself!

Usefully, John, the adjudicator, had given us a tip... to work on sustaining energy throughout the production.

In our next rehearsal we would do a runthrough to figure out when it dipped. Should we change something to lift it... or... just focus on sustaining energy?

With the Easter Holidays taking up the next two weeks, there wasn't a lot of time to rehearse before the Western Area Final.

We were SOOOO excited!

---

[51] The reference to the word "shit" was quoting something I'd say to YT members (with a big smile) if things weren't going as well as I expected! It tended to get results.

VERBATIM - The Fun of Making Theatre Seriously by Mark Wheeller

In the Western Area Final we performed at the Verwood Hub in a big hall that was very different to our more intimate space.

The stage was raised with the audience on the flat floor spreading back forever it seemed. It was wide like our theatre but not at all deep, unlike ours.

Like all the other competitors, we had half an hour to familiarise ourselves with the space, forecast potential issues and do a sound/light check.

We were up against it and I stressed how important it was to enunciate words as it was such a big space. We were the only youth group to have qualified into what was also the AETF semi final.

Once the cast went back stage to change and the audience started to come in, I had a wonderful surprise. Claire Jeffrey, who had been in the 1987 OYT production, was in the audience. We hadn't seen one another for ages! What would she make of it? She helped calm my nerves as we nattered about what she'd been up to in the intervening years.

> I was so pleased to have found Mark on Facebook. Reconnecting brought back all the extraordinary memories of OYT, a period of my life that was incredibly important to me.
> Mark had posted on FB that a production of Graham was going to be on so, I bought a ticket and went along.
> As I sat down I saw Mark and, feeling like teenager again, I waved to get his attention. We had a brief chat. I was thrilled to support and was excited to see a new production of something I'd been in many years before.
> It started.
> Great opening, great young actors. It was very different to when I was in it and…
> … where are the songs?
> Why aren't they dancing?
> I was absolutely captivated!
> The audience were so engaged. You could hear a pin drop. It brought back so many memories. Choral speaking, the way we used our bodies to create settings, the team-work and above all, the friendship between the actors.
> **Claire New (née Jeffrey)**

This **was** a very different production.

The cast were confident and took to the stage to present an impressive performance.

VERBATIM - The Fun of Making Theatre Seriously by Mark Wheeller

Then came the adjudication from a more senior GODA adjudicator, currently (2021) GODA's Chair so he definitely knew what he was talking about.

> *This is a very moving play on the page.*
>
> *The way you used those white sticks was impressive and imaginative, a golf club, other pieces of sporting equipment, a counter, a barrier, strong sunshine and many more - it shows how you can stretch an audiences imagination with very simple things. All the audience laughed and cried at some point during the play.*
>
> *The director got the very best out of the young actors, individually and in the ensemble work. The movement was one of the strongest elements of the staging, so much works well; the slow-mo section, the soldiers, the office/telephone scene, the hit-and-run, the toilet-brush joke, and the swimming were all well done and made a huge contribution to the "professionalism" of the piece.*
>
> *The delivery of the "we're not going to employ you" messages didn't quite work. I don't think they needed to pull an embarrassed face each time, just coldly deliver the obvious pathetic excuses with no embarrassment, will make it even more shocking and effective!*[52]
>
> *The awesome copulating dogs was a great highlight and the hand-shake, a masterful touch. I enjoyed the rain scene - really enjoyable enthusiasm by the squirter, Charlie Wheeller, whose physical comedy was excellent throughout.*
>
> **Graham - Michael Mears**
> *A splendid performance. I loved the enthusiasm you brought to the character, indeed the enthusiasm that Graham obviously had as a real person. Strong physical acting and strong facial expressions. It is hard because you are on camera the whole time with no chance to relax. A very touching ending, well acted. Above all else, you were totally believable in the role.*
>
> **Mark - Simon Froud**
> *Very strong to-audience delivery, you established a relationship with us early on. Good volume and good projection. Your concentration and focus was excellent during your inactive periods on stage and you were really likeable.*[53]
>
> **cont...**

---

[52] This was another recurring feature of our adjudications - 'less is more'... gradually we were listening and learning.

[53] Another key point here that I would repeatedly make to my casts was that reactions make the other actors' acting seem better. I would demonstrate this by asking one of the cast to pretend to thump me in the stomach. The first time I don't react. The second time, I do. Clearly the second punch seems better but the only difference was the reaction. Well done Simon!

VERBATIM - The Fun of Making Theatre Seriously by Mark Wheeller

> *In Summary*
> *This was a delightful performance, with strong teamwork, good discipline and innovative grouping/choreography. Try to make the energy and purpose apply to the moments where you move into position as well as the acting when in position.*
> **Chris Jaeger**

We were delighted by this adjudication which was delivered with passion and much lively humour.

We LOVED his reference to our 'copulating dogs'... in fact, he went on to award both the dog and the bitch (Matt Griffiths/Charlie Wheeller) the Adjudicators Award for the best moment (in his opinion) of the festival!

So... that scene and how it came to be an 'award winning' scene serves to illustrate my development over the 25 years since I started work on **Race**.

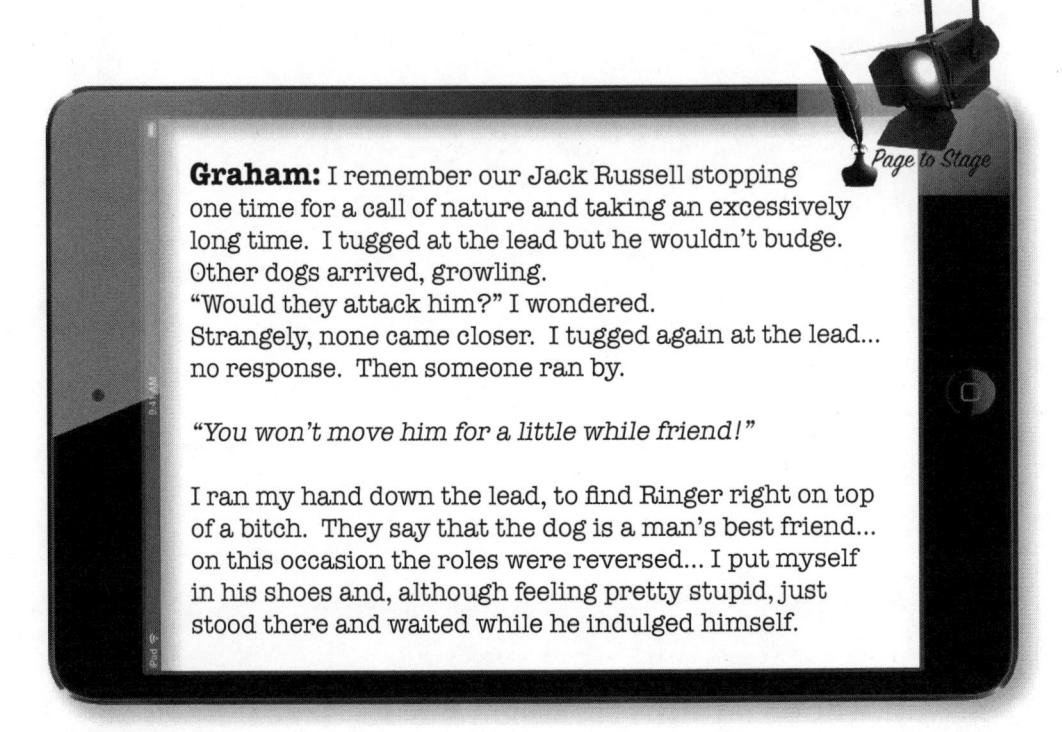

Graham: I remember our Jack Russell stopping one time for a call of nature and taking an excessively long time. I tugged at the lead but he wouldn't budge. Other dogs arrived, growling.
"Would they attack him?" I wondered.
Strangely, none came closer. I tugged again at the lead... no response. Then someone ran by.

"You won't move him for a little while friend!"

I ran my hand down the lead, to find Ringer right on top of a bitch. They say that the dog is a man's best friend... on this occasion the roles were reversed... I put myself in his shoes and, although feeling pretty stupid, just stood there and waited while he indulged himself.

VERBATIM - The Fun of Making Theatre Seriously by Mark Wheeller

When Epping Youth Theatre first did this in 1984, we simply had Graham saying the lines and gently demonstrating what he was saying with no dogs on stage. It was underplayed. It got a decent laugh so we were happy.

At Oaklands in 1987 I did much the same and Jason, who like Matthew was a strong performer, carried it off brilliantly.

When Tim Ford directed the EBYT version, he had the idea to have a boy and a girl playing the dog and bitch, gently acting the copulation as Graham narrated the story. This worked and gained a better reaction.

I decided this was what we would do but felt it would be difficult to impose on anyone, so asked for volunteers to experiment with the idea as we rehearsed it.

My son Charlie and Matt Griffiths came forward without any hesitation AT ALL!!! Both were confident with physical theatre. I asked them to decide who should be 'on top'. They made that decision. Matt was on top!

I asked them to go into a side room to figure out what they'd do with Michael (playing Graham) narrating the story to them. I was of the opinion that if it didn't work we could just go back to what I'd done before.

I should never have had any doubt!

I don't know the exact sequence of events but, after they'd shown us, Simon (playing me) said he thought it needed a bit more wellie!

He asked me to read the lines while he and Michael spontaneously acted it out (Simon on top) with a vigour no-one anticipated... least of all Michael!

Everyone was in stitches. It was repeated so that someone could video it. We described it as being X rated!

I knew this was the genesis of something... but we would have to tone it down a bit.

Charlie and Matt were absolutely 'up for it'!

Straight away they performed a far more 'vigorous' copulation scene.

This would get a huge laugh!

VERBATIM - The Fun of Making Theatre Seriously by Mark Wheeller

Then...

Simon, who was standing, watching said...

'I think you should add a very formal handshake at the end.'

We tried it and the idea added icing onto the already very tasty cake!

This process is typical of how we worked... one idea led to another with everyone open to an end point being different to what we originally imagined.

I always say it's important for me not to limit anyones ideas by setting a ceiling as to what we might achieve. Had I told them what to do, we would have ended up with far duller scene. I needed that imaginative, organic input and the cast needed the right atmosphere to inspire experimentation with no fear of failure. That's why I asked for volunteers for this simulation. Not everyone would be willing... but some would absolutely relish the opportunity and go for it!

We were awarded 84/100 and won the Festival!

We had now qualified for the FINAL of the All England Theatre Festival!!!

We could not believe it.

The photo that appeared in the paper failed to capture the rapturous atmosphere when we heard. There's a reason for that. It had been taken before the performance... just in case we won. Every group had one taken pretending to celebrate it was all a bit fake!

The Final was in Grays, Essex!

Oh my word!

What a place.

Totally grey!

The next time I heard about Grays would be in 2018 when commissioned to write **Game Over**, the tragic story of the murder of Breck Bednar. Grays was the location of his gruesome murder.

VERBATIM - The Fun of Making Theatre Seriously by Mark Wheeller

The Thameside Theatre was amazing and we were met with a big smile by John Scowen, who had adjudicated us back at the TDF. It was his home theatre.

The Totton Drama Festival crew were there to support us. This was the first time any group from Totton had reached the Final.

Marie Salmon was there too with her friends. She wouldn't have missed it for the world but it was something we realised she would watch with conflicting feelings.

Bernadette Chapman was also there, the first time she'd seen the play since being our singer at the Edinburgh Fringe with EYT back in 1984. Danny had sampled her singing and so, unbeknown to her, she would hear her voice in the pre-recorded soundtrack.

> I was honoured and shocked when you invited me along. I hadn't realised my voice was still a part of what was such a poignant part of my youth. A lovely surprise.
> Being involved with Race to be Seen and being a small part of Graham and Marie's life was a privilege.
> I met the cast back stage and Mark asked me to sing "the" song. I couldn't as I hadn't sung it for years. I wish I had now.
> I felt so humbled watching the performance... and so proud I had been a part of making it happen.
>
> **Bernadette Clere (née Chapman)** ♥

Other than our personal memories of this momentous day there is also a video recording that Barrie Sapsford (from the original EYT production in 1984) made to accompany the planned multi-camera DVD release he'd made of the play.

Inspired by my enjoyment of watching the VHS of the 1987 OYT production I decided, for the first time ever, to watch the Thameside DVD. I had watched the four-camera shoot. This proved to be so much better and I have included my Director's Commentary in the Appendix of this book which will give you some understanding of how we made this a metaphorical firework display of a show!

Race To Be Seen had become the joyous celebration I always it to be!

We didn't win the final but we really (honestly) weren't upset by this.

We had performed at the English Final and represented our region. That was enough!

However...

VERBATIM - The Fun of Making Theatre Seriously by Mark Wheeller

I remember a conversation soon afterwards where I said:

'It leaves us something to be won... and next time, I will want to!' And we did... although OYT had become Oasis[54] Youth Theatre by then...

Our next entry, **One Million to STOP THE TRAFFIK** won the AETF and qualified for the British Final.

We didn't win that... but again, we weren't fussed. Honestly. Getting there, representing England, and being treated so magnificently by the Scottish hosts provides a wonderful memory for us all.

Our next production also, remarkably, reached the English Final. This was a no words/physical theatre production of **Jack** based on Jack and the Beanstalk. We didn't qualify for the British Finals because of an outrageous judge. I did mind that![55]

It was an amazing hat-trick of OYT appearances in the AETF after years of not progressing. It just goes to prove... never give up!

The golden ticket had proved to be enunciation, along with an amazing adult backstage team who had gradually gathered around me. They, bringing their experience, shared my passion and determination to bring out the best in the young and supremely committed casts we were so fortunate to have... for free!

Along with the ongoing contribution of Danny Sturrock, another ex-OYT performer returned as an adult helper. Carley Sefton-Wilson, who amongst other things had been a tv producer, became my assistant. She was able to offer not only crucial, informed quality control for our work but also a level of admin I would never have been capable of in a world that was increasingly seeing this as necessary. Other adults seemed to gather around us. We eventually had our own photographer, costume and set designer(s)! These proved to be incredibly fruitful creative years.

---

[54] The Oasis Academy chain decided to keep OYT and supported it until I left in 2017. Sadly, despite my having a succession plan, Oasis allowed both youth theatre and curriculum drama to fade into oblivion. I never believed that could happen as quickly as it did but when the powers that be withdraw support, things can no longer flourish. I am so grateful for the support I received in my time at both Oaklands and Oasis!

[55] The adjudicator in question was a senior one... Scott Marshall. Following our performance, he asked the audience whether they had understood the play or not and to indicate this by raising their hands. The manner in which this was done was, we felt, belittling. We had courageously used few words to tell our physical theatre story. There may have been problems but, with an equally incomprehensible (to me) Shakespeare play, he didn't raise that question. We felt cheated! It DID matter! Both **Jack** and **Stop the Traffik** are available as streamed productions from SalamanderStreet.com so you can judge for yourselves!

VERBATIM - The Fun of Making Theatre Seriously by Mark Wheeller

This run of success served to energise the final years of my youth theatre career under the Oasis banner and consolidated the myth that seemed to be generating about the quality of my playwriting.

The cast of **Graham** achieved more than we could have hoped for at the start.

Half remained in OYT and the other half, including Mike, moved off to live the rest of their lives... but they certainly didn't disappear completely. Many remain in touch. When I asked Mike to write his memories of his involvement in **Graham**, I was not surprised but moved to read this, his final paragraph.

> I remember the feeling of group unity and the friendships born from OYT. I'm still in touch with many cast members, having been a best-man and brides-man at two of their weddings. It's safe to say many of my lasting friendships stem from OYT. My involvement in it continues to ripple positively through my life.
> **Michael Mears**

Following our appearance in the AETF Final two things happened to ensure it was seen by a wider audience.

1: Zinc re-editioned the shorter version of **Graham - World's Fastest Blind Runner.**

2: Edexcel approached me to write a scheme of work to support what was, then, a newly released GCSE specification in their official resource book.

This scheme is one I'm supremely proud of and have developed it to support the new **Race To Be Seen** script (Salamander Street 2021 edit) with additions by Tracy Dorrington (Drama Matters) to assist with something that didn't exist back then... ways of working when social distancing is in force! (Thank you Tracy)

These two factors led to more schools becoming aware of the play and of Graham and his key role in Paralympic history. This, in turn, generated wonderful productions and reactions from teachers, such as this:

> "I didn't ever need convincing that **Graham** was an ideal piece to challenge my group and that it ticked all the boxes for A' level work but, if I ever needed justification, then the results have certainly given it. In the breakdown of the Unit 2 marks i.e. the performance of 'Graham', all seven candidates were awarded 100%. It's worth noting that the external moderator was accompanied that evening by her senior examiner! Thanks again for the material and thanks to Graham, such an inspirational person!"
> **Mike Fleetwood** - Parkside Arts College

VERBATIM - The Fun of Making Theatre Seriously by Mark Wheeller

Race To Be Seen is a play, for me, that has everything.

It has challenge in the staging of scenes that once seemed all but impossible.

It has:

- a challenge, particularly for the performer playing Graham
- an incredibly interesting storyline for performer and audience alike
- drama
- a lot of humour (unusual for my plays)
- TRUTH!

The challenge for an actor to play Graham is an interesting one. I am only too aware of the move to be inclusive in casting. Within the small world of our school/youth theatre we never had the opportunity to cast someone who was blind. Had we have done, I would have jumped at the chance. It would have been preferable.

I am always keen to use appropriate outreach settings to offer relevant experience (not to mention motivation). In this instance it was to play football etc. with Graham or with visually impaired (young) people we arranged to meet in the course of our rehearsal period.

However, I am aware the role of Graham (and Pete etc) offer a fantastic opportunity for a sighted person to step into the shoes of someone who is visually impaired. You can see, from the accounts of the actors I cast to play this role, how they approached it with a level of commitment to finding their truth and took on all sorts of research. I have never known other roles in any of my plays which led to such experimentation. It offers a huge and invaluable opportunity.

My hope is that the play and Graham will offer increased opportunities to inspire many more people.

VERBATIM - The Fun of Making Theatre Seriously by Mark Wheeller

Chapter 15: Legacy and The Fun Of Being a Serious Playwright

"My obsession with authenticity, while it occasionally went overboard, was probably my greatest asset... a quality of relaxed intimacy with contributors, how they felt licensed to express themselves... something real, almost magical was taking place... but... what appeared untoward was to have achieved success with a programme that hinged on nothing I'd done."
Louis Theroux - *Gotta Get Theroux This.*

The pixie was standing good and proud at this point, wearing appropriate clothing and seeming to accept his place in this fairy tale world.[56]

When I'm asked: 'Why do you write verbatim plays?' My answer is to motivate my cast to perform truthfully. My verbatim plays <u>always</u> achieve this.

Truth is so important on stage.

Truth is so important in relationships either in the real world or in the world of school/youth theatre.

How can you explore a play about a real person without being truthful?

It's a prerequisite of the performance.

I had proved with **Hard to Swallow** that I could invent dialogue, albeit based on the outline of a situation in Maureen Dunbar's biography. This proved to me, at least, that I could actually write!

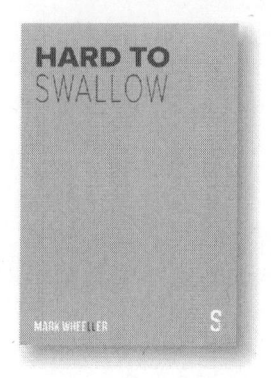

---

[56] Note to self. No more pixie analogies!

VERBATIM - The Fun of Making Theatre Seriously by Mark Wheeller

With **Chicken!** I went further. I had developed a story and turned it into a play with original dialogue.

With **Legal Weapon** I wrote dialogue and superimposed a fictional story on a factual car accident described verbatim.

Finally, with **Arson About** (later re-branded **Butcher, Butcher Burning Bright**), I had invented a structure, a storyline and dialogue I was completely satisfied with which proved commercially successful. It was published and toured professionally in UK schools extensively.

This said, when I reverted wholeheartedly to my verbatim roots with **Missing Dan Nolan** in 2002 I felt totally at home and fully in control of what I was doing… I didn't want help putting this together, like I had at the start of **Race**.

Nevertheless, somehow I still couldn't view it as a 'proper' play.

In 2008, as we completed our work on **Graham**, I applied to join a playwriting course at the Nuffield Theatre (Southampton) run by John Morley. I had never had any training and I felt this might help me become a better ("proper") playwright.

John couldn't understand why I wanted to enrol. He said I had created a niche for myself which was clearly (to him) proving successful.

I started the course with the best of intentions but didn't complete it.

I enjoyed it immensely at the start and was learning a lot.

VERBATIM - The Fun of Making Theatre Seriously by Mark Wheeller

In 2009, after having committed fully for an academic year, I withdrew. There were three main reasons for this.

- I was struggling with the increased pressure of my 0.8 teaching job in the new merger Academy where the workload was increasing.

- I was also struggling with a task we had been given to write: a 50 minute radio play. John was unimpressed by my efforts and I wasn't enjoying trying to please him when I wasn't sure what he wanted! I became frustrated and knew that around the corner was the task of writing a three act play!!![57]

The third reason is hugely significant as part of this story but somewhat faded into the background in the light of these more weighty reasons.

- One evening in John's course he gave us some source material from interviews and asked us to create a scene from this, using only those words.

Wow! This was a recognised way of writing a play and being a playwright?

My 'guilt' had been misplaced all these years.

In 2011 the feeling was lifted completely when the National Theatre presented **London Road** by Aleky Blythe and Adam Cork... a verbatim musical!

Suddenly, my work became part of a genre I didn't know existed... Verbatim Theatre.

It gave my work a new lease of life and consolidated my feeling of this being a 'proper' form of theatre.

From this point on, my output became almost exclusively verbatim and I benefited from the more interesting structural ideas I had been introduced to by John on his course.

Something else I started to do from this point on (after losing my self-consciousness following the success of the 2008 **Graham** production) was to include myself in some plays. This was inspired by London Road's uber-authentic use of er's and um's. I felt the inclusion of my questions and even, at times the relationship I had with the subjects, brought the authenticity of the original interview setting of the verbatim nature of my work to the forefront of those plays.

---

[57] I used the start of my radio play to write my immersive play **This Is For You** but did need help to complete it which I got from fellow course member Matt Beames, who, by coincidence, had played me in the EBYT (2000) production of **Race to Be Seen**!

VERBATIM - The Fun of Making Theatre Seriously by Mark Wheeller

London Road also inspired me to write a couple of lyrics which the composer/musical director at Oasis Youth Theatre Paul Ibbott set to music. He was equally enamoured by Adam Cork's setting of the verbatim material in the above-mentioned National Theatre musical.

We completed two (verbatim) songs, one of which appeared in the 25th anniversary production of **Too Much Punch For Judy**. You can hear it (sung beautifully by OYT's Kelly Lambert) on the promo for and in the DVD/Stream of OYT's 25th anniversary production.

Vi's Theme
Music by Paul Ibbott. Lyrics by Mark Wheeller using the words of Vi Poulton.

Be careful in the car. Just be careful!
They were the last words I said to her.
Be careful in the car. Just be careful!

She was beautiful,
To put her into words is impossible.
Everyone said... "Oh, ain't your Jo a lovely girl!"
She was beautiful.

Be careful in the car. Just be careful!
They were the last words I said to her.
Be careful in the car. Just be careful!

No way in the world do I blame you Judy.
I love you very, very much Judy...
I need you as much as you need me.

Be careful in the car. Just be careful!
They were the last words I said to her.
Be careful in the car. Just be careful!

The opportunity has not arisen so far but both Paul and I would love the opportunity to write a full scale verbatim musical at some point.

Meanwhile, I was being kept busy with a succession of increasingly exciting commissions.

My charmed life continued.

VERBATIM - The Fun of Making Theatre Seriously by Mark Wheeller

A Legacy Of Kindness *(co-written with Cate Hollis)*

I was commissioned along with Cate Hollis to write a (verbatim) play for the professional TIE company Voices of the Holocaust telling the story of Susan Pollack MBE, a Holocaust survivor.

I remember being somewhat overawed by the subject matter about which I knew no more than the basic headline information but Cate reassured me, saying that I could rely on her expertise… as indeed was the case.

Cate offered to run the interview for me but I was keen to take this on, saying something to the effect of: 'I need to ask all the naive questions as that is the position our audience will be in.' It was at this moment that I realised something I mentioned earlier in the book… I had never pre-researched the stories I told and from this point forward this became a conscious strategy.

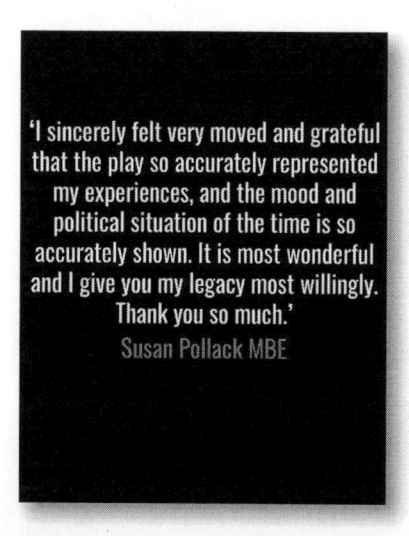

> 'I sincerely felt very moved and grateful that the play so accurately represented my experiences, and the mood and political situation of the time is so accurately shown. It is most wonderful and I give you my legacy most willingly. Thank you so much.'
> Susan Pollack MBE

KINDNESS: A LEGACY OF THE HOLOCAUST
A verbatim play based on the testimony of Holocaust survivor Susan Pollack MBE, with additional material by Cate Hollis and Voices of the Holocaust
Commissioned by Voices of the Holocaust
CATE HOLLIS AND MARK WHEELLER

As I listened to Susan, I remember thinking how history had been mis-sold to me in school as a dusty, academic subject. The Holocaust was simply a story… a horrific and appalling story but eminently readable… and, like other plays I'd worked on, told of people thrown into an exceptional situation. It had happened, actually happened to these real people. For the first time I regretted being put off history at school with its cloak of academia, making it appear distant and therefore not about real people like you and me.

The same can be said about theatre and playwriting. I hope this book serves to offer some demystification and encourages more people to have a go regardless of perceived "appropriate experience".

VERBATIM - The Fun of Making Theatre Seriously by Mark Wheeller

I used Susan's words exclusively to lay out her story, allocating some of them to others she referred to in her narrative.

I remember one structural idea I had (the exploration of structure was a key focus of John's playwriting course) was that gradually the other characters would disappear (as they tragically did) leaving Susan alone on stage delivering a monologue. This didn't happen in the final versions of the play but the idea of being gradually and heartbreakingly isolated from those she loved is something I ask directors to consider when staging the play.

Chequered Flags to Chequered Futures, **Scratching The Surface** and the full version of *I Love You, Mum - I Promise I Won't Die* played with the chronology of events.

Photographs from the Samuel Ward Academy Production of Chequered Flags to Chequered Futures.

VERBATIM - The Fun of Making Theatre Seriously by Mark Wheeller

In *Chequered*:

- The first scene is Chris's story from his schooldays.
- The second is Jane's story from the day of (her daughter) Shelley's tragic car accident.
- The scenes continue, alternating between Chris's and Jane's story until the moment Chris gets in Shelly's car and the two stories merge.

Scratching the Surface:

The structure merges the central story of a self-harmer with a school drama group talking about their experiences of self-harm. The fluid movement between the two separate stories present wonderful opportunities for a director to stage this play.

Production photos from Alderbrook School's premiere of Scratching The Surface

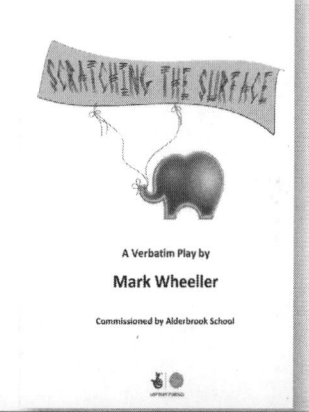

I Love You, Mum - I Promise I Won't Die.

Act 1: Tells the story of Daniel Spargo-Mabbs' tragic death following an ecstasy overdose from the perspective of his friends. It begins with them meeting him at school and ends with the aftermath of his death.

Act 2: Tells the same story from the perspective of his family and his girlfriend's family. It starts with the sentencing of Daniel's supplier and moves backwards from his funeral to the moment of his passing, saying goodbye to his parents and girlfriend as he leaves for his night out and then back to memories of him as a teenager and child. Our production ended with video footage of Daniel as a baby.

VERBATIM - The Fun of Making Theatre Seriously by Mark Wheeller

John, as he enrolled me on his course, said he wanted to give me a 'voice'. I'm not sure he achieved that but I would never have had these structural ideas had I not participated in the course. I felt bad about dropping out but want him to know how useful it was, not only regarding this but also in giving me confidence and self-respect as a writer rather than someone who simply used other people's words.

OYT's production of I Love You, Mum - I Promise I Won't Die.

Now I believe the way I work has an 'artistry' to it and the layer of structure produces special work I am proud to have created.

These structures make each of these (end of career) plays, in my opinion, more interesting to watch/study than the more simplistic "start at the beginning and more forward sequentially to the end" manner in which my pre-2009 plays were generally written.

VERBATIM - The Fun of Making Theatre Seriously by Mark Wheeller

My final (thus far) verbatim plays have more interesting structures than the early version of **Race** and others I wrote in the '80s and early '90s. Two more followed:

Can You Hear Me Major Tom?

Tells the story of David Bowie's career and unexpected death from the emotional distance of six fans (one of them me) and one person who worked with him. Their stories, like **Scratching**, run from one to another but are held together by the chronology of David's career and passing. The challenge to pull them together is in the director's hands and when I directed it with RSCoYT we enjoyed the considerable challenge.

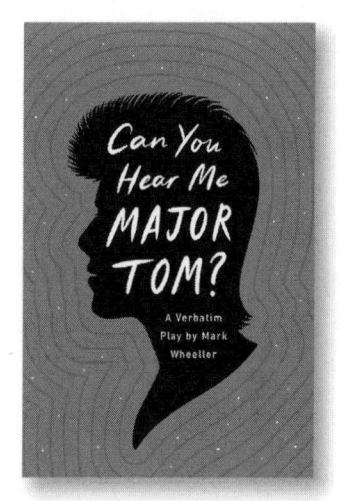

The standing ovation at the end of the production with Bowie fans from all over the country watching was a superb and unexpected reward. It rates as one of the most fulfilling and exhilarating reactions I've experienced at one of my performances. A huge regret is that we didn't record it on DVD because I wasn't confident enough to invest in hiring a videographer to film the production. A Bowie fan took a photograph that captures the cast on stage, not knowing where to put themselves, as the ovation wouldn't stop.

This is a play where any performing group can have the opportunity to capture this reaction... just invite passionate Bowie fans. I assure you, they will always be the same. Even better, tie it in with a significant Bowie date... go on... have a look at the play and test out my theory!

VERBATIM - The Fun of Making Theatre Seriously by Mark Wheeller

Game Over

This commission offered me a perfect opportunity to meaningfully expel some of my ghosts from Lincoln using the contemporary story of Breck Bednar's grooming and horrendous murder.

The chronological structure is fairly simple but the experimental idea I used arrived in my mind from the moment Breck's mum Lorin said:

I didn't feel whole, missing parts and I can't function properly. Torn apart.

Immediately I had the idea of dividing her role into five.
This had the advantage of:

1. Her being able to talk/fight with herself

2. Illustrating how Breck might have felt (and certainly how LD, Breck's murderer, perceived her to be), surrounding him with her opinions, love and frustration

3. Preventing one character from hogging the stage with long monologues that may lack movement.

Lorin and the five girls portraying her in Beaumont School's premiere of Game Over.

VERBATIM - The Fun of Making Theatre Seriously by Mark Wheeller

I made Lorin (without a number) the original Lorin from her time with Breck, prior to LD tearing her world apart. With LD's arrival in her world the other Lorins appear, becoming increasingly concerned, even paranoid about the situation. The number allocated to the character increases and indicates the level of anxiety Lorin faces.

Once again, this offers the director/ensemble of/in this play opportunities for magical creativity and interpretation.

Zoom Productions/Socially Distanced Performances

These plays, because of the original interview setting, have proved to be a perfect vehicle for Zoom productions or socially distanced performances. This development, like so much of what has happened with my plays, was totally unintended but they are now perceived to be perfect for this purpose and directors and school students are bringing much invention to the table.

As I am involved in developing this more recent work I am often reminded of how it all began with ***Race***.

The elements I loved about that remain in all of these plays:

- The true story inspired talented young people to offer their time to each phase of the work.

- The opportunity to lead a group who care so deeply about the work we undertake to develop a fulfilling and memorable performance.

- Many moments of discovery when we surprise ourselves with a way of presenting something that, at the start of the process, we feared may not even be possible.

- The relationships with the real people who are the subject of each play and are then in the room watching us in rehearsal. I have never found a more effective way of motivating people to perform to the best of their ability... and often beyond!

- Becoming the focus of the school, community and sometimes well beyond that, as the performances start.

VERBATIM - The Fun of Making Theatre Seriously by Mark Wheeller

- The 4-dimensional experience for everyone of having the real people in the audience to watch them. Nothing surpasses the unique experience of watching the subjects of my plays reacting to their story on stage.

- The plays taking off in their own way and seeing the different ways they can be interpreted, particularly by those who weren't able to see the original production.

- Finally, the continuing and sometimes lifelong relationships that develop between the real people and the production team.

Some of our cast from **Race** back in 1984 still remain in contact with Marie.

I keep in touch with many involved in my productions while Marie and Graham became lifelong friends. Many attended my memorable retirement from teaching 'bash'. As I looked around the venue I saw ex-YT members from each era of my career, sitting together and laughing. They all knew each other because they had their youth theatre experience in common. Most knew one another well because they had met up at various productions over the years - in the case of one, Dave Nurse, for a period of nearly 40 years and almost every production!

Dave back in the early 90's bonding with Graham as he had a go at guide running.

They became a new sub-group of my youth theatre life and their loyalty to both myself and our work is still treasured. One of them has designed this book and a previous one... such commitment beyond the call of YT volunteering duty! These relationships were authentic from the outset.

The morning after my retirement from teaching party. Some of those who straddle the years from 1979-2016, Shiny Hussain, Dave Nurse & Mark Eagle.

VERBATIM - The Fun of Making Theatre Seriously by Mark Wheeller

Fiona Spargo-Mabbs (mother of Daniel) jokes that I have used playwriting as my way of making friends... she may have a point. Most of my long-lasting friends are either subjects or former cast members of my (often verbatim) plays!

I have been delighted to witness in more recent productions, the friendships struck up in the virtual world between cast and subjects. In *I Love You, Mum - I Promise I Won't Die*, I remember our cast 'friending' on Facebook and then organising actual rendezvous with Dan's friends.

After the production of **Game Over** (which wasn't performed by my own Youth Theatre group) I watched the real Carley and Chloe having their photos taken with those who played them and then becoming Insta (or whatever it was... snapchat?) followers of each other. Delightful!

My involvement in Verbatim Theatre scaffolded my confidence as a writer. The pre-existing story gave a natural shape to the play. That extended to the lines. I knew they were right because they were what the person remembered.

I always cite the line Maud says when she is told her 18-month-old toddler has to lose his second eye. As a writer, what do you put that doesn't seem too cheesy?

What Maud said was perfect... because it was correct.

'Couldn't we give him one of our eyes?'

No one can argue with this.

These lines gave me confidence to write.

Mark and Maud at Marie's 60th birthday party.

VERBATIM - The Fun of Making Theatre Seriously by Mark Wheeller

Luke Abbott, my Head of Drama and curriculum mentor at Stantonbury, talked about 'protecting students into role'. He would use strategies to make taking on a role more gentle and therefore easier for his students.

Verbatim theatre protected me into writing and, if it can do this for me, with a CSE grade 2 in English Literature (equivalent to a GCSE grade D), it can do so for someone who has the interest and commitment to read this book... and well done for getting this far... we're nearly at the end...

This idea of protecting people into action has got me thinking.

In 1982, Dorothy Heathcote (Luke's mentor), explained how she created moments of "theatre" with young people – without asking or expecting them to do this in the same way as trained actors:

> *"... my particular skill as a teacher has always been to make good theatre with children who may not have any knowledge of theatre skills at all and I do it by a process of taking their minds off themselves and not expecting them to be actors or behave like actors, but to create such significance out of something else that it turns into theatre. Paradoxically, I do the very opposite that the actor does - I take the children's minds off themselves so they behave significantly."*
>
> From ***Dancing with a Whirl Wind***, Dorothy Heathcote's interview with Tony Goode, in: ***Heathcote at the National, NATD publications, 1983***.

This way of thinking was so embedded in my practice, from my time at Stantonbury, that I now realise this was also how my youth theatre practice was developed.

In another article she talks about protecting students from 'being stared at...'

VERBATIM - The Fun of Making Theatre Seriously by Mark Wheeller

> *"The actor in the theatre has made a contract to allow people to stare at them, but children have not made that contract. Teachers of drama who take for granted the children have given them this permission, spend useless time eroding the embarrassment which happens during drama lessons where children feel stared at. The obvious way of avoiding this is to give them something so attractive in the room, that they feel they are staring at it. The teacher protects individual privacy, always.*
> *This should operate no matter what you're doing.*
>
> *Dorothy Heathcote* - From Video Series D: ***Teacher intervention and strategies in the four levels of drama progression.*** Dorothy Heathcote Archive, Birmingham City University; except from "***Signs (and Portents?)***, SYCPT Journal 9 (April 1982).

The focus in my productions was on the story/person we were telling rather than how good we were (or weren't). It shifted the perspective of both cast member and audience. People said to me how professional my youth theatre casts were. I was often asked how we did it. I never had a definitive answer but, reading this, perhaps I do now. We simply focused on the stories we told, rather than ourselves. In this way we lost the self-consciousness that befalls poor student theatre.

It also relieved me from having to be good at control. The play rather than the teacher becomes the controller. For example, in **Race**, we had to present a 400-metre race. That became the control. It had to be staged. I often wasn't in the room for a rehearsal of a specific scene. I was never the controller. The interest in what we were staging was my control mechanism as was the content of my drama lessons in school. I rarely had discipline problems. There was nothing magical about this. It was genuine interest in what we were trying to accomplish and a group commitment to complete the task. This was the control... not me!

Verbatim Theatre had many significant benefits for me... a failed rock star.

It has, over a sustained period of time, allowed me to feel successful at something. This doesn't always mean it has been easy and I hope this book makes that clear.

VERBATIM - The Fun of Making Theatre Seriously by Mark Wheeller

It also made some additional spending money... not a massive amount but more than I expected... and although, this was never originally a motive in itself it was always welcome. Money making is an attractive motivator for young people and one I am happy to refer to but they should also be aware that there are never any guarantees of this happening. More often than not I see playwrites on Facebook etc. bemoaning that their work is never noticed... which brings me to my advice to budding playwrights.

Get your work performed and reviewed.

Plays aren't to be read in isolation. I generally refuse to do this... but I will go to see a production... that's what theatre is about, whether it's verbatim or anything else!

Try to make your play interesting... not only in content but in the way you perform it.

I co-wrote **This Is For You** with local playwright Matt Beames. It's one of my few predominantly naturalistic plays. It tells the story of a teenage love affair resulting in an unplanned baby back in the 1970s. The father of the baby didn't know of the baby's existence til many years later.

When he dies and, after a large amount of money is left to his ex-girlfriend, the previously unknown story tumbles out. It is a really tender play but could, I feared, be a little static as much was set in a cafe... more like the radio play it was originally intended to be.

To make it more interesting (and it really worked) we turned our drama studio into a cafe. The audience came in, sat at tables and the performance happened all around them, sometimes at their table! It made the production very special. You can see the whole thing on YouTube and see how this immersive production works. It was a simple idea that made a wonderful production even more so... and it became such a talking point.

As you will know, originally I wanted to be a rock star and then tried to write hit musicals... neither of these attempts were particularly successful. The 'hits' I have had were never really intended to be. Nothing could be planned meticulously but I realise, looking back, they were very much, the result of determination, persistence and solid hard work.

VERBATIM - The Fun of Making Theatre Seriously by Mark Wheeller

Who would have thought my youth theatre productions could ever be selected by exam boards as their set texts? The timing of the first two was perfect... just as I retired from teaching!

Consequently, my plays have offered me a second career as a playwright/workshop leader in schools here and abroad. This has afforded me travel to far flung places I may never have visited: New Zealand, Dubai and Hong Kong to name but three.

OYT's immersive production of This Is For You with the audience clearly visible around the cast.

In these visits and in more recent Zoom sessions I've been interviewed for real. These are not so different from those I did alone in my garden when I was much younger. They're not about my favourite goal but about my favourite play or favourite scene I wrote or directed. I love doing these and am flattered by the continued interest in my work!

I appreciate my good fortune and the wonderful people, young and a bit older, whom I have had the chance to work alongside.

VERBATIM - The Fun of Making Theatre Seriously by Mark Wheeller

It was always important for me to leave a written legacy. I remember thinking this in my schooldays as I filled exercise books with stories and manuscript books with songs. I was always in awe of anyone who had achieved this.

A few years ago I went to the National Theatre to see a Verbatim Theatre play about Brexit. 48% of the words were anti and 52% pro-Brexit. What a great idea! I was excited to see the production and paid good money to do so. As I walked in I saw stools dotted around the stage and my heart sank. I thought... are they going to move? They did, but hardly at all. It was two hours of talking heads. They had ignored the theatre part of Verbatim Theatre... yet these were top professionals. In all our 'amateur' productions we worked relentlessly to avoid delivering lines from a fixed position and to present Verbatim Theatre... theatrically.

Verbatim theatre has allowed me to leave a legacy I am proud of. I'm thrilled that the bulk of my back catalogue (not to mention this book) has been taken on from 2020 by Salamander Street, a specialist theatre publisher.
I'm tempted to make a pixie reference here... but will resist.

As I often say to the young people I work with:

I engaged in my youth theatre work for the fun of making theatre seriously.

In the final analysis...

...Verbatim Theatre made it a bit more serious...

...but a lot more fun!

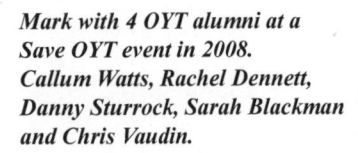

Mark with 4 OYT alumni at a Save OYT event in 2008. Callum Watts, Rachel Dennett, Danny Sturrock, Sarah Blackman and Chris Vaudin.

VERBATIM - The Fun of Making Theatre Seriously by Mark Wheeller

Afterword: Race To Be Seen (2021 edit)

"I'm not dead yet!"
Monty Python And The Holy Grail

It amuses me to hear that some students exploring my plays are shocked to discover I'm still alive.

That said... over the last year everything I seem to be doing regarding Wheellerplays seems to be putting things in order before my death...not that I have any plans for that.

This has happened as a result of a number of things colliding.

Firstly COVID 19 came along and teachers needed online resources, so I decided to film my recollections of my Wheellerplays story on YouTube (and create a Mark Wheeller Channel with accessible, well organised playlists). The success of that (over 100 episodes) led to a suggestion that I should do something similar with respect to my songs which I started in the 2021 lockdown. These leave well documented accounts of literally everything I have done creatively throughout my life.... perhaps too much!

In the early weeks of Covid, and as a direct result of it, my then publisher Zinc, unexpectedly (and very suddenly) closed their play publishing arm. I wasn't sure what would happen to my plays. It looked like most might become a weird casualty of Covid-19.

Salamander Street stepped in, literally days after Zinc announced their closure, bringing forward their projected launch (which I was never previously a feature of) by a few months to ensure schools could access my plays easily, particularly as e-books, in a time when teachers were under a lot of extra pressure.

VERBATIM - The Fun of Making Theatre Seriously by Mark Wheeller

Salamander Street also offered to take on most of my back catalogue over time... and publish this book. It was an unexpected and welcome intervention and one that led me to undertake updates and revisions to almost all of my plays and musicals.

A tour of my *I Love You, Mum - I Promise I Won't Die* play was postponed (due to COVID) and eventually cancelled. Fiona Spargo-Mabbs had the amazing idea to use the funding for the tour to create a 'virtual performance'. Tie It Up Theatre Company (who have been touring a fantastic production of **Hard To Swallow**) boldly stepped up to the challenge of this in these incredible times, and created a beautiful high-end studio version of the play which will, I am sure, become the go-to film of this production.

Tie It Up filming the virtual production of I Love You Mum I Promise I Won't Die

Amy Balmforth as Catherine in Tie It Up's streamed production of Hard To Swallow

The success of this led to a similar 'virtual' production of **Hard To Swallow**. These two films will show exemplar versions of the way in which my verbatim scripts can be performed with maximum impact and ability to engage a young (indeed any) audience. I am so fortunate to have professionals of the quality of Tie It Up[58] continuing to support my playwriting.

This book, which was originally intended to be an exploration of my first playwriting venture, morphed into a Verbatim demystification exercise and involved me in even more looking back. I've enjoyed it but it has made 2020-2021 seem to me as though I'm preparing for death.

---

[58] Particular thanks to Elliot Montgomery and David Chafer who have been the super-friendly power-houses behind the amazing Tie It Up Theatre Company team.

VERBATIM - The Fun of Making Theatre Seriously by Mark Wheeller

Thankfully, I am also engaged in developing two new commissions over the next few months of 2021. One of these is a musical. I am finally returning to my musical roots. Too late to be a rock star? So, I can confirm at the time or writing... I'm very much alive!

One of the plays to update... one of the most important in my view... has been **Race To Be Seen** - yes, I've reverted to the original title. It has benefitted from my study of it in this book. As I watched the various productions I noted moments that worked or didn't to ensure the 2021 edit included everything that makes it my favourite Wheellerplay. I was not restricted in this version to a particular time limit but also know very well what did and didn't work over the various versions.

I hope that the new 2021 edit of **Race To Be Seen** is the definitive edit and will never need to be updated again.

Race To Be Seen has bookended my career and this version will benefit from the enthusiasm of youth and the experience of age. It has been produced at all times with much love and much deference to a true hero. I know my storybook man would be excited to see it being upgraded. It is important to me that, alongside my work, Graham's story lives on and he is recognised as the inspiration and influence he was.

Graham showing Mark his European Championships Gold Medal in 1984. Happy times.

259

Appendix 1: School Report - from my Head of House 50 years on

I first came to know Mark Wheeller in about September 1975.

He was a pupil and I had become a Head of House, a Pastoral role, in the recently opened Marlwood School, Alveston. On the first day in my new appointment, Mark came to my office to introduce himself as the House Captain, having been elected prior to my appointment. I had been aware of him up to that point but had no knowledge of him beyond the fact that his father occasionally gave my wife a lift to the School where they both worked.

It was common then for House Captains to have made a name for themselves on account of their sporting prowess. But this was not a notable feature of Mark's achievements. There was something else lurking in the background – an aspect of his life that was to emerge shortly.

Mark's personality had something just a bit different, but it was not to be a drive for academic success. So, sport = not really, academia = not a lot of that either! Crikey, I thought, what have I let myself in for?!

The truth was soon to emerge, and it was quite a surprising reveal. Mark's drive was for drama, the musical variety, a passion which hitherto had lain under-employed because the school had no proper drama teacher – only an elderly (but a very nice) lady who loved classical music, so taught that (sort of) even though she was actually a nurse!

Mark's enthusiasm, his passion for House productions was so well established that it continued after he left the school. I use the word 'era' for his output was to impact on the lives of many other pupils and other aspects of school life in ways that could never have been imagined.

Mark showed a precocious talent for embellishing simple scripts with catchy music and lyrics – a feature of his output that has brought great success in his mature and adult years. The plots, now with their key messages, e.g. **Too Much Punch for Judy** have doubtless matured with greater complexity, but the popular appeal has been retained.

The Marlwood School, 'Harwood House' programme evolved rapidly and came to embrace a Christmas Pantomime, an Easter Musical, and a Summer term

VERBATIM - The Fun of Making Theatre Seriously by Mark Wheeller

'Strawberries and Wine' musical event – all of the entertainment carefully crafted by Mark to suit the performers and also the occasion. The pupils were involved in picking the strawberries the day before, and some of them made it to the evening's refreshment the next day!

The key to his great success as a social leader at school was his infectious enthusiasm which ensured always a queue for active participation and a full house on performance nights. He was a popular leader and lent his enthusiasm to all aspects of House functions. I recall saying to Mark when he first came to negotiate the possibility of doing a pantomime:

'If it is to be done, then it has to be done properly, and well.'

There was never any fear of a failure in that respect. There was always a thorough and criterion-related expectation of his work, which involved many hours outside of normal school work. His momentum fed into the ensuing success for the new, young drama teacher who took on her role as Mark's time in the sixth form neared its end.

We have remained in good contact in the many years since. I have admired his substantial professional output, his ambition for those he is teaching, both pupils and colleagues on INSET days, and the drive and love of life he still exudes. He has been a friend whose life I am proud to have observed.

David Goldring (Head of Harwood House - Marlwood School, Alveston Bristol in the era of Mark's sixth form)

Appendix 2:
Magic Moments by Johnny Carrington.

When I started Oaklands Community School as a newly qualified teacher (or baby teacher as Mark would call all newbies), I joined with two roles. Half my timetable was teaching humanities (I did my PGCE in history) and half teaching lower school drama (my second subject was drama). Moreover, I came into Oaklands with what I would now call a traditional background in theatre. However, following an inspirational trip to the NSDF with our school (now, unfortunately, a festival that prohibits school children from attending), I moved to full time drama teaching.

I had been a member of Maskers Theatre Company since being knee-high to a grasshopper, and my experience had very much been, for want of a better term, 'normal plays'; although I had taken part in some spectacular large scale outdoor shows, most of my experience inside a theatre had been traditional. So, when I came to Oaklands, I experienced verbatim theatre for the first time.

When Mark first told me about the story of a boy called Daniel Nolan from Hamble who went missing and how he was writing a play about the circumstances behind his disappearance, I was intrigued by the process… and the emotional connection. Here were real people, talking about real events… something I hadn't encountered before in theatre. Mark wrote the play over the summer holidays. I came in, watched a few rehearsals, gave feedback occasionally[59] and witnessed the show evolve. When it was first performed, there was still no evidence that Dan was deceased, and the play helped raise awareness and contributed in pushing the police to re-designate their investigation into his disappearance.

There were even plain clothes detectives in the audience for that first performance, looking out for potential suspects. But for me, the most emotional moment of the evening was watching the Nolan family, who came to see the play, watching 'themselves'; particularly Dan's mum, Pauline, watching someone playing her son. Although this must have been traumatic, Pauline was adamant that this play be shown and fully supported it. Not only at first when still trying to find Dan but also, tragically, after it was established he was dead. The play had full support from the Nolans and was being used to raise awareness about the issues raised from the story.

---

[59] As I read this I realise what a large part Johnny's feedback played in my OYT output. In all productions subsequent to this, he would come at a late point in rehearsals to provide an expert outside eye to help us improve our work and to offer a reason for reaching performance standard well before the actual performance. I would offer the same "service" for him and both of us for Danny Sturrock. It was part of our excellent teamwork which I remain very proud of.

VERBATIM - The Fun of Making Theatre Seriously by Mark Wheeller

Over the years I have been privileged to witness many similar touching moments from Mark's work. Never intrusive, almost therapeutic. I have only ever heard positive remarks from people who have been kind enough to volunteer their testimonies; their stories often helping to raise awareness and hopefully preventing some tragedies from happening again.

Watching Mark's work inspired me to write plays myself. At first, fictional, but I always felt I was just waiting for the right subject to come along. When Mark and I decided to work on a project together, we approached the Maskers Theatre Company to see if they would commission a play. With us living in Southampton, I suggested writing something about the Spitfire (it was designed and first flew from here in 1936), thereby giving a local connection to the work (it was originally a play with music, with Mark writing the lyrics and our Head of Performing Arts, Paul Ibbott, writing the music). Thankfully, The Maskers agreed; being a pilot myself, Mark often remarked that I was 'born to write it'.

Alex Chalk as Bob Doe

It certainly was a labour of love. Travelling over the country and interviewing Battle of Britain pilots, ground-crew, women who worked at the Supermarine factory and a lady who, as a young girl, witnessed the first flight and, not to mention, the son of RJ Mitchell (the designer), Gordon. I felt honoured to hear their stories, but also a sense of responsibility to write their tales in a sensitive but honest manner. This was more than a play about a machine, it was a tribute to the men and women, across all walks of life, who were inspired by this national icon to acts of great bravery.

VERBATIM - The Fun of Making Theatre Seriously by Mark Wheeller

And soon I had my own 'moment'… well, actually three. Watching Pat Viney watching herself as we re-enacted her witnessing the first flight of the Spitfire, talking to the Mitchell family (RJ's grandchildren) after that same performance and watching Alex Chalk reciting the Battle of Britain ace Bob Doe's moving words about the Spitfire, whilst touching… a Spitfire. This is a project that I have very fond memories of and a sense of pride at recreating these stories for future generations, and none more so than when it was published in July 2020.

Without the encouragement from Mark and witnessing first-hand the very special moments that can be created using verbatim theatre, this would never have happened. I would like to think that I have brought to my work the truth and honesty that is so abundant in Mark's. It is this combination that I feel, is needed above all else for verbatim theatre to create those magic theatrical moments… moments that enhance and 'celebrate' the stories they represent.

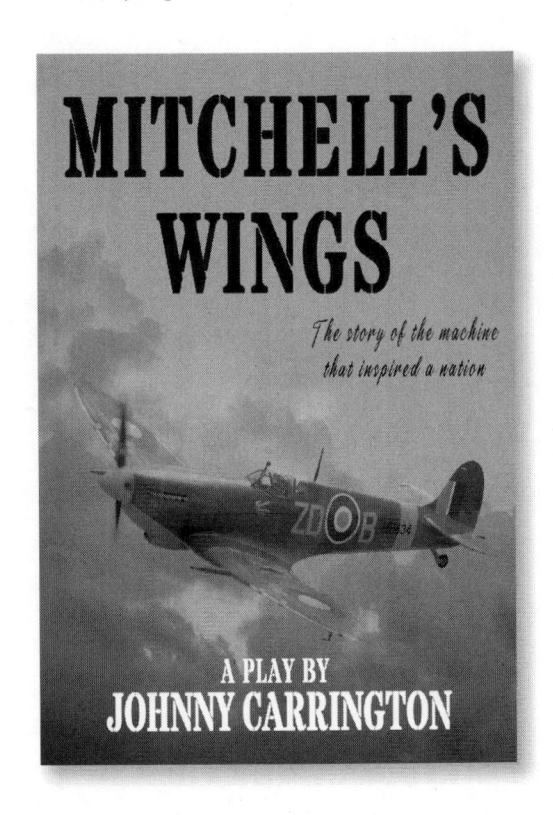

VERBATIM - The Fun of Making Theatre Seriously by Mark Wheeller

Appendix 3: Director's Commentary
Race To Be Seen 1984 Epping Youth Theatre (VHS)

I hadn't planned to watch this but after having been so thorough watching the others, I decided I must. I have had this VHS since it was filmed in 1984 but, to be honest, have never watched it. It came as something of a relief that it was very good and much better than I remembered, particularly the final 400 metres race.

Frustratingly the video of this production was made as a last minute effort with a hurriedly put together cast on the basis of availability. Some were not available.

We had a stand-in actor playing Susan and two stand-in singers who only performed for this performance and one bonus touring production organised as a result of the Edinburgh Fringe. I was incredibly surprised to witness myself stepping up to sing one of my songs! I say performance... this VHS was a private dress rehearsal for the bonus production.

The Set (such as it was!)
The most striking thing I noticed as I watched this performance was the lack of care and effort about the setting (my laziness). We were performing in our school Drama Studio and behind the actors is a noticeboard still displaying various notices. There is nothing on stage other than the actors and a simple portable screen onto which the slides were projected.

The vast number of photographs available for this production were used to complement it and attract the audience's interest in a time where multi-media wasn't really a thing. For example, the image of Graham on his tricycle caused a huge guffaw of laughter.

I am fascinated by how slides highlighting the real people somehow make the audience engage with the actor more closely. They add to 'belief' in the stage action.
The reality of the slides seem to make the stage fiction more real!

Complex... contradictory maybe, but, psychologically ***very*** interesting!

VERBATIM - The Fun of Making Theatre Seriously by Mark Wheeller

The stage is literally a black space. That would change in every production I did after this!

Despite it being a different script from the one now available, these notes will prove useful to anyone studying and/or performing any of my plays just to see little ideas as to how we did things.

Blackouts

This production had a blackout between every scene because, at this point, I thought that was a rule! Later, when presenting ***Chunnel of Love*** at the ***NSDF (National Student Drama Festival)*** we (OYT) were absolutely slated for our scene change blackouts.

They said that every time there was a blackout we allowed the audience to switch back into their own world and we had to work hard to re-gain their interest. From that point on my productions became fluid and never had blackouts. This offered an additional benefit of forcing creativity to make a transition between every scene or section.

Diction

Interesting to note that the diction of some of the performers was not so good, something that if you have read the book you will know I worked hard on in the early 2000s (but not until then despite it being picked up by numerous reviewers, adjudicators, etc.). Oasis Youth Theatre and RSCoYT members will remember me calling out "t"s whenever someone didn't pronounce a 't'!

Opening Moments

It was striking to notice that I had written a very low key downbeat song as the opening number. The songs were, I remember, an attempt of mine to copy the the folky style used in Roy Nevitt's documentary plays.

In my next production 'Too Much Punch For Judy' I would learn that the audience needs to be grabbed by a lively upbeat opening. This downbeat song gave the cast an uphill struggle from the off as the opening scenes in this earliest version of ***Race*** are the equally downbeat scenes where Maud and Harry are coming to terms with the problems associated with their baby Graham. I would not have been able to diagnose this issue back then. I don't remember anyone else commenting on it either.

All later versions begin with a more animated opening to draw the audience in. In the 1987 version it was nothing to do with me. Clearly, Brian Price who wrote the opening number for that show, knew about grabbing the audience from the start!

VERBATIM - The Fun of Making Theatre Seriously by Mark Wheeller

Maud & Harry Scenes

The opening scene showed Maud & Harry deliver their speeches unsupported by anyone/anything. The performers were exposed and there was little atmosphere. Again, I'm glad that now I would do something to support them with ensemble performers (as Tim did in 2000 and as I did in all other productions I put on) or underscored music... or something!

My focus, at this point, was very much on the spoken word (which I believe has always been a considerable strength of my productions). The delivery of certain lines was outstanding. I insisted that cast members said them as though they were their own words. Nick (Jones), playing Harry offered a great example of this:

    Harry: At 3:30 we had to leave.

The line is underpinned with a good deal of frustration. It was never just a line to be regurgitated. After about 5 minutes of Maud and Harry speaking out to the audience there was a different stage picture, albeit with the same two characters. Maud is sitting down, Harry is standing.

    Maud: Couldn't we give him one of our eyes?

Maud's (beautiful) line came out of the shadows on stage... effectively from nowhere when the focus had been entirely on Harry at the front of stage in conversation, alone with the consultant. It was as though humanity suddenly shone through the awful "bad news" scene.

Nice injection of 'quicker' vocal delivery pace...

Harry:	Were we being selfish keeping him alive?
Maud:	Would all this pain and suffering affect him?
Harry:	Our heads were, like, bursting with questions:
Maud:	What'll happen when he's an adult?
Harry:	Will he make friends?
Maud:	Will he find a wife, a job?
Harry:	And how will we cope?
Maud:	We'd never met a blind person before...
Harry:	... yet Graham was to be our responsibility.
Maud:	Little did we know how proud we'd become of our Graham.

At the end of this section the pace was slowed again. It showed that an injection of pace, when done with clear intention, is just as effective as a changing stage picture.

Graham

When Matthew (Graham) appeared on stage there was an instantly warm relaxed atmosphere surrounding his performance which seemed to spread to the cast! The performance lifted from this point onwards.

Schooldays Scenes

The introduction to the RE lesson scene (which I have returned to the 2021 edit) was presented interestingly. The class enters in a regimented manner attached from arm to shoulder. This was further highlighted by the teacher clapping a regular rhythm to control the speed of their footsteps. As they arrived the teacher issued two faster claps to indicate a desk opening routine. This swiftly established a regimented school of this era with excellent visual interest.

The military nature of the (Linden) Headteacher was established by Jeremy Turner by use of accent and a super-aggressive persona. He achieved a guffaw of laughter from his delivery of the 'stupid songs' line.

Great introduction from Matt (Graham) to establish athletics at Linden Lodge School. As Bill (his PE teacher) narrates, Graham removes his track suit top revealing England athletics shirt. He also established his athleticism by doing a leap-frog over a fellow actor contextualising the scene.

The scene where sports activities are described at Linden was thoughtfully set with the ensemble all participating in warm-up activities.

The scene where Pete Young talks about Marie fancying Graham- was staged wonderfully with him and Graham both engaged in an arm wrestle. Nice setting for the words. Pete wins at the very moment Graham gives in and agrees to ask Marie out.

When he went to talk to her in the dormitory, he used the sound of the zipper on his track suit to alert her to his presence.

Graham unpacked his white stick to exit, only to be called back by the Worcester teacher to talk about his commitment to school. Nice idea to offer the stage exit as the motive symbolising the real one.

Graham's **King Of The College** song without the shoobe-doo-wah's lacked excitement but the staging of the scene with Graham and the ensemble telling the story worked brilliantly. Having seen the other productions the missing shoo-be-doo-wah's were a significant loss.

VERBATIM - The Fun of Making Theatre Seriously by Mark Wheeller

The Sporting Sections

There is an elongated scene in this original script communicating the aims of the Metro Sports and Social Club. It is pure information giving. To offer visual interest, the stage is set up as though Graham is in a gym using the ensemble as different pieces of equipment. It's a great example of making the best use of virtually nothing... not to mention contextualising dry material.

The tannoy announcements are amusingly done with people holding their fingers over their nose and cupping their mouths to amplify their voices.

The choral repetition of the word 'ninth' in the Bulgaria 100m record underscored Graham's concern that he might not do well at this European Championships. It was an effective use of voice.

Interesting to see how I wasn't yet aware of using tableaux to illustrate this section:

Roger:	The sun was blazing down on Varna Stadium.
Marie:	Graham and Roger climbed to the back of the stands to find some shade.
Roger:	We talked about friends at home...
Mark:	Mark and the Epping Youth Theatre waiting eagerly for the results of this race before completing their play...
Maud:	His mum...
Harry:	... and dad...
Maud & Harry:	... nervous and very proud.
Mark:	He thought of Marie...
Harry:	Marie, who worked so hard and sacrificed so much for his success...
Maud:	... who always had the right words when things went wrong...
Mark & Maud:	... who was so completely dedicated.
Marie:	He knew how much a gold medal would mean to her.
All:	He had to win.

Instead, I had the ensemble shaped in a simple semicircle saying the lines. It's good for me to see how my directing skills have developed over the years... though this set a very low bar for that to happen!

The songs were, interestingly, not integrated into the play. The action stopped and the stage was often blacked out as the songs were sung. If I were doing this now I would ensure that there was a transition on stage or in some way the cast were highlighting the lyric. I suspect one of my thoughts was: this was the singers' moment and I didn't want to take the audience's attention away from them. I was also keen for my songs to be in the foreground.

The Final 400 Metres

The staging of the European Final (400 m race) was simple but more effective than I remember.

It showed Graham and Roger using an upper body running action with their feet planted firmly to the floor. They make four quarter turns through (nearly) 360° and, on the final turn, face towards the audience, at which point their running arm motion went into slow motion and the audience saw them seemingly approach the finishing line. Matthew and Christian Ignatiou's performances as Graham and Roger were particularly committed. Behind them, in the shadows, were another couple of ensemble performers representing the competitors. They ran (using the same upper body running action) for the first quarter of the race and the final section but didn't turn, just dipped out of view/audience focus for the middle section of the race. For the final few seconds of the race Roger and Graham return to their full tilt running action with the two in the background doing the same.[60]

The medal ceremony at the end of the play was interesting. We staged it side on, so the audience could see Graham dip down to receive his medal and freeze as one of the ensemble said:

'I don't think you'll be able to manage the stairs.'

It proved an incredibly effective ending.

---

[60] You can see this section of this scene on my Mark Wheeller YouTube channel.

VERBATIM - The Fun of Making Theatre Seriously by Mark Wheeller

Appendix 4: Director's Commentary
Race To Be Seen 1987 Oaklands Youth Theatre (VHS)

Despite being a different script from the one now available, this will prove useful to anyone studying and/or performing any of my plays.

The Set
A rostrum was diagonally positioned to dominate SR (how arty!) It was 2 metres square and 0.5 metres high.

USL had a smaller raised area (again, diagonally positioned), the same height but 1 metre square. (Great for monologues).
This was repositioned on top of the SR rostrum for the final 400 metres race which offered a new stage picture and also a raised area (for Graham and Roger to be a focus) on top of a raised area for the competing athletes to do their step ups.

There was a large open area in the middle of the stage. Performers brought movable cube blocks into this area. When not used these cubes resided at the back of stage.

Beside the smaller SL block the cast, while not on stage, were seated in two lines from the back wall to the front row of the audience.

Behind these lines, Brian and his keyboards were situated.

At the front of the stage far SL, with two microphones, in front of Brian, were seated two female singers who stood up when they sang. These non-acting roles offered singers opportunities if they weren't interested in acting a major role. Equally there were major roles for actors who weren't interested in solo singing.

I was only introduced to the use of levels around the time of ***Too Much Punch For Judy*** (1986). I remember I booked a professional performer to lead a workshop on levels. Following that we bought some rostra! I hadn't even considered the use of levels for the original 1984 EYT production of ***Race***. Incredible eh?

VERBATIM - The Fun of Making Theatre Seriously by Mark Wheeller

We had moved away from using actors as furniture and were using cubes, brought on during the songs in blackouts. (See the note about these in the 1984 production)

Centre stage, just in front of the back wall, was hung a large screen for projections. This was quite dominating. We were fortunate that our Theatre doubled as a Cinema!

The cast were all on stage and visible throughout. They were wonderfully disciplined. It's also worth mentioning that it makes managing offstage discipline far easier when no one is off stage!

Ideas For The Graham Salmon Actor

In this production, as in the original EYT production, Graham as a young boy was played by a younger actor (in this instance Chris Vaudin, Year 9). Graham the teen/adult was played by an older teenager (Jason Eames aged 17).

Graham as a toddler effectively appeared in the mind's eye of both his parents on stage, whose performances made his existence "real" for the audience.

However, I noticed something very interesting. Through the toddler years, we had Graham & Young Graham, clearly in view, on the front corner of the SR raised area. Little Graham was sat in front of/beneath Graham on the floor.

This gave the appearance of the scenes beside/behind them happening in their minds. They looked in the general direction of action that happened beside them. If behind them, they looked forward, as though imagining what the audience were seeing.

At one point, Maud put her arm around the bigger Graham's shoulder as she and Harry talked about baby Graham's pain following the radiotherapy. This stylistic split scene idea worked beautifully.

Once Little Graham became a visible, moving character, adult Graham leaves the stage so the audience focus on Little Graham. There was a wonderful exception to this and a really nice touch:

As the uncle told Little Graham about the 100 metre world record in the Guinness Book of Records in the centre area, adult Graham entered and stood on SR rostra block, to face the back. In silence, he put on his Great Britain track-suit top, then turned to bow and accepted his medal, foreshadowing that climatic moment!
A fantastic non-naturalistic moment.

VERBATIM - The Fun of Making Theatre Seriously by Mark Wheeller

Even when they moved in the scene changes, both Grahams maintained the illusion of being blind. Either an ensemble member guided them or they kept their hands out in front of them to be prepared for obstacles. When near the rostrum they used their leg or (later) a white stick to establish its location.

Equally important was that both Grahams focused their eyes just above the person they were addressing (or the audience) to sustain the illusion of blindness. They never made eye contact with other characters, nor the audience.

Jason (Graham) offered a wonderful, cheeky performance when he asked Marie out. He used the zipper on his track suit to alert her to his presence as per the 1984 production.

Marie was offering a wonderful mime making beds with zero props. Graham's delivery of the final three words before the actual 'ask':

'I went ahead... and did it!' This was said with a real excitable zeal and higher pitch. This gained an audible response from the audience.

To accentuate Graham's awkwardness, I directed Graham to climb onto the raised area to reach Marie.

Marie, it was important to note, always found Graham's hand, in holding hands scenes! It was so important to maintain every aspect of Graham's 'blind' illusion. These things are best discovered by Graham rehearsing in a blindfold to establish where these nuances occur... so he must learn lines early!

The Songs & Music

I noted early on how the music & larger cast had made the production more exuberant.

We were blessed with two talented singers. Schools often have these... make use of them!!!

That said, there was nothing like the full ensemble joining in, either offering backing vocals or full on vocals!

Talking of full on vocals...

Graham's rock 'n' roll song **King of the College** with a huge cast is **WONDERFUL**. Visually I preferred the more storytelling version EYT did, rather than choreography that ignored the story. A mix of both would be perfect!

This led to a fantastic climax for Act 1 (in this still 2-act version of the play)!

The audience certainly left wanting more in this production.

The song before the Bulgaria scene added status to the European Championships. It gave time for the significance of the event to be more clearly established.

Ideas For Maud and Harry Actors and the Salmon Family

In this section where Harry buys Maud a mantle clock, it was impressive how Maud continued placing the clock in her front room (all mimed) as Harry continued to talk about Mr Mason. This offered a visual background context. Harry, in our time, Maud back then - multiple time-frames co-existing!

Interesting to see that I kept the idea of Maud & Harry being physically separate as they talk about 'sitting there waiting' for the operation, making it emotionally strained for them both. She joined Harry when the doctor revealed the devastating news.

It was interesting that I also asked the performers to remain physically separate on the line:

'It brought us together.'

I'm not sure about this. It seems to contradict the actuality. I'm not keen on doing that just for the sake of theatre so I doubt I'd do the same now… but it's a good example of how a director can illustrate a line (incorrectly?).

Maud created a good relationship with Junie simply by being tactile with her. An example of this was when she asked what Graham would look like following his operation. This was beautifully and sensitively performed (well done Debbie Batt).

I like the way we had the family appearing together even when Junie or Susan had no specific lines. It gave a sense of family. A particular example of this was when the two sisters appear with Little Graham as he talks about his childhood & toys.

Other Points Of Interest

- Not having a body-prop bike was a surprise. I relied on this to cause added humour but the audience guffawed loudly despite the non-appearance of any bike body-prop or otherwise, largely due to the slide of the real Graham.

- The military style classroom entry (from 1984 production) was replicated to great effect.

- Although we did get a big laugh, the Ringer scene was yet to be perfected!

- Marion, who is typing in the office but doesn't tell the stories, was clearly enjoying what Graham's and her friends were saying as she was (intentionally) distracted from her (mimed) typing! Lovely little cameo before we knew why this character was there. Excellent work Sarah Blackman, who went on to play Catherine in the original **Hard to Swallow**.

- The nightmare following Ron Murray's line:
'The worst thing you can do is to run the final in your mind.'
This was brilliantly executed and raised the stakes for the importance of the big final. The cacophony of voices (mean words from the track officials as Graham struggles to run the race exaggerated in slow motion) ended menacingly with everyone turning towards Graham, laughing at him.

- As Graham waits for the Final in the stadium there are flashbacks over his life. The tableaux were fantastic, showing his memories and led into the wonderful Marie 3rd person speech.

'Marie, who had worked so hard, sacrificed so much for his success.'

… despite that line not even being allocated to her. It will in the 2021 edit… that's for sure!

Reactions

The reaction to the performance on the VHS was amazing. A long-lasting standing ovation with loud and persistent cheering.

Amazing!

VERBATIM - The Fun of Making Theatre Seriously by Mark Wheeller

Appendix 5: Writer's Commentary
Graham - World's Fastest Blind Runner 2001 Eastleigh Borough Youth Theatre performance (VHS)

My involvement in this was zero other than going to see/support it but I watched the video of the production and my notes illustrate the highlights, as I saw it, of the EBYT production.

The production was a 'back to basics' one using body props (albeit more selectively) which was a lovely nod to the original EYT performances.

A cast of 9.

The Set
Visually, the Tara Whiting/Tim Ford set was simple but effective. A screen at the back (used for projections) with two stripes running across the whole width, red white and blue, the colours of the GB team. There was a small plinth either side at the back of the stage with steps. There were flashes of red & blue stripes in the part of the step facing the audience. Typically for a Tim Ford production this was all beautifully conceived.

Physical Theatre
He used interesting physical theatre ideas that developed from those I had seen SNAP use. I wonder if, by this time, Tim had witnessed groups such as Frantic Assembly (I hadn't). The production seems to suggest he had.

For example, the ensemble created moving tableaux (rather than static body props like we'd had) to support the spoken word more symbolically.

In this section:

      Harry: Maud returned at about twenty past one. She was crying…
      Maud: They've got to take his eye out.
      Harry: Do what?

VERBATIM - The Fun of Making Theatre Seriously by Mark Wheeller

Maud: Take his eye out.
Harry: What for?
Maud: He's got a tumour. I wanted you to be there Harry.
Harry: Can't they do anything else?
Maud: That's what they told me!
Harry: I've been telling you for weeks there's something wrong! You told me they thought we were making a fuss.
Maud: I've been in that hospital for over four hours with Graham crying almost all the time... it's not my fault...

The ensemble stand behind Graham who is kneeling and facing forward. They are linked to each other in a line facing the back and curling round behind him. As Maud and Harry talked Graham enacts excruciating pain and the line of actors moved so as to signify the throbbing tumour.

There is another lovely moment of physical theatre (and using supportive vocal sounds) as when the ensemble illustrate the climax of Harry's frustration with anger boiling up inside him.

Harry: It made me so angry!

These moments offered much needed contrasting visual and aural dynamic.

Songs

In my original version, I included complete songs at certain points, which halted the action, at times needlessly. Here, they added to the emotion pointedly and with no extraneous 'fluff'. Tim cleverly split up the lyrics of the **Race To Be Seen** song and used a couple of lines sung plaintively to highlight important moments. For example, the moment where Graham was being inspired by the lines from the Guinness Book of Records these lines were sung:

> *There's a race at the local running track... no tickets to be sold*
> *There'll be no famous runners there... there'll be no winners gold.*
> *But their determination to succeed will surely mean...*
> *They will be part of a race to be seen.*

It worked beautifully.

Graham's lively **King Of The College** song proved a highlight again, especially the shoo-be-doo backing vocals. In this production Tim added a few extra 'snoops' after the line about the history teacher was sung.

> *Until the History Teacher came snooping around (snoop snoop snoop!)*

VERBATIM - The Fun of Making Theatre Seriously by Mark Wheeller

The 'Marie' Moment
A highlight for me was the moment where I (Mark) step out of the play to talk about Marie. This device allowed Marie to have her part in the story underlined with great potency. I would have liked this highlighted even more with Mark coming off stage and entering the audience area. (As you can see I was sitting there thinking of how I would do it… if that were ever to happen). Watching a play offers so much more than reading the pages one has written. which is why I rarely offer to read anyone else's plays. I just can't see them.

Comedy
The staging of the sponsored swimming, which was an innocuous scene at first was, fantastic as they added a fabulous comic idea. Everyone was swimming normally apart from Graham who was enacting a manic doggy paddle. After the others relaxed, having finished their 30 lengths, Graham slowly put out his hand to touch the edge of the pool and said the word…

'One'

… indicating he had just finished his first lap. That was a little joke I kept in the script but I know was EBYT's invention.

They also had two humans playing Ringer and the bitch… which I had never imagined. Genius!

The 400 Metres European Final
The final 400 metres was based strongly on my description in the (2000 edition) script but was tidier than our 1987 version. It proved to me, it was possible for someone other than us to stage this scene and that was super-important for the future of the play.
Wonderful.

VERBATIM - The Fun of Making Theatre Seriously by Mark Wheeller

Appendix 6: Director's Commentary
Graham - World's Fastest Blind Runner: OYT at the AETF Final 2008 - Thameside Theatre.

Barrie Sapsford (also in that original EYT production back in 1984) filmed OYT's performance in the AETF final to accompany the planned four-camera DVD of the original performance four months previously.

The production had improved so much but he had to do this on one camera due to restrictions made by the Thameside Theatre/AETF. It provides a fantastic memory of the occasion and shows how much the group's performances had improved.

Inspired by my enjoyment of watching the VHS of the 1987 OYT production I decided, for the first time, to watch this recording. I had watched the four-camera shoot previously. This really was so much better despite the lack of multi-camera angles.

This production is the joyous celebration I had always wanted it to be!

As I watched the DVD, I wrote these notes to provide a **Director's Commentary** on the 2008 version and I hope, these will prove useful to anyone performing or exploring the new 2021 edit of *Race To Be Seen*.[61]

I am immediately reminded we had a false start which the cast dealt with perfectly. Normally they walked on in a blackout to adopt their pre-set positions, the music starts and the lights go up. I like the audience to see the mechanics of the production and to have that 'distance' from the outset.

The Festival organisers decided the safety curtains had to be closed before the production began. So the cast prepared themselves behind the curtains. As they

---

[61] This DVD is available from SalamanderStreet.com. There are two versions. A four-camera shoot at the start of the run and a single-camera one shot at the AETF Final. I used the latter as it was the better performance in my opinion.

VERBATIM - The Fun of Making Theatre Seriously by Mark Wheeller

opened, the lights should come up, together with the music, which in turn cues the choreographed opening sequence to start.

The music didn't materialise.

The lights were on, the curtains opened and there the cast remained in their pre-set position for what was probably 30 seconds but seemed like an eternity.

No one twitched.

The audience knew there was a problem.

Our hearts went out to the cast.

Should I stand up and ask them to start again? I wasn't sure what to do. (I was internally echoing Graham's thoughts when the question over the lane allocation in the 400 metre final was being questioned by the officials).

I froze.

My dilemma was resolved, as I hoped it would be. The music began and allowed my cast to do their best… and they did!

What a relief!

My nerves were jangling!

I was incredibly proud!

INCREDIBLY!

The Opening Scene
The music Danny (Sturrock) had provided used Bernadette's **Race To Be Seen** song from EYT's production, sampled together with brief extracts from Graham Salmon interviews and underscored by a rhythmic drum n bass style backing. It offered a fantastic high energy opening.

The opening movement sequence established Graham & his family centre-stage, surrounded by the ensemble, playing old fashioned playground games.

Graham was dressed in white, contrasting with the ensemble in black (with white gloves). Each was equipped with a white stick collected from and deposited in two buckets at the rear of the stage to use from time to time. In this sequence the white sticks were used

VERBATIM - The Fun of Making Theatre Seriously by Mark Wheeller

as skipping ropes, race track lines, a finishing tape and, to end this sequence, a selection of golf clubs.

Our white sticks were broom handles painted white (very cheap).[62]

Graham's blindness was highlighted by Maud putting a pair of dark glasses on him.

This sequence clearly established the stylistic nature of the production.

Behind the action a screen showed moving pictures of the real Graham Salmon in race mode.

Opening Exchange
In the opening scene, which maintains a high energy, Mark tells the story of Graham from 1984 to the present day. The sticks (after being used as Graham's crutches) took on a more symbolic use. They became a barrier (representing geographical distance) to close contact. This enabled a potentially static exchange to be energised with the Mark character running from place to place around the semicircle of ensemble trying to break through the barriers to talk with Graham. I note how the ensemble added energy by the manner they close the barriers. This was such a contrast with the slow paced EYT opening scene.

Poignant moment
There was a poignant moment where Charlie Wheeller, aged 16, played himself as an 8-year-old, asking Graham who'd just had his leg amputated to play football. I found it interesting to note that the real Charlie turned to look at the screen showing a photo of him as a little boy with the real Graham, on the day he was referring to in the script. Focusing the audience on this slide, in a Brechtian manner, reminds them that what's happening on stage is not real but it does refers to a true story. As I have said previously, I believe this inexplicably makes the stage action even more 'real'. The addition of the real person playing himself is an added psychological wow factor!

Use of Accents
Gemma Aked Priestley (16), played Maud (Graham's mum) and used an Essex accent. It's unusual in my Youth Theatre for an actress to choose to do this. Gemma wanted to highlight the difference from her as a real person. Gemma's was an outstanding and caring portrayal. Her relationships with characters on stage were all beautifully drawn and in this case the use of accent helped both her and her characterisation.

---

[62] By this time in OYT we had the invaluable resource of Kat Chivers who was a totally committed props and costume lady/stage manager. She ensured that everything was just so and that the idea I had suggested from Cathy's production was implemented with bells and whistles! Back in EYT days I (and of course the cast) was doing everything... some things, such as props and costumes, not that well.

VERBATIM - The Fun of Making Theatre Seriously by Mark Wheeller

Use of Song
In all productions of **Race/Graham** I used solo singers humming or singing to underscore lines in the play.

In the scene where Graham as a baby, is at the hospital being diagnosed, a solo singer (my daughter Daisy, aged 14) sang **Rock-a-Bye Baby** and added a beautiful emotive quality to this scene.

Ideas For Direction Of Baby/Toddler Graham
The actor playing Graham also portrayed 'baby Graham' even more actively than in the EBYT 2000 production.
On SL Harry tested Graham's eye. Two sticks, held horizontally by ensemble actors, represented the outline top edge of the cot where Graham lay in front of Harry. There was no baby… he was imagined. On SR an ensemble actor passed a stick in front of Graham's eyes. Gemma (Maud) floated between the two scenes, referring to one or the other, as she narrated using the second setting as a close up/magnified scene. It worked superbly!

In the hospital Mike (playing Graham at six months old) walked in with Maud. A nurse walked him away and sat him on the floor to comfort him as Maud was being given details of the procedure. I find it interesting that the audience were able to suspend their disbelief in such an extreme manner with Michael (17) representing a baby. It undoubtedly added to the emotional intensity of the presentation of this scene.

In the hospital and home scenes where Maud and Harry reacted to the news that his eyes had to be removed Michael as Graham underscored their words with his sobbing. I used this idea in **Too Much Punch For Judy** (1986) where, after Duncan rescues Judy, he narrated the scene underscored by her sobbing. It proved equally effective here at creating a tension. It is an interesting use of split scene.

Body Scenery
The scene where Harry bought Maud a mantle clock was beautifully staged. The cast used the sticks to create a grandfather clock complete with moving pendulum. This established the location of the clock shop together with an ensemble soundscape of different 'tick-tock's.

VERBATIM - The Fun of Making Theatre Seriously by Mark Wheeller

Creativity And The White Sticks
The white sticks were used to represent the radium going in to Graham's head. It highlighted the aggression and the power of these rays over a tiny baby, represented by 17-year-old Michael. The precarious way these sticks were balanced from around Michael's shoulders added to the sense of danger, in what was at that time in history a new and risky treatment.

Making The Most Of Comic Moments
We created a lovely moment as Graham asked Marie out.
Unbeknown to Graham, Marie moved to SL, to make a different bed. He turned to SR to deliver the line asking her out. She, and the audience, saw this and as he heard her response behind him he realised his error. The audience responded with a big laugh and it was a fantastic little set piece under the dialogue.

The cast made a fantastic end to the unemployment scene during which different prospective employers offer Graham all manner of ridiculous reasons for not employing him because he is blind. The final reason offered was:

'I don't think you'll be able to manage the stairs.'

This was followed by a revelation contradicting the given excuse.
This was imaginatively contextualised by the cast, who repositioned themselves behind Graham in a small square shape (as though inside a full lift). One of the workers approached the lift and pressed the (imaginary) call button and said:

'Boing.'

… at which point the ensemble turned, the doors opened and they shout at him:

'There was a lift!'

A fantastic way to point the joke and it elicited another loud guffaw of laughter from the audience.

It's also good to note that the appalling comments were much better for being underplayed, as suggested by the semi-final adjudicator.

Imaginative Take On The Hit And Run
In this scene Graham witnessed a hit-and-run car accident. It transpired he was the only witness.

This was cleverly set up. Three of the ensemble took on the role of commentators improvising a horse race commentary quietly (but audibly) behind Graham as he narrated the story. The car that caused the accident entered in the form of a horse and rider and gradually morphed into the car to hit the victim child.

The Definitive 400M Final… Finally.

Remembering John Rowley's (1984) exercise when he tired himself out in front of all of us was, once again, my starting point for the staging of this scene.

Michael, who was fit (an accomplished basketball player), ran on the spot behind me as I talked to the group about the scene for ages… and Michael's extreme effort had the desired effect on the ensemble watching… it altered their breathing.

They saw the potential in the idea.

I explained what OYT had done in 1987 and how effective it had been but my reservation was that it didn't look like a race.

'Does anyone have any ideas?'

Someone piped up:

'A bleep-test.'

Once again, it's the question that led to the idea, rather than being reliant on the ceiling of my knowledge for the answer.

I'd never heard of a bleep-test!

Someone demonstrated.

Yes! This could work.

We lined up four volunteers either side of Mike. I asked him to run (on the spot) in slow motion (together with Matt, his guide runner), with the rest of the ensemble counting from 1-55.

I said Graham and Matt needed to make their way to the front of the stage while the four athletes either side of them do a repeated mini-bleep-test run from their position at the back of the stage to the front of stage and return etc etc.

It worked!

VERBATIM - The Fun of Making Theatre Seriously by Mark Wheeller

I'd set aside 9 hours' rehearsal time to figure this out. In the end we had it in the bag after the first 3! Amazing!

It had taken 20 years!

I can see from the DVD that we went on to implement some additional and important tweaks.

- Graham and Roger ran on the spot, not in slow motion but at full energy, throughout the 55 seconds, adding to the intensity of the 'work-out'.

- Graham and Roger started their running action a moment or two prior to the ensemble either side of them on the word 'Run!'.

- The ensemble counted from 1-55 immediately after the 'Run!' line and the two neighbouring bleep-test runners started their epic 55 second marathon!

- The outer two bleep-testers started their run at 11 seconds, to allow a build of activity in the stage picture.

- At regular intervals, worked out by Mike (Graham) and Matt (Roger) they moved one pace forward in unison, edging closer to the front of stage.

- At 37 seconds the outer two runners stopped running to show how out of breath they were, and to highlight the distance between them and Graham/Roger (and the other two neighbouring bleep-testers).

- Gradually the others either side of Graham and Roger dropped out, audibly panting.

- From about 48 seconds on, the focus was solely on Graham and Roger as they became the only two remaining runners, while the panting of the others continued to underscore the scene!

- The final 5 seconds saw Graham and Roger move, in slow motion, to win the race. The ensemble continued counting to 55.

- As they ended the race there was a moment of no dialogue when the breathing/panting of the runners was the only sound to be heard.

- The quiet was broken by a loud (very loud and energetic) cheer and much commotion around Graham as he was congratulated.

VERBATIM - The Fun of Making Theatre Seriously by Mark Wheeller

My one, minor reservation, looking back at this today, is that the runners either side of Graham ran alone. We didn't try it with guide-runners linked because we felt it would look untidy, particularly on the quick turns. This dramatic license was acceptable, particularly as the effect of the scene was so powerful.[63]

The production was received positively and won the AETF (Rex Walford) Award for Creativity, cementing the wonderful memory of this production.

---

[63] This scene can be seen on the DVD of the production and also as a separate edit on my Mark Wheeller YouTube Channel. It's well worth a look.

Appendix 7: Where Are They Now?
What happened to the contributors?

Lisa Andreae (né Beer - 1984 era EYT)
Lisa gained a BA Hons in History & French from the University of Exeter, and her love of drama led her to a career in television. She worked on the inaugural, and subsequent, seasons of BBC2 hit series Two Fat Ladies, then became Head of Production at leading UK production company Optomen Television, whose shows included Jamie Oliver's The Naked Chef, Police Camera Action, and Gordon Ramsay's Kitchen Nightmares. Lisa and her husband Simon (also a producer), moved to Los Angeles in 2005 and, between raising a family of four children, started an independent production company The Incubator, making shows for Discovery Channel, National Geographic and many others. Lisa took over sole responsibility in 2010 and executive produced several high profile documentary and reality shows, including Morgan Freeman's Emmy-nominated series Through the Wormhole. She, Simon and the children returned to the UK in 2013 and now divide their time between London and Wiltshire, where she continues to raise the family and consult on selected television projects.

Matthew Allen (1984 era EYT)
Matt worked at the E15 acting school and Harlow Playhouse followed by 3 years' study at the Guildford School of Acting. Before graduating, Matt set up the Ape Theatre Company which toured educational theatre across the UK for 25 years to well over a million students. Ape produced Mark Wheeller's plays **Too Much Punch For Judy** and **Legal Weapon** together with two of his own **Pills and Thrills** and **Vicious Circle**. During Ape's early years Matt also enjoyed a solo acting career, mostly theatre including some West End. Over the years international travel has played a major part in Matt's life and, in 2014, he moved to Nepal to work as a Tandem Paragliding Pilot, taking tourists for pleasure flights in the Himalayan Mountains. Currently Matt is back in London where he lives on the South Bank.

Bernadette Clere (né Chapman - 1984 era EYT)
"Being part of Race To Be Seen and Epping Youth Theatre was the best foundation for me as a teenager. My love for music and theatre was encouraged and inevitably led me to my English and Drama degree later in life. Singing was always my passion which I have shared with many since those days".

VERBATIM - The Fun of Making Theatre Seriously by Mark Wheeller

Robbie Currie (1984 era EYT)
"I've moved through several careers since leaving school. Currently (2021) I'm the Sexual Health Programme lead for the London Borough of Bexley in South East London, but I've worked professionally in the arts, mostly dance, and in Physical Theatre. I became a teacher and lived in the far East for nearly 10 years and got involved with Health Promotion for a variety of organisations to improve health and wellbeing. But throughout my career(s), I've always been involved in HIV prevention. As a young gay man who grew up in the 1980s, HIV was such an important and influential backdrop to my community I got involved whenever I was, whatever I was doing, which led me to my current role. I did a Dance and Drama Degree, but my Masters was in Science. But, without doubt, my educational grounding in the arts has enabled me to progress and develop my life and career in extraordinary ways: team work, deadlines, diversity, creativity, compromise, curiosity, etcetera, etcetera. Although I'm no longer involved in the arts more formally, I volunteer to promote and champion the arts. I want others to reap the benefits and transformative powers of exploring the arts, but theatre and dance in particular".

Jason Eames (1987 era OYT)
"I moved from the dream of wanting to become an actor to the reality of people management, and have held Operations Directorships for global corporates and built smaller brands both here and abroad. The experiences in Theatre, especially OYT, genuinely gave me the ability to become the person I am today, to identify ability, develop and enable people in an engaging way and in a style that's been, I believe, subconsciously taken and adapted from the stage. It was a godsend!"

Ali Garner (Cedar School/Branch Out 1990's)
"In 2004 I reduced my hours when I started my family in 2004. I continued to work part time there until my daughter PJ was 7 years old. In 2011 (after 20 years at Cedar) I took up the position of Nurture Group leader at Hollybrook Junior School. I moved to Kings Copse Primary to support pupils with visual impairment. In 2013 I became the Senior Learning Mentor at Ludlow Junior School. I incorporated performing arts into my thinking and planning in all these roles. I also took the opportunity to integrate therapy into my work, so Hamish, my labradoodle, has joined me on my journey. I continue to work at Instep as workshop leader and am still involved in youth theatre work alongside young people with additional needs".

Paul England (Cedar School 1990's)
Since leaving the Nuffield Theatre Paul has has worked in the Utilities and Financial Services businesses. He is a successful people manager and recently has taken a role in the charity sector in Service Delivery. Outside of work Paul still enjoys theatre and music. Paul is a Southampton FC season ticket holder. Paul says "never say never" and would love to work with Mark again if the opportunity were to arise.

VERBATIM - The Fun of Making Theatre Seriously by Mark Wheeller

Michael Mears (2008 era OYT)
"I'm currently living in Suffolk and working out of a local FE college as a tutor. I run a Youth Theatre which is looking to produce its first production in the spring of 2021 (COVID permitting).
- Went to Chichester University to study Performing Arts
- PGCE in Theatre
- Professional Theatre work
- Theatre Teacher at FE for 4 years
- Currently heading a youth theatre named Suffolk Youth Players.

Created in 2019, we have started to develop original work and will be working to produce our first production in the spring of 2021".

Barrie Sapsford (1984 era EYT)
When I left school, my involvement in EYT continued. My first job in an art, design & printing company was heavily influenced by my involvement with EYT. The company had done the printing of the **Race To Be Seen** posters and the owner was a massive Am-Dram fan. However, within less than a year, I embarked on a 2-year European backpacking adventure and entered the world of catering. Hands-on experience included being a waiter, chef, baker, barman and even karaoke host (which played to my theatrical strengths) and took me through the ranks from barman to bar owner. Taking various qualifications en route led to running my own nightclub in Naples, Italy.

Returning to the UK, I continued the catering career path and started exploring the hotel industry, swiftly moving up the ranks although my confidence was far greater than my knowledge. Bizarrely this led me straight back to my original career choice of art & design when the director of a graphics company pitched me regarding hotel marketing. Not only did he get the contract but he got me as well!

I continued pursuing my creative side, learning amazing skills in copywriting, advertising layouts, graphic design and - what was to become my ticket to independence - designing pages for the internet! After attaining the various qualifications needed to become a marketing expert, I joined a fledgling Contract Catering company as their Business Development & Marketing Manager and in a few short years gained a reputation as a go-getter, turning the company into a multi-million pound success story.

I achieved personal goals, getting 'by Royal Appointment' on my letterhead and eating in the top five restaurants in the country. The team were great and we even made a 20-minute video parody of Jamie Oliver's **The Naked Chef**, aptly named **Chef in Bad Pants**. We used it as in-house promotion and on our website, and one of the chefs used it as an audition piece for Breakfast Time TV. During that period I dined

VERBATIM - The Fun of Making Theatre Seriously by Mark Wheeller

with royalty, drank cocktails with movie stars and champagne with pop stars.

In 2001, with the birth of my first child (I have 2 boys), I started my own Marketing Consultancy and moved to the Kent countryside. I added video and film production to my repertoire and have been behind the scenes launching many successful businesses and getting products to the market. Twenty years later, with a handful of published works under my belt and a whole suite of marketing skills, having made and lost a million pounds, I continue to help companies and individuals achieve their goals. Whilst expressing my excitement and reminiscing over various chapters of this book, my wife said to me:

"You seem to have this rose-tinted view of a wonderful school life."

I replied that this wasn't school... it was youth theatre... we had so much fun.

Mark Wheeller

"You have heard enough about me after reading this book so I shall say no more other than what a joy it has been to revisit my past life in these pages (and that as a child I also enjoyed imaginary worlds inhabited by pixies). I hope the book has proved interesting and will be useful to you".

Mark with Dusty

VERBATIM - The Fun of Making Theatre Seriously by Mark Wheeller

www.salamanderstreet.com